The EU and Effective Multilateralism

This book investigates the extent to which the EU has defined and operational-ized the notion of effective multilateralism.

Reform has dominated the agenda of the EU in recent years with the adoption and implementation of the Lisbon Treaty. However, various international organ-izations have also been in reform mode in an attempt to adjust their structure to the changing polarity and counter criticisms about a lack of legitimacy, account-ability and effectiveness.

The EU and Effective Multilateralism examines the EU's intention to make multilateral settings more effective, as formulated by the European Security Strategy in December 2003. Firmly grounded in new empirical research, it pro-vides a balanced account of the fit between internal reform (the institutional reform within the EU, notably following the entry into force of the Lisbon Treaty) and external reform (the institutional reform of the international settings in which the EU operates).

This book will be of much interest to students of EU politics, European security, international organizations, foreign policy and IR in general.

Edith Drieskens is Assistant Professor of International Relations at Leuven International and European Studies (LINES) at KU Leuven, Belgium. She is co-editor of *The Sage Handbook of European Foreign Policy* (2014).

Louise G. van Schaik is Senior Research Fellow at the Clingendael Institute in The Hague. She is author of *EU Effectiveness and Unity in Multilateral Negotia-tions: More than the Sum of Its Parts?* (2013).

Routledge Studies in European Security and Strategy
Series Editors:
Sven Biscop
Egmont Royal Institute for International Relations, Belgium
Richard Whitman
University of Kent, UK

The aim of this series is to bring together the key experts on European security from the academic and policy worlds, and assess the state of play of the EU as an international security actor. The series explores the EU, and its member states, security policy and practices in a changing global and regional context. While the focus is on the politico-military dimension, security is put in the context of the holistic approach advocated by the EU.

Tactical Nuclear Weapons and Euro-Atlantic Security
The future of NATO
Edited by Paolo Foradori

The EU and Military Operations
A comparative analysis
Katarina Engberg

The EU and Effective Multilateralism
Internal and external reform practices
Edited by Edith Drieskens and Louise G. van Schaik

The EU and Effective Multilateralism

Internal and external reform practices

Edited by Edith Drieskens and Louise G. van Schaik

Routledge
Taylor & Francis Group

LONDON AND NEW YORK

First published 2014 by Routledge

2 Park Square, Milton Park, Abingdon, Oxfordshire OX14 4RN
711 Third Avenue, New York, NY 10017

Routledge is an imprint of the Taylor & Francis Group, an informa business

First issued in paperback 2018

Copyright © 2014 selection and editorial material, Edith Drieskens and Louise G. van Schaik; individual chapters, the contributors

The right of the editors to be identified as the authors of the editorial material, and of the authors for their individual chapters, has been asserted in accordance with sections 77 and 78 of the Copyright, Designs and Patents Act 1988.

All rights reserved. No part of this book may be reprinted or reproduced or utilised in any form or by any electronic, mechanical, or other means, now known or hereafter invented, including photocopying and recording, or in any information storage or retrieval system, without permission in writing from the publishers.

Notice:
Product or corporate names may be trademarks or registered trademarks, and are used only for identification and explanation without intent to infringe.

British Library Cataloguing in Publication Data
A catalogue record for this book is available from the British Library

Library of Congress Cataloging in Publication Data
The EU and effective multilateralism : internal and external reform practices / edited by Edith Drieskens, Louise G. van Schaik.
    pages cm. – (Routledge studies in european security and strategy)
    Includes bibliographical references and index.
    1. European Union countries–Foreign relations. 2. European cooperation. 3. International agencies–European Union countries. 4. National security–European Union countries. I. Drieskens, Edith, editor. II. Van Schaik, Louise, editor.
    JZ1570.A5E85 2014
    341.242'2–dc23   2013030919

ISBN: 978-0-415-71311-5 (hbk)
ISBN: 978-1-138-37745-5 (pbk)

Typeset in Times
by Wearset Ltd, Boldon, Tyne and Wear

Contents

Contributors

Samantha Battams is Course Director, Faculty of Medicine, University of Geneva, and senior lecturer at Flinders University. She is also a private consultant in public and global health. She was research/visiting fellow at The Graduate Institute of International and Development Studies, Geneva. She has worked in academia as a lecturer and researcher in public health and has experience as a member of government boards and legal panels. Prior to entering academia, she worked for ten years in the community and health services sector.

Laura Davis has a PhD in Political Science from the University of Ghent, Belgium. Her academic work focuses on peace and justice in EU foreign policy. She examines the relationships between principles, policy and practice, focusing on the EU's engagement in the Democratic Republic of Congo, its relationship with the International Criminal Court, and the EU as peace mediator. In addition, she works with non-governmental organizations and governmental agencies on peacebuilding and transitional justice issues, including supporting peace processes.

Peter Debaere is a research fellow at the Ghent Institute for International Studies at Ghent University. His research focuses on the relationship between the EU and the G7/G8/G20, as well as on the reform of the IMF. Recent publications include 'The European Union in the G20: What role for small states?' (*Cambridge Review of International Affairs*, 2012) and a chapter on the EU in the Gx-system for the *Routledge Handbook on the European Union and international institutions* (Routledge, 2013).

Tom Delreux is associate professor of Political Science at the Institut de Sciences Politiques Louvain-Europe at the University of Louvain (Louvain-la-Neuve, Belgium). His research interests include European environmental policy and policy-making, the external dimension of the EU's internal policies, and inter- and intra-institutional relations in the EU. He is the author of *The EU as international environmental negotiator* (Ashgate, 2011) and of various international publications, including 'Taking the lead: informal division of labour in the EU's external environmental policy-making' (*Journal of European Public Policy*, 2013, with Van den Brande).

Margriet Drent is a senior research fellow at the Research Department of the Netherlands Institute of International Relations Clingendael and assistant professor at the International Relations Department of the University of Groningen. She specializes in international security issues with particular attention on the EU as a security actor. She is also a member of the Peace and Security Committee of the Advisory Council on International Affairs. Until 2004, Margriet Drent was the executive director of the Groningen-based Centre for European Security Studies.

Edith Drieskens is assistant professor of International Relations at Leuven International and European Studies (LINES) at KU Leuven, Belgium. Taking an institutional perspective, her work explores the regional and multilateral dimensions of global governance and looks into the implementation of the Lisbon Treaty in various UN contexts. Her findings have been published in various international journals and edited volumes. She is co-editor the *Sage Handbook of European Foreign Policy* (Sage, 2014, with Jørgensen, Laatikainen, Kalland and Tonra).

Johanne Grøndahl Glavind is an assistant professor at the Department of Political Science and Government at Aarhus University, Denmark. Her research areas include EU non-proliferation policy, nuclear weapons and disarmament and international law and the use of force. She is the author of *Can great powers change fundamental norms? A theoretical and empirical assessment of the strength of fundamental norms in post-2001 international society* (Politica, 2011).

Judith Huigens is a doctoral candidate at the University of Amsterdam. Her work explores the role of the EU in informal global governance and focuses on the EU's functioning within the context of the G8 summit. Writing together with Arne Niemann, her findings have been published in *Cambridge Review of International Affairs* (2011), *Journal of European Public Policy* (2011) and in *The European Union in the G8*, edited by Larionova (Ashgate, 2012).

Robert Kissack is assistant professor of International Relations at the Institut Barcelona d'Estudis Internacionals, Spain. Recent publications include *Pursuing effective multilateralism: the European Union, international organizations and the politics of decision making* (Palgrave, 2010), 'The EU's Performance in the International Labour Organization' (*Journal of European Integration*, 2011), as well as a chapter on the European Union and multilateralism in the *Routledge Handbook on the European Union and international institutions* (Routledge, 2013).

Dries Lesage is professor of Globalization and Global Governance at the Ghent Institute for International Studies at Ghent University, Belgium. His main research interest is the architecture of global governance, with a focus on reform of international organizations, the G8/G20, energy, taxation and sustainable development. He co-authored *Global Energy Governance in a Multipolar World* (Ashgate, 2010) and has published in journals such as *Global Governance, Energy Policy* and *Development Policy Review*.

Arne Niemann is professor of International Relations at the Johannes Gutenberg University in Mainz, Germany. He is author of *Explaining Decisions in the European Union* (Cambridge University Press, 2006) and has published in several journals, including the *Journal of European Public Policy* and the *Journal of Common Market Studies*. His research focuses primarily on the European integration process and European Union policy and politics. Recurrent themes and aspects of his research include neofunctionalist and constructivist approaches to theorizing EU integration, EU negotiations and decision-making, EU external relations, EU migration policy, Germany in the EU and the Europeanization of football.

Jan Orbie is a professor at the Department of Political Science of Ghent University, Belgium. He is the co-director of the Centre for EU Studies, which forms the political science pillar of the Jean Monnet Centre of Excellence at Ghent University. He teaches and researches the soft dimensions of the EU's external relations and on the EU's role as a civilian and normative power. He has published various articles and book chapters on EU external trade policy, EU development policies, the EU's global social role and EU democracy promotion.

Yf Reykers is research fellow at Leuven International and European Studies (LINES) at KU Leuven, Belgium. Funded by the Research Foundation Flanders, he studies the role of regional actors in the UN context by taking a principal-agent perspective and looking into the EU, African Union and Arab League.

Laura Van Dievel is research fellow at Leuven International and European Studies (LINES) at KU Leuven, Belgium. Her research focuses on the role of observers in international relations, including the EU, Palestine and the Holy See.

Louise G. van Schaik is a senior research fellow at the Netherlands Institute of International Relations, Clingendael, in The Hague, the Netherlands. Over the past ten years, she has extensively analysed the EU's international performance in the fields of health, climate change and food standards, as well as related topics such as EU external action after the Lisbon Treaty, EU development cooperation and scarcity of natural resources. In addition, she has managed several training courses for (international) diplomats and civil servants. She recently published *EU effectiveness and unity in multilateral negotiations: more than the sum of its parts?* (Palgrave, 2013).

Niels van Willigen is assistant professor of international relations in the Institute of Political Science at Leiden University, the Netherlands. His professional fields of interest include theories of international relations, foreign policy analysis and security studies (more in particular peace operations, arms control and European security). Recent publications include a book chapter on evaluating diplomacy in the *Routledge Handbook on the European Union and international institutions* (2013, with Kleistra) and *Peacebuilding and international administration: the cases of Bosnia and Herzegovina and Kosovo* (Routledge, 2013).

Foreword

At the turn of the twenty-first century, 'effective multilateralism' was at the top of the global agenda; it informed both the first ever European Security Strategy and the UN Secretary-General's report *In Larger Freedom* which sought to reform and reconceptualize collective security. Partly this reflected long-term dynamics, as reforms were seen as necessary to accommodate an enlarging membership (the EU) or shifting configurations of global power and new security challenges (the UN). And partly it reflected more immediate concerns stemming from the perceived need to address the challenge posed to the multilateral system by the Bush Administration in the US (as seen in the US rejection of the International Criminal Court or its rush to go to war against Saddam Hussein's Iraq). At the UN, this culminated in the major 2005 Summit which affirmed the norm of the Responsibility to Protect, created a Peacebuilding Commission, and transformed the UN Commission for Human Rights into the Human Rights Council, all of which were EU priorities. Major reform of the UN Security Council, however urgently needed, was scrapped. For its part, the EU embarked on a significant institutional reform project with the drafting of the Constitutional Treaty, which after being rejected by voters in France and the Netherlands had to be repackaged as the Lisbon Treaty – and eventually entered into force in 2009. It was the EU that created a relationship between the two processes when it proclaimed in the 2003 European Security Strategy that it would bolster multilateralism, particularly by supporting UN reform.

An indisputable outcome of this emphasis on effective multilateralism is that it spawned an avalanche of research over the past ten years, particularly on EU multilateralism. This book is a welcome and very important addition to this literature because it focuses centrally on the EU and international institutions generally. It fills an important gap in the literature on the EU and international institutions (done by us and others) that has largely focused on the EU's *internal* effectiveness (a single voice, coherence of the EU) and one dimension of *external* effectiveness (EU influence). This volume tracks the impact of the Lisbon Treaty on EU representation and coherence in international organizations, as well as the reform processes in international institutional settings more broadly, to assess whether the EU makes international organizations more effective. A decade after we first proposed this internal/external characterization of effective multilateralism, it is striking how rarely scholars have investigated the EU's contributions, or lack thereof, to broader multilateral processes. It is refreshing that the contributors to this volume have taken up the challenge.

Ten years after the launch of effective multilateralism, evidence for increasing internal effectiveness abounds. The Lisbon Treaty, as is well documented in this volume, has introduced reforms that once fully implemented are likely to impact the EU's effectiveness rather dramatically. However, by including the external dimension so clearly, the contributors paint a mixed picture of the EU's contribution to global governance more generally. The Lisbon Treaty may make EU multilateralism more coherent and it may make the EU more influential, but it is not at all clear that this will contribute to more effective multilateralism across the international institutional landscape. While EU diplomats celebrated the hard-won passage of a 2011 UN General Assembly resolution that upgraded the EU's observer status and enabled the EU delegation to represent the EU in the UN General Assembly in line with the Lisbon Treaty, the lingering resentment of small states and other regional organizations (such as the Caribbean Community) that opposed such a change – and are resistant to the presence of this new institutional actor alongside EU member states in the UN General Assembly – continues two years later.

The emergence of a new European External Action Service composed of Commission, Council and national diplomats, a highly visible EU 'foreign minister' who is not a member of a government, a Council President without a polity ... the list of EU multilateral innovations emerging from Lisbon is extensive. Yet these internal reforms are increasingly bumping into the external multilateral order which seems somewhat allergic or incapable of such far-reaching reform – because the implications of a shifting diffusion of power in the international system are resisted by some or are still not clear for others. This is not to say that change or evolution does not occur in broader multilateral processes; but the legalistic, treaty-based reform process that has characterized EU multilateral change over the past few decades stands in stark contrast to evolutionary change in broader multilateral processes that more often emerges from politics or practice. The tensions inherent in these different realms suggest that despite the EU's commitment to effective multilateralism, what we may be witnessing is *diverging* rather than *intersecting* multilateralism. This volume goes a great distance in launching that conversation.

Katie Laatikainen
Adelphi University
Karen E. Smith
London School of Economics

Acknowledgements

The idea for this volume comes from a workshop that was organized at the Clingendael Institute in February 2012 on the EU's external representation after the entry into force of the Lisbon Treaty. The workshop revealed much continued interest in the EU's functioning in international *fora*, both in academic and policy circles, but also that the EU's contribution to the reform of those settings was vastly under-explored, unlike the reform of the EU within those settings. Early drafts of most contributions were presented and discussed at the workshop, and we are indebted to the Clingendael Institute for hosting the meeting and to the *LISBOAN – Erasmus Academic Network* for the financial support.

We are most thankful to Routledge for sharing our enthusiasm for this project. More specifically, we would like to thank Series Editors Sven Biscop and Richard Whitman, Senior Editor Andrew Humphrys and Senior Editorial Assistant Annabelle Harris for their support. Also, we are grateful to Zsuzsa Erdős for language editing and preparing the index. In addition, we would like to extend our sincere thanks to Katie Verlin Laatikainen and Karen E. Smith, for writing the foreword, but also for being constant sources of academic inspiration. Above all, we would like to thank the contributors for their excellent cooperation. We are most grateful to be surrounded by a strong community of creative and supportive minds.

The genesis of this volume coincided with new life coming into being, but also with life coming to an end. Dave Allen was our guest at Clingendael and, together with David Spence, had keenly started to explore the EU's post-Lisbon functioning at the WTO before passing away in October 2012. Our discipline has lost a true pioneer and a warm personality. We cherish how extremely generous he was with his time and knowledge.

Edith Drieskens
Louise G. van Schaik

Abbreviations

3G	Global Governance Group
ACP	African, Caribbean and Pacific (countries)
ACT	Allied Command Transformation (NATO)
Adapted CFE-Treaty	Adapted Conventional Armed Forces Europe Treaty
AFRO	Africa (as a WHO region)
AMRO	the Americas (as a WHO region)
ASP	Assembly of States Parties (ICC)
AU	African Union
BRIC	Brazil, Russia, India and China
C-10	committee of ten African states that negotiates on behalf of the African countries (UNSC)
CAR	Central African Republic
CARICOM	Caribbean Community
CBD	Convention on Biological Diversity
CBRN	chemical, biological, radiological and nuclear
CFSP	Common Foreign and Security Policy
CGPCS	Contact Group on Piracy off the Coast of Somalia
CICC	Coalition for the International Criminal Court
CIS	Commonwealth of Independent States
CMPD	Crisis Management and Planning Department (EEAS)
CoC	Committee of the Conference (FAO)
CoE	Council of Europe
COJUR-ICC	Public International Law Working Party (ICC)
COP	Conference of the Parties (UN conventions)
COSCE	Council's Working Party on the OSCE and the CoE
CPCC	Civilian Planning and Conduct Capability (EU)
CSCE	Conference on Security and Cooperation in Europe
CSD	Commission on Sustainable Development (UN)
CSDP	Common Security and Defence Policy
CSP	Country Strategy Papers
CSTO	Collective Security Treaty Organization
DRC	Democratic Republic of Congo
DROI	Subcommittee on Human Rights (EP)

E3	France, Germany and the UK
E3+3	France, Germany, UK and US, Russia and China
EB	Executive Board
EC	European Community
ECAP	European Capability Action Plan
ECOSOC	Economic and Social Council (UN)
EDA	European Defence Agency
EEAS	European External Action Service
EEG	Eastern European Group (UNSC)
EFC	Economic and Financial Committee (EU)
EIDHR	European Instrument for Democracy and Human Rights
EMRO	Eastern Mediterranean (as a WHO region)
ENP	European Neighbourhood Policy
EP	European Parliament
ESDP	European Security and Defence Policy
ESS	European Security Strategy
EU	European Union
EUDEL	EU Delegation to the United Nations
EUMS	EU Military Staff
Euratom	European Atomic Energy Community
EURO	Europe (as a WHO region)
EUSR	EU Special Representative
FAO	Food and Agricultural Organization
G20	Group of Twenty
G-4	Group of Four (Germany, Japan, India, Brazil) (UNSC)
G8	Group of Eight
GAERC	General Affairs and External Relations Council
GESDPE	green economy in the context of sustainable development and poverty eradication
HCNM	High Commissioner on National Minorities (OSCE)
HLPF	High Level Political Forum (UN)
HR	High Representative
IAEA	International Atomic Energy Agency
IAI	International Affairs Institute (Rome)
ICC	International Criminal Court
IEE	Independent External Evaluation (FAO)
IFSD	institutional framework for sustainable development
IGO	inter-governmental organization
IHL	international humanitarian law
IMF	International Monetary Fund
IMFC	International Monetary and Financial Committee (IMF)
INC	Intergovernmental Negotiating Committee (UNEP)
IO	international organization
IPA	Immediate Plan of Action (FAO)
JIU	Joint Inspection Unit (UN)

L.96	refers to draft resolution A/61/L.96 (UNSC)
LMG	Like-Minded Group
MDGs	Millennium Development Goals
MEA	multilateral environmental agreement
MERCOSUR	Mercado Común del Sur
NAC	North Atlantic Council (NATO)
NAM	Non-Aligned Movement
NATO	North Atlantic Treaty Organization
NCD	non-communicable disease
NGO	non-governmental organization
NORDEFCO	Nordic Defence Cooperation
NPT	Non-Proliferation Treaty
ODA	Official Development Assistance
ODIHR	Office for Democratic Institutions and Human Rights (OSCE)
OECD	Organisation for Economic Co-operation and Development
OEWG	Open-Ended Working Group (on the Question of Equitable Representation on and Increase in the Membership of the Security Council and Other Matters Related to the Security Council)
OPCW	Organisation for the Prohibition of Chemical Weapons
OSCE	Organization for Security and Cooperation in Europe
P5+1	France, UK, US, Russia, China and Germany
PBC	Peacebuilding Commission
PfP	Partnership for Peace
PISM	Polish Institute for International Affairs
PSC	Political Security Committee (EU)
PSC+7	briefing of non-EU NATO members
PSC+9	briefing of non-EU NATO members and candidate countries
REIO	regional economic integration organization
RFOM	Representative on the Freedom of the Media (OSCE)
RIE	Elcano Royal Institute (Madrid)
S-5	Small Five (Costa Rica, Jordan, Liechtenstein, Singapore and Switzerland)
SADC	Southern African Development Community
SANCO	DG for Health and Consumers (EU)
SCIMF	sub-committee on IMF related issues (EU)
SEARO	Southeast Asia (as a WHO region)
SG	Secretary-General
TCF	Technical Cooperation Fund
TRIPS	Trade Related aspects of International Property rights
UfC	Uniting for Consensus
UI	Swedish Institute of International Affairs (Stockholm)

UNCED	UN Conference on Environment and Development
UNEA	United Nations Environment Assembly of UNEP
UNEO	United Nations Environmental Organization
UNEP	United Nations Environment Programme
UNFCCC	United Nations Framework Convention on Climate Change
UNGA	United Nations General Assembly
UN-HABITAT	UN Human Settlements Programme
UNSC	United Nations Security Council
WEOG	Western Europe and Others Group (UNGA)
WEU	Western European Union
WHA	World Health Assembly
WHO	World Health Organization
WMD Strategy	EU Strategy against the Proliferation of Weapons of Mass Destruction
WPIEI Global	Council Working Party on International Environmental Issues/Global (EU)
WPRO	Western Pacific (as a WHO region)
WTO	World Trade Organisation

1 Introduction

A framework for analysing effective multilateralism

Edith Drieskens

Introduction

This volume builds upon a workshop that was organized by the Clingendael Institute in February 2012. Bringing academics and policy officials together, the workshop explored the European Union (EU)'s functioning in international settings following the entry into force of the Lisbon Treaty. In their contributions, most participants discussed processes of coordination and representation to evaluate whether or not the EU's newest treaty makes it a more effective international actor. Doing so, they gave the notion of reform a predominantly internal interpretation.

Bringing an external reform dimension into the picture and addressing the question what has become of the EU's intention to make multilateral settings more effective, as formulated by the European Security Strategy (ESS) in December 2003, this volume aims to provide a balanced empirical account of the fit between internal and external reform.

The purpose of this introductory chapter is to set the scene, introduce the focus, outline the framework of analysis and provide an overview of the various contributions. It starts with discussing the main characteristics of the reform dimensions around which this volume is structured, namely internal and external reform. The former covers institutional reform within the EU; the latter refers to the institutional reform of the international settings in which the EU operates.

Dimensions

Looking from an EU perspective, the Lisbon Treaty (in full: *Treaty of Lisbon amending the Treaty on European Union and the Treaty establishing the European Community*) can be seen as the most comprehensive internal reform effort for many years. Signed in Lisbon in December 2007 and in force since November 2009, its main aim is to increase the EU's coherence and consistency on the international level, thus transforming the EU into a more effective international actor. To this aim, it introduces a more permanent system of external representation, at least for matters falling within the Common Foreign and Security Policy (CFSP). In the old system, the EU was represented for those issues by the member state holding the rotating presidency, thus by a different country every six months, which resulted in criticisms of inconsistency both in academic and policy circles.

Somewhat ironically, then, the new set-up includes more faces than before. Probably most visible are the appointments of Herman Van Rompuy as first permanent President of the European Council and Catherine Ashton as first High Representative for Foreign Affairs and Security. The President of the European Council convenes and chairs the meetings, sets the agenda, takes care of the follow-up and represents it vis-à-vis the other EU institutions. Also, he represents the EU at the level of heads of state and government with third countries, including in multilateral settings. Merging three roles into one, the High Representative for Foreign Affairs and Security combines the functions of the former High Representative for the CFSP (a position held by Javier Solana between 1999 and 2009), the Commissioner for External Relations and the foreign minister of the country holding the rotating presidency (Kajnc *et al.* 2012; Vanhoonacker *et al.* 2012). As High Representative, Ashton has to contribute to the development of the CFSP and ensures the implementation of the decisions adopted by the European Council and the Council of Ministers of the European Union. In addition, she has to ensure the unity, consistency and effectiveness of the EU's action, represents the EU for CFSP matters, presides over the Foreign Affairs Council, takes part in the work of the European Council and is vice-president of the Commission. Also, being first, Ashton had to manage the complex logistical operation of establishing the European External Action Service (EEAS), which is to support her work.

The EEAS was officially launched in September 2011, but has known a slow start also because the organizational set-up was a main focus in the first year of operation. Slowly but surely, however, the new diplomatic service has changed the EU's functioning not only in Brussels, but also around the world (Drieskens 2012). The delegations of the European Commission in third countries and at international organizations – about 140 offices worldwide – were upgraded to EU delegations and became responsible for representing the EU at the local level. Exploring the EU's post-Lisbon functioning in seven centres for multilateral diplomacy – Brussels, Geneva, Nairobi, New York, Rome, The Hague and Vienna – this volume shows that the introduction of the Lisbon Treaty is still work in progress, not least because the implementation has created resistance from both the EU member states and third countries.

Unfinished business and criticism notwithstanding, the EU decided to go one step further in December 2012. Without giving it much publicity, the EU embarked on a campaign to progressively improve its status in various international organizations, aligning it with the objectives of the Lisbon Treaty. When this volume was submitted to the publisher in June 2013, it was too early to evaluate the campaign, but the Arctic Council had given a first indication that it would not be smooth sailing for the EU. Permanent access to the meetings of this body is seen as increasingly important following the melting of the Arctic ice and the subsequent availability of transport routes and mineral resources. However, while the EU's request for permanent observer status was affirmatively received at the meeting in Kiruna on 15 May 2013, a final decision was postponed. By contrast, China, India, Japan, South Korea, Singapore and Italy managed to secure their seats. Like the EU's upgrade in the UN General Assembly (UNGA; see Chapter 2), the course of events illustrates that the EU may have the ambition to upgrade its status internationally, but that it can only do so by virtue of its international partners. Most probably, to realize its ambitions at the Arctic Council, the EU will have to accommodate Canada and meet its concerns over trade in seal fur.

Awareness that international status requires external recognition may seem to grow rather slowly within the EU, but there was a large consensus during the negotiations of the Lisbon Treaty on the need to define the underlying principles and general objectives of the EU's external action in a way that would be clear to the EU's partners (European Convention 2002: 2). Defining those principles and objectives would make it easier to define common interests and to agree upon a strategy to defend them. Echoing the consensus, the Lisbon Treaty determines that the EU has to develop relations and build partnerships with regional and international organizations and third countries sharing the EU's principles. In that regard, it underlines the EU's adherence to multilateral cooperation and stipulates that the EU shall promote multilateral solutions to common problems, as well as an international system based on stronger multilateral cooperation and good governance. Laatikainen (2013: 472) has aptly summarized this duality in the EU's strategic approach:

> it embraces two somewhat contradictory visions of international order, one based on rule-based multilateral order supported by international organizations and rule of law, the other an explicitly political order wherein great powers jointly coordinate among themselves issues of bilateral and collective concern.

The question is then not only whether multilateralism and multipolarity are compatible organizing principles, but also if the EU's external partners are as like-minded as the EU wants them to be. Recent research shows that they embrace different meanings of what multilateralism entails and how it should be operationalized (see, for instance, Grevi and de Vasconcelos 2008; Bouchard and Peterson 2011; Keukeleire and Bruyninckx 2011; Renard and Biscop 2012; Bouchard *et al.* 2013). Also, they have a different understanding of how multilateralism should be organized. Questioning the Western-centred set-up of multilateral settings, they often demand more inclusiveness. In other words, reform may have dominated the agenda of the EU in recent years with the adoption and implementation of the Lisbon Treaty, but various international organizations have been in reform mode as well in an attempt to adjust their structure to the changing polarity and counter criticisms about a lack of legitimacy, accountability and effectiveness.

Exploring the compatibility between internal and external reform, this volume defines the notion of effectiveness in terms of goal achievement (Jørgensen *et al.*

2011). As explained below, the achievement standards are the objectives on the reform of multilateral settings as specified by the ESS. Doing so, this volume aims to generate new insights for scholars and practitioners with an interest in the EU, but also for those interested in the reform dynamics of global governance more generally.

Scope

Both types of institutional reform are moving targets, yet the tenth anniversary of the introduction of the concept of effective multilateralism offers a unique opportunity for stocktaking. Indeed, it has been ten years since the EU defined its long-standing choice for multilateral cooperation in terms of *effective multilateralism* with the ESS calling for 'an international order based on effective multilateralism' (European Council 2003: 9). Since the genesis of the notion has been well documented, we limit ourselves here to highlighting the main findings (Bailes 2005; Biscop 2005; Biscop and Drieskens 2006; Koops 2011).

Various scholars have traced its origins to the discussions at the UN on the intervention in Iraq in early 2003, which painfully displayed a fundamental lack of agreement between the EU member states serving at the UN Security Council. In an attempt to close ranks, Javier Solana, the EU's then High Representative for Common Foreign and Security Policy, was tasked to elaborate a *strategic concept* at the meeting of the foreign ministers in Kastellorizo on 3 May. A few weeks later, he presented a first draft at the meetings of the External Relations Council (16 June) and the European Council (19–20 June), where he was asked to draft a *security strategy* for adoption at the next European Council meeting. In the following months, the text, which was drafted by a small team headed by Solana, was discussed at expert seminars in Rome (19 September), Paris (6–7 October) and Stockholm (20 October). Deliberations with the EU member states and the Commission were organized as well. On 12 December, the European Council adopted the final text – a 14-page document titled *A Secure Europe in a Better World* and subtitled *European Security Strategy*. Solana was congratulated for the work accomplished and, together with the incoming Dutch Presidency, mandated to elaborate concrete proposals for implementation. Four issues were selected in that regard, including *effective multilateralism with the UN at its core*.

In the years following its adoption, the notion *effective multilateralism* became an important symbol for, even synonym with, the ESS and the EU's intention to reaffirm itself as a coherent and capable international actor (Koops 2011). Providing a unifying concept for the EU's foreign policy objectives, the term has been the guiding principle of many foreign policy documents issued by the EU, notably in relation to the UN. Yet the notion does not have European roots: Robert Kagan introduced it in 2001 to define and delineate the American view of multilateralism. In an opinion article in the *Washington Post* (headlined 'Coalition of the unwilling'), he noted that the real debate was not between unilateralism and multilateralism, but rather between 'effective multilateralism' and 'paralytic multilateralism' (Kagan 2001). In his view, a precondition for an effective form of multilateralism is a unilateral determination to act, as exemplified by the Gulf War coalition of the early 2000s. By contrast, Clinton's attempts at providing a collective response to the Bosnian crisis in the early 1990s were regarded as the example of paralytic multilateralism. In other words, the original meaning of effective multilateralism does not reflect the EU's long-standing preference for and practice of common solutions – a reality that has been explained even in genetic terms suggesting that multilateralism is part of the EU's DNA (see, for instance, Jørgensen 2009).

The ESS suggests that effective multilateralism should be read as *enforceable* multilateralism, but lacks a clear operational definition of the term (Biscop and Drieskens 2006):

> In a world of global threats, global markets and global media, our security and prosperity increasingly depend on an effective multilateral system. The development of a stronger international society, well functioning international institutions and a rule-based international order is our objective.... We want international organisations, regimes and treaties to be effective in confronting threats to international peace and security, and must therefore be ready to act when their rules are broken.
>
> (European Council 2003: 9)

This bold but imprecise language may help explain why the term has drawn considerable scholarly attention, particularly from researchers exploring EU–UN relations (Kissack 2010; Bouchard and Drieskens 2013). As the growing group of scholars exploring the impact of the Lisbon Treaty illustrates, the increase of research on the EU's international functioning often stems from changes to the rules governing the EU's functioning – be it in the form of amendments to the treaties or policy documents. The ESS is then no different. Importantly, while new rules have been added in the meantime, the notion of effective multilateralism continues to inspire scholars ten years later (see, for instance, Krause and Ronzitti 2012; Bouchard *et al.* 2013; Lucarelli *et al.* 2013). As explained below, more recent work examines the EU's practice and performance in various multilateral settings, but also analyses whether the EU's interpretation of multilateralism fits with the changing global multilateralism.

Focus

Laatikainen and Smith (2006) may have underlined the importance of combining internal and external variables when explaining the EU's functioning in international settings already in 2006, but scholarly knowledge has increased only more recently (see Foreword). A growing group of scholars acknowledges that the study of the EU in international affairs cannot be limited to EU variables only and that the variety in and success of the EU's approach are not only determined by the EU's internal decision-making procedures and dynamics, but also by contextual factors (see, for instance, Jørgensen 2009; Kissack 2010; Blavoukos and Bourantonis 2011; Costa and Jørgensen 2012; Laatikainen 2013). Or, as argued elsewhere, the EU may have the ambition of being a *structural* power, but it is also a *structured* one, defined by the international context in which it operates (Drieskens 2009; Delreux *et al.* 2012).

It is within this emerging strand of literature that the present volume is to be situated. Contributors were asked to incorporate an external dimension into their analysis by comparing the EU's perspective on institutional reform with that of its external partners. Some of the volumes mentioned above discuss the issue of reform, but they tend to do so only in passing by. Unlike the present volume, they do not systematically analyse the compatibility between (the international demand for) external reform and (the EU's supply of) internal reform. In fact, few of the scholars that have explored the notion of effective multilateralism, and the ESS more generally, have looked directly at the question of whether the EU has made multilateralism more effective through reform, despite the ESS explicitly formulating that ambition.

More specifically, the ESS stipulates that the EU aims for well-functioning institutions and that strengthening the UN by equipping it to fulfil its responsibilities and to act effectively is a European priority. Regarding the widening of the membership of international organizations, the text refers to the World Trade Organisation (WTO) specifically and to the international financial institutions more generally, stating that the membership of such bodies should be widened 'while maintaining their high standards' (European Council 2003: 9). In a similar vein, the *Report on the Implementation of the European Security Strategy*, which was adopted in 2008, recognized that the international system, as created at the end of the Second World War, 'faces pressures from several fronts' and that the EU's representation has come under question (European Council 2008: 12; see also Conclusion). It was argued that the International Monetary Fund (IMF) and other financial organizations should be adapted 'to reflect modern realities'. Also, the EU should continue the reform of the UN system, seizing the 'unique moment to renew multilateralism' and playing a leading role therein.

> Key institutions in the international system, such as the World Trade Organisation (WTO) and the International Financial Institutions, have extended their membership. China has joined the WTO and Russia is negotiating its entry. It should be an objective for us to widen the membership of such bodies while maintaining their high standards.
>
> (European Council 2003: 9)

> The international system, created at the end of the Second World War, faces pressures on several fronts. Representation in the international institutions has come under question. Legitimacy and effectiveness need to be improved, and decision-making in multilateral fora made more efficient. This means sharing decisions more, and creating greater stake for others.... We should continue reform of the UN system, begun in 2005, and maintain the crucial

role of the Security Council and its primary responsibility for the maintenance of international peace and security. The International Criminal Court should grow further in effectiveness, alongside broader EU efforts to strengthen international justice and human rights. We need to mould the IMF and other financial institutions to reflect modern realities. The G8 should be transformed.

(European Council 2008: 12)

These grand statements raise the question as to what concrete action the EU has taken regarding the reform of the international settings with the aim of making them more effective, as well as to what effect. To provide a balanced answer to this question, this volume explores the EU's functioning in a variety of formal and informal settings both inside and outside of the UN, and is firmly grounded in new empirical research. Most contributors interviewed policy officials to substantiate their claims. No direct quoting will occur, however. The community of diplomats involved is often very small, as a result of which it was often impossible to include names, and also positions or affiliations, both for reasons of informant confidentiality and issue sensitivity.

Contents

The contributions are built around the twin pillars of external and internal reform, and a common set of questions. Contributors were asked to introduce their case by providing a snapshot of the past ten years, notably of the main debates, developments and actors. They discuss the question of external reform by looking into the position of the EU and its member states regarding the reform of the setting studied, the rationale behind the positions as well as their evolution since the ESS was adopted in December 2003. The chapters provide an overview of the concrete initiatives that the EU and its member states have taken in terms of operationalization and evaluate the effectiveness of these measures. Finally, they evaluate to what extent the Lisbon Treaty answers the reform questions that have been raised by the external context. To explore the question of internal reform, contributors look into the effectiveness of the EU's coordination and representation practice and evaluate the EU's *sui generis* nature. Closing the circle, each chapter discusses how the Lisbon Treaty influences the EU's practice and performance. Not only actors and procedures, but also more substantial policy modifications are to be analysed in that regard. In the concluding section, authors summarize the main findings by reflecting upon the fit between internal and external reform. Also, they explore the way forward in terms of how the EU could achieve effective multilateralism in the setting studied.

Chapter 2, by Edith Drieskens, Laura Van Dievel and Yf Reykers, assesses the compatibility of UN and EU reform by looking at what are probably the best known principal organs of the UN, i.e. the UN Security Council (UNSC) and UNGA. Taking a comparative stance, the chapter analyses the EU's answer to the UN's continued search for inclusiveness and revitalization. It develops the argument that while the EU's discourse has been one of effective multilateralism, its practice has been rather selective. More specifically, it demonstrates that the EU has given the notion of effective multilateralism a mainly internal interpretation, equating it with effective participation. It shows that the EU's focus on improving the effectiveness of its participation within those multilateral contexts has continued to prevail after the Lisbon Treaty entered into force, particularly in the context of the UNGA, where the EU tabled a resolution requesting additional observer rights under the guise of strengthening the UN system and encountered an unprecedented high degree of external resistance. The authors conclude that a better balance between internal and external reform would demonstrate that the EU does not only speak about enhancing the effectiveness of multilateral organizations, but also acts accordingly. More to the point, a more constructive attitude on the reform of the UNSC would demonstrate that the EU is as serious about strengthening the UN as it is about strengthening its own position therein.

In *Chapter 3*, Louise G. van Schaik and Samantha Battams examine the complementarity between external and internal reform by looking at the World Health Organization (WHO). The global health landscape may have become increasingly crowded, but this specialized agency still enjoys a special position because of its central role in combating infectious diseases and its global membership. At the same time, it faces financial difficulties as well as criticisms about its structure and its attitude towards the private sector. Exploring the reform process that started in early 2010, the authors demonstrate that the EU has engaged rather cautiously in the debate on WHO reform, focusing on operational rather than substantive questions. The EU has presented common positions, but also brought its own governance experience to the table, notably on matters like stakeholder engagement and transparency. However, it has been punching below its weight. The chapter offers four explanations to explain this state of affairs: internal disagreement on the EU's authority in the field of health, a lack of trust in EU actors taking care of external representation, absence of strong positions on key issues and the EU not engaging in behind-the-scenes diplomacy. Exploring the way forward and providing a glimpse behind the scenes of EU's functioning in Geneva, the authors paint a rather negative picture. Major stumbling blocks are the foreign policy implications of health as a policy domain and the luring question of enhanced status.

Chapter 4 by Robert Kissack assesses the EU's policy of effective multilateralism within the Rome-based Food and Agricultural Organization (FAO). Like the WHO, the FAO is a specialized agency of the UN, but it is unique insofar as the EU has been a fully-fledged member since 1991. Presenting a detailed study of the EU's involvement in the reform process undertaken by the FAO between 2005 and 2012, Kissack finds that the long-established formal institutions of coordination between the member states – both in Brussels and in Rome – served as a useful platform from which to influence the working groups that were charged with reform within the FAO. Even if the EU's initial engagement was seen as leaving the initiative in the hands of the less reform-oriented South, the outcome was widely welcomed across the FAO's membership and very close to the EU's preferences. According to Kissack, the EU may not have been a very visible leader throughout the process, but it deserves recognition for its discrete support, particularly for its roles as bridge builder and facilitator. At the same time, the successful reform of the FAO, and the role of the EU member states in it, has complicated the implementation of the Lisbon Treaty in Rome. Kissack concludes, however, that the shadow of success will not hang over the implementation of Lisbon Treaty forever, because the national diplomats involved in the reform process will literally move on, improving thus also the chances for a better acceptance of the European External Action Service.

Chapter 5, by Tom Delreux, concentrates on the EU's contribution to the reform of the institutional framework for environmental governance and sustainable development. Taking as starting-point that the EU's adherence to multilateralism is very apparent in the environmental domain, it discusses the involvement of the EU and its member states in two decisions that were taken at the Rio+20 summit in June 2012: the decision to strengthen the Nairobi-based United Nations Environment Programme (UNEP) without transforming it from a programme into a specialized agency, and the decision to replace the UN Commission on Sustainable Development with a High Level Political Forum on Sustainable Development. Looking beyond UNEP's failed institutional upgrade, Delreux demonstrates that the EU was rather effective at the Rio+20 summit because its concerns over universal membership and stronger financing were met. The same goes for the creation of the High Level Political Forum on Sustainable Development. Explaining why the EU expressed disappointment notwithstanding these achievements, he lists various contextual factors. More generally, his empirical analysis of the EU's functioning within two international environmental negotiations (i.e. the 10th Conference of the Parties to the Convention on Biological Diversity (Nagoya, October 2010) and the 16th Conference of the Parties to the United Nations Framework on Climate Change (Cancún, November–December 2010) shows that not only external factors, but also internal ones, and particularly the inter-institutional tensions linked to the implementation of the Lisbon Treaty, influence the EU's effectiveness in a rather negative way.

Analysing the development and amendment of the Rome Statute, Laura Davis, in *Chapter 6*, evaluates the EU's contribution to the reform of the International Criminal Court (ICC). The ICC is not formally part of the UN, but has a working relationship with various UN organs. Arguing that the EU's effectiveness is to be situated in the informal sphere, Davis shows that the EU has operationalized its commitment to a more effective ICC by supporting the principles of universality, complementarity and cooperation in its dealings with third countries, notably with African Union members. Exploring the EU's representation and coordination practices, the chapter argues that the Lisbon Treaty has had little impact on the EU's contribution to a more effective organization. Davis recognizes that the new delegations engaging with the host countries on ICC-related business may have a positive effect, but challenges the assumption that one EU voice in the formal bodies of ICC would be the most effective way for the EU to achieve that objective. She demonstrates that EU unity could come at a high price for the ICC because it may reduce the engagement of the more activist member states and result in a lowest-common-denominator approach. In a similar vein, the introduction of regional seats may reduce the ability of the EU member states to build alliances and would likely silence the pro-ICC voices within the African Union. Other initiatives, like the new Special Representative for Human Rights, may have a bigger impact in terms of effectiveness. Put differently, EU effectiveness at the ICC is likely to be discreet.

Chapter 7, by Johanne Glavind, addresses the EU's contribution to the reform of the International Atomic Energy Agency (IAEA). The IAEA, which is based in Vienna, is often seen as the UN's nuclear watchdog because of its inspection activities in countries like Iran. However, like the ICC, it is not formally part of the UN. The organization has been characterized by tensions between North and South, with the North concentrating on security, safety and safeguards, and the South claiming more technical assistance. Glavind shows that the EU does not support grand political reforms because of diverging interests, but tries to affect the IAEA indirectly by supporting smaller reform initiatives. Importantly, the EU's support is not limited to financial and technical measures, yet also has a political dimension, as illustrated by the EU's position regarding the safeguards system resolution and Iran's nuclear programme. Increasing the EU's visibility and influence in the decision-making bodies of the IAEA, the Lisbon Treaty seems to have a positive effect on the interaction between not only the EU delegation and the EU member states, but also between the EU and third countries. The Lisbon Treaty did not change the formal status of EU within the IAEA, though more recent developments suggest that the EU aims for such upgrade. Pointing at the likely risks of external and internal resistance, Glavind writes that formal speaking rights for the EU do not automatically improve the effectiveness of the EU or the IAEA and that the EU's indirect and combined approach to reform should be continued.

Focusing on the relationship between the EU and the North Atlantic Treaty Organization (NATO), in *Chapter 8*, Margriet Drent observes a significant gap between the wording of the ESS and its implementation. The ESS explicitly refers to the importance of a strategic partnership with NATO, but the actual relationship between the EU and NATO has been characterized by political and functional rivalry. Defining this relationship in terms of selective multilateralism, even nihilateralism, she writes that it has remained largely unaffected by the Lisbon reforms of 2007 (EU) and 2010 (NATO) and that it should be understood within the broader trend towards a more pragmatic and flexible approach to security. She develops this argument by assessing four stages (competition, formalization, impasse and informalization) and three fields (crisis management, capability generation and the proliferation of informal contacts) of cooperation. In her view, making effective multilateralism a reality requires a grand bargain with politicians following the example of the staffs of both organizations who have already shown their flexibility in this regard. More generally, Drent raises the question if (effective) multilateralism still has the same meaning as it does in the ESS. After all, multilateral cooperation has become much less institutionalized and formalized, and crisis management settings like the EU and NATO are being used in a rather selective way.

Staying in the security sphere, Niels van Willigen, in *Chapter 9*, explores the EU's contribution to the reform of the Organization for Security and Cooperation in Europe (OSCE). The EU and the OSCE have been seen as natural partners, but the former has been one of the main actors fuelling the identity crisis within the latter, mainly because of decreased financial commitments and an increased focus on the human dimension. Exploring, like Glavind, the EU's functioning in Vienna, van Willigen finds that the EU's internal effectiveness was not seriously harmed by the competences debate that surrounded the implementation of the Lisbon Treaty. In fact, its effectiveness seems to have increased with common positions being the rule rather than the exception. Even if these positions often resemble the lowest common denominator, the EU's coordinated practice seems to enhance its impact on the OSCE's agenda. In terms of reform, however, the EU has taken a rather pragmatic stance by focusing on concrete issues. A grand strategy is lacking. Importantly as well, while the EU has played an enabling role in various projects and missions, it has mainly used the OSCE for its own foreign policy objectives. The *status quo* being one of unequal partners, van Willigen concludes that a less instrumental and more genuine use of the OSCE as a platform for cooperation and dialogue could benefit the EU's policy of effective multilateralism.

Bringing Drent's conclusion on the increased informality of multilateral cooperation to the forefront, the next two chapters focus on the EU's implementation of the notion of effective multilateralism within specific groupings. *Chapter 10*, by Judith Huigens and Arne Niemann, explores the EU's contribution to the reform of the Group of Eight (G8). Following a narrow reading of the ESS, one could argue that informal governance only indirectly contributes to effective multilateralism because it lacks enforcement rules. Moreover, it constitutes a form of interest-based rather than norm-based multilateralism. However, practice shows that the G8 has been able to stimulate and facilitate formal cooperation in various ways, including through reform. Looking into the reconfirmation of the G8 after the creation of the Group of Twenty (G20), the authors find that the EU has worked towards a more effective facilitating role for both the G8 and G20, mainly by strengthening the informality of both settings. This should be no surprise, because the informality of the G8 setting has facilitated the formalized necessity of the EU's presence. The authors conclude that it is not so much the G8 context that challenges the EU's ability to pursue effective multilateralism, but rather the EU's internal arrangements. This holds true after Lisbon, even though its implementation has improved the consistency of the delegation representing the EU within both the G8 and G20.

Chapter 11, by Peter Debaere, Dries Lesage and Jan Orbie, discusses how the EU has been moving closer to the G20. Like Huigens and Niemann, the authors start with the question whether the G20 format is compatible with the notion of effective multilateralism, pointing at both its informal nature and exclusive membership. In order to explore the question of external reform, the chapter first examines the settings' upgrade to the level of heads of state and government and the broadening of its agenda beyond economic and financial issues. The authors write that the EU has only gradually accepted the G20 as a forum for global governance, but now sees it as a stepping-stone towards multilateralism, prioritizing thus 'effective' over 'multilateralism'. Then they look into the run-up to the decision that was taken by the G20 in Gyeongju in October 2010 to reduce the number of European seats on the Executive Board of the IMF. They find that the EU has been rather reluctant to reinforce the IMF despite official proclamations to the contrary. The concluding section shows that the EU's internal reform has largely consisted of flexible and ad hoc responses to the G20 context, particularly in terms of coordination. Like Huigens and Niemann, however, the authors find that the impact of the Lisbon Treaty is limited to streamlining the EU's representation.

Finally, in *Chapter 12*, I summarize the main findings and explore the way forward. Drawing evidence of the empirical chapters in this volume, this concluding chapter provides a balanced picture of the realities of external and internal reform and their complementarity. The proposals that were put forward with regard to the revision of the ESS in preparation of the European Council meeting of December 2013 serve as stepping-stones for the discussion.

Conclusion

The purpose of this introductory chapter was to provide a context for, and an overview of, the empirical chapters that follow. It defined the research focus in terms of reform and outlined the questions that have framed those chapters. It was argued that reform is an important research focus within the field of EU studies, but that it has been given a mainly internal interpretation.

Taking the EU as point of departure, most scholars have concentrated their analysis on the EU's effectiveness in multilateral settings and explored the implementation of internal reform measures like the Lisbon Treaty. Few have taken those settings as point of departure and analysed the EU's response to the growing demand for making those settings more effective.

The following chapters will explore the compatibility between internal and external reform in a systematic way. Doing so, this volume aims to contribute to a more comprehensive understanding of the notion of effective multilateralism, particularly of its operationalization in the decade following its introduction in EU foreign policy.

References

Bailes, A.K. (2005) *The European Security Strategy: an evolutionary history*, Stockholm: SIPRI (SIPRI Policy Paper No. 10).

Biscop, S. (2005) *The European Security Strategy: a global agenda for positive power*, Aldershot: Ashgate.

Biscop, S. and Drieskens, E. (2006) 'Effective multilateralism and collective security: empowering the UN', in K.V. Laatikainen and K.E. Smith (eds) *The European Union at the United Nations: intersecting multilateralisms*, Basingstoke: Palgrave Macmillan, pp. 115–32.

Blavoukos, S. and Bourantonis, D. (eds) (2011) *The EU presence in international organizations*, New York: Routledge.

Bouchard, C. and Drieskens, E. (2013) 'The European Union in UN politics', in K.E. Jørgensen and K.V. Laatikainen (eds) *Routledge Handbook on the European Union and international institutions: performance, policy power*, London: Routledge, pp. 115–27.

Bouchard, C. and Peterson, J. (2011) *Conceptualising multilateralism: can we all just get along?* MERCURY E-paper no. 1, January 2011. Online. Available http://mercury.uni-koeln.de/fileadmin/user_upload/E-paper_no1_r2010.pdf (accessed 15 May 2013).

Bouchard, C., Peterson, J. and Tocci, N. (2013) *Multilateralism in the 21st century: Europe's quest for effectiveness*, London: Routledge.

Costa, O. and Jørgensen, K.E. (eds) (2012) *The influence of international institutions on the EU: when multilateralism hits Brussels*, Houndmills: Palgrave Macmillan.

Delreux, T., Drieskens, E., Kerremans, B. and Damro, C. (2012) 'The external institutional context matters: the EU in international negotiations', in O. Costa and K.E. Jørgensen (eds) *The influence of international institutions on the EU: when multilateralism hits Brussels*, Houndmills: Palgrave Macmillan, pp. 58–74.

Drieskens, E. (2009) 'Walking on eggshells: non-permanent members searching for an EU perspective at the UN Security Council', in J. Wouters, E. Drieskens and S. Biscop (eds) *Belgium in the UN Security Council: reflections on the 2007–2008 membership*, Antwerp: Intersentia, pp. 175–85.

Drieskens, E. (2012) 'What's in a name? Challenges to the creation of EU delegations', *The Hague Journal of Diplomacy*, 7(1): 51–64.

European Convention (2002) *Final report of Working Group VII on External Action* (CONV 459/02). Online. Available http://european-convention.eu.int/pdf/reg/en/02/cv00/cv00459.en02.pdf (accessed 15 May 2013).

European Council (2003) *A Secure Europe in a better world: European Security Strategy*, Brussels, 12 December 2003.

European Council (2008) *Report on the implementation of the European Security Strategy: providing security in a changing world*, Brussels, 11 December 2008.

Grevi, G. and de Vasconcelos, A. (eds) (2008) *Partnerships for effective multilateralism: EU relations with Brazil, China, India and Russia*, Chaillot Paper no. 109, Paris: Institute for Security Studies.

Jørgensen, K.E. (ed.) (2009) *The European Union and international organizations*, London: Routledge.

Jørgensen, K.E., Oberthür, S. and Shahin, J. (2011) 'Introduction: assessing the EU's performance in international institutions – Conceptual framework and core findings', *Journal of European Integration*, 33(6): 599–620.

Kagan, R. (2001) 'Coalition of the unwilling', *Washington Post*, 17 October 2001.

Kajnc, S., Jans, T. and Courtier, A. (2012) 'The Belgian Presidency and the new leadership architecture under Lisbon', in S. Van Hecke and P. Bursens (eds) *Readjusting the Council Presidency: Belgian leadership in the EU*, Brussels: ASP, pp. 221–42.

Keukeleire, S. and Bruyninckx, H. (2011) 'The European Union, the BRICs and the emerging new world order', in C. Hill and M. Smith (eds) *International relations and the European Union*, Houndmills: Palgrave Macmillan, pp. 380–403.

Kissack, R. (2010) *Pursuing effective multilateralism: the European Union, international organisations and the politics of decision making*, Houndmills: Palgrave Macmillan.

Kissack, R. (2013) 'The European Union and multilateralism', in K.E. Jørgensen and K.V. Laatikainen (eds) *Routledge Handbook on the European Union and international institutions: performance, policy power*, London: Routledge, pp. 405–15.

Koops, J. (2011) *The European Union as an integrative power?* Brussels: VUBPRESS.

Krause, J. and Ronzitti, N. (eds) (2012) *The EU, the UN and collective security: making multilateralism effective*, London: Routledge.

Laatikainen, K.V. (2013) 'EU multilateralism in a multipolar world', in K.E. Jørgensen and K.V. Laatikainen (eds) *Routledge Handbook on the European Union and international institutions: performance, policy power*, London: Routledge, pp. 472–87.

Laatikainen, K.V. and Smith, K.E. (eds) (2006) *The European Union at the United Nations: intersecting multilateralisms*, Houndmills: Palgrave Macmillan.

Lucarelli, S., Van Langenhove, L. and Wouters, J. (eds) (2013) *The EU and multilateral security governance*, London: Routledge.

Renard, T. and Biscop, S. (eds) (2012) *The European Union and emerging powers in the 21st century: how Europe can shape a new global order*, Farnham: Ashgate.

Vanhoonacker, S., Pomorska, K. and Mauer, H. (2012) 'Belgium at the helm of EU external relations: a successful "non-presidency"', in S. Van Hecke and P. Bursens (eds) *Readjusting the Council Presidency: Belgian leadership in the EU*, Brussels: ASP, pp. 65–78.

2 The EU's search for effective participation at the UN General Assembly and UN Security Council

Edith Drieskens, Laura Van Dievel and Yf Reykers

Introduction

This chapter analyses the EU's reading of the notion of effective multilateralism by exploring the EU's contribution to the reform of two principal organs of the UN, i.e. the UN General Assembly (UNGA) and UN Security Council (UNSC). Assessing the compatibility of UN and EU reform, it develops the argument that the EU has given the notion a mainly internal interpretation, equating it with effective participation. Rather than focusing on the reform of the UN as a multi-lateral setting, the EU has concentrated on improving the effectiveness of its participation within that setting. This internal focus has continued to prevail after the Lisbon Treaty entered into force, particularly in the context of the UNGA, where the EU tabled a resolution requesting additional observer rights under the guise of strengthening the UN system.

The chapter consists of three parts. The first part discusses the EU's position and performance regarding the question of reform, both for the UNSC and UNGA. The second part analyses the EU's effectiveness within those organs. It discusses the mechanisms for coordination and representation, and evaluates the impact of the Lisbon Treaty. By linking the questions of external and internal reform, the concluding part summarizes the main findings and explores the way forward.

The seemingly never-ending story of UN reform

This chapter looks into the setting whose functioning spurred the introduction of the notion of effective multilateralism in the European Security Strategy (ESS), i.e. the UNSC. The split over the intervention in Iraq in early 2003 and the deci-sion of the US to bypass this body made the EU redefine its long-term history of multilateral cooperation in terms of effective multilateralism (Biscop and Drieskens 2006; see Introduction). More specifically, calling for an 'international order based on effective multilateralism', it defined the UN Charter as the funda-mental framework for international relations and confirmed that the UNSC holds the primary responsibility for the maintenance of international peace and security (European Council 2003: 9). During the crisis, the EU was very visible within this body, though in a negative way, with France and Germany diametrically opposing Spain and the UK over the question of intervention. Javier Solana, who acted as the EU's High Representative for the Common Foreign and Security Policy between 1999 and 2009, explained the course of events by pointing at the EU's representation, stating that

> [t]he EU is not represented by one seat in the UN.... What makes it difficult for the EU and me is that the EU has four members in the UNSC.... The lesson we learnt is that Europe is losing influence when it does not speak with one voice.
>
> (Die Welt 2003: para. 4; authors' translation)

In doing so, he touched upon a recurring theme in the debate on UN reform, i.e. the EU's perceived overrepresentation at the UNSC.

As explained in the Introduction to this volume, the ESS emphasizes that the EU aims for well-functioning institutions and that strengthening the UN by equipping it to fulfil its responsibilities and to act effectively is a European priority. However, as regards the widening and the deepening of the membership of international institutions, the text only refers to the World Trade Organisation and the international financial institutions. In comparison, the *Report on the Implementation of the European Security Strategy*, which was adopted five years later in 2008, recognizes that the international system, as created at the end of the Second World War, faces 'pressures from several fronts' and that the EU's representation in international institutions 'has come under question' (European Council 2008: 12). It was argued that the EU should 'continue' the reform of the UN system, without specifying organs or bodies. Focusing on the reform of the UNGA and UNSC, this chapter demonstrates that it has done so in a rather selective way. The discourse has been one of effective multilateralism; the practice of selective multilateralism.

Importantly, the Iraq debacle did not only spur reflection in Brussels, but also gave a new impulse to the reform discussions in New York. Those discussions gained momentum when the UN was approaching its 60th birthday in 2005, at least for a short time. Expressing his view in *Foreign Affairs* in May 2005 and referring to the city where the UN was established, then UN Secretary-General Kofi Annan called for 'a new San Francisco moment' (Annan 2005: 65). Encouraging the members to make 'the most-far reaching reform' in UN history, he laid out a broad agenda (Annan 2005: 74). At the same time, he admitted that reform would be incomplete without changing the composition of the UNSC. The latter holds the primary responsibility for the maintenance of international peace and security, and its decisions are binding for all UN members. Discussions started almost immediately after its setup, yet it was particularly following its increased activity after the end of the Cold War that the reform question gained momentum (Bourantonis 2005). However, the composition of the UNSC changed only once, in 1963, when four non-permanent members were added. Ever since, the UNSC has had 15 members, of which five have a permanent seat including veto rights. As a result, the UNSC is often portrayed as a relic of the past. Virtually everyone seems to agree that the membership of the UNSC should be given a more representative nature and be aligned with current political realities. The question is, however, how this can be done.

The membership of the UNSC may be the hardest nut to crack, but the reform agenda includes a diversity of items, including also the relationship with the UNGA. The latter is often seen as the main deliberative organ of the UN (Karns and Mingst 2009). It has been negatively portrayed as a talking shop, yet has binding decision-making power regarding elections and budget, as well as for amending the UN Charter. More positively, the UNGA has been portrayed as a model of representativeness because every UN member has a seat of its own as well as the right to vote. Since the end of the Cold War, however, and especially following the reactivation of the UNSC, the demand for reform has grown. A resolution on revitalizing the UNGA is now adopted every year. As for the UNSC, change has occurred, often through small improvements in working methods, but substantial reform remains lacking, mainly because of fundamental differences in opinion between North and South.

Looking at the last ten years, the first part of this chapter explores the reform of both organs and the EU's contribution thereto. The second part raises the question if and how that contribution has been influenced by what could be seen as the EU's latest internal reform measure, i.e. the Lisbon Treaty. Doing so, it aims to evaluate the compatibility of both types of reform. A bonus of this dual perspective is that it allows for answering the question that was raised by Mario Monti during the confirmation hearing of Catherine Ashton at the European Parliament on 11 January 2010, namely whether the EU should have its own seat at the UNSC. Seemingly taken by surprise, Ashton did not come further than the following answer: 'I don't know. This has not even crossed my thinking. You've caught me out. Well done' (Barber 2010: para. 12). As we explain below, the parameters that define the answer to the question raised are clear and have not changed in recent years. Sticking with the facts, Ashton could have simply replied that the support for introducing regional seats at the UNSC is limited, both within the UN and the EU, and that the Lisbon Treaty does not point in such a direction – quite the contrary. That said, the question could have been expected because of the European Parliament's maximalist position on the EU's functioning at the UN, but also because of the EU's ambitions regarding the implementation of the Lisbon Treaty in the UNGA.

We start building our argument by discussing the *status quo* of the reform of both the UNGA and UNSC in 2013, and the main developments that have characterized the decade following the 2003 introduction of the notion of effective multilateralism.

External reform: the search for inclusiveness and revitalization

The *Open-Ended Working Group on the Question of Equitable Representation on and Increase in the Membership of the Security Council and Other Matters Related to the Security Council* (OEWG) was established in 1993 to channel the discussions on the reform of the UNSC. When the members started their deliberations one year later, they were convinced that the reform would be completed the following year, just in time before the UN's 50th anniversary. Twenty years later, however, there is still no agreement, even if various initiatives were taken. Luck writes in this regard that the typical cycle of UN reform begins with political leaders denouncing the *status quo* and calling for new initiatives (Luck 2005). In a following step, a high-level commission is established to substantiate their concerns. Next, the commission's vision for the future is translated into policy measures for consideration by the membership. Closing the circle, a culminating event is organized, preferably at a symbolic moment. Remarkably, while little reform is usually accomplished, officials tend to present the conclusions as a breakthrough. At the same time, they recognize that the work is unfinished and express renewed dedication, laying thus the basis for a new round of discussions. Each cycle of reform has left its imprint, 'even if only because its unsettled issues have laid the basis for the next one' (Luck 2006: 653).

Echoing this pattern, three main episodes can be distinguished in the last ten years. The first one starts with Kofi Annan setting up the *High-Level Panel on Threats, Challenges and Change* in November 2003. Bringing together eminent persons and chaired by the former prime minister of Thailand, Anand Panyarachun, the panel was given the task to formulate recommendations about the changes necessary to ensure effective collective action, including also a review of the principal organs (United Nations Secretary-General's High-level Panel 2004). Unable to reach an agreement, the panel presented two models for the reform of the UNSC in December 2004. Both of them were endorsed by Annan in his *In Larger Freedom Report* in March 2005. In the same report, he wrote that a decision on the reform of the UNSC had to be reached before the start of the Millennium Review Summit in September 2005 (United Nations Secretary-General 2005). He preferred a decision taken by consensus, but he did not exclude a vote. However, it was only a matter of weeks before alternative proposals began circulating again. Unable to regain the momentum lost, the Millennium Review Summit failed to produce concrete results regarding the reform of the UNSC.

Haya Rashed Al-Khalifa made a new attempt when she presided over the UNGA during the 61st session (September 2006–7). She invited the membership to start consultations around five key issues and appointed five permanent representatives as facilitators: the size of an enlarged Security Council (Muñoz of Chile), the categories of membership (Hachani of Tunisia), the question of regional representation (Mladineo of Croatia), the question of the veto (Mavroyiannis of Cyprus), the working methods of the Security Council and the relationship between the Security Council and the General Assembly (Majoor of the Netherlands). In April 2007, after three months of consultations, a report was issued proposing a *transitional* or *interim* stage of reform. In terms of follow-up, the permanent representatives of Chile and Liechtenstein were asked to conduct further negotiations. In their report of June 2007, they confirmed that a temporary arrangement might be the best option, perhaps even the only one, because views diverged on how to proceed. As a result, Al-Khalifa's chairmanship came to an end without the much-hoped breakthrough.

The latest episode started in September 2007, when the UNGA adopted a resolution stipulating that the reform of the UNSC should be considered during the next session so that further concrete steps could be achieved, including through intergovernmental negotiations. The latter negotiations were established in September 2008 and have been chaired ever since by Zahir Tanin, the Afghan ambassador to the UN. More than four years later, Tanin could present a 31-page inventory document that compiled a multitude of options and was written in resolution-format (Tanin 2011). A reform proposal that is supported by the required majority at the UNGA was still lacking.[1] In fact, the discussions held in 2012 were not characterized by negotiations on the inventory document, but rather by lengthy discussions on five different proposals from five different groups. Despite the slow progress, Tanin was re-appointed as chairman of the negotiations in November 2012.

The five proposals that were discussed in 2012 were the ones of the following groups: G-4, UfC, L.96, C-10 and S-5. The last proposal (by the Small Five, i.e. Costa Rica, Jordan, Liechtenstein, Singapore, Switzerland) concentrates on the reform of the UNSC's working methods; the others on the membership. The G-4-proposal (by the Group of Four, i.e. Germany, Japan, India, Brazil) supports the expansion of both permanent and non-permanent seats. Unsurprisingly, those countries request a permanent seat for themselves, but also for Africa. By contrast, the UfC-proposal (by the Uniting for Consensus group) does not add permanent seats, but introduces a new category of seats with a longer term of up to six years and increases the number of non-permanent seats. It is no secret that the UfC-movement symbolizes Italy's protest against Germany's bid for permanent membership and includes countries who fear becoming second-rank powers in their respective neighbourhoods when the G-4 have permanent seats. Referring to draft resolution A/61/L.96, the L.96 plan is supported by countries from Africa, Latin America and the Caribbean, and suggests an expansion of both permanent and non-permanent members. Finally, the proposal of the C-10 (i.e. the committee of ten African states that negotiates on behalf of the African countries) supports the common position on UN reform that was adopted by the African Union (AU) in March 2005 and is better known as the Ezulwini Consensus. In the UNSC, the African countries want at least two permanent seats and five non-permanent ones.

The AU's organization and representation in the ongoing intergovernmental negotiations contrasts with the EU. Unlike their African counterparts, the EU member states do not have a common position or a specific representative who negotiates on their behalf. The EU has repeated insistently that it supports a comprehensive reform of the UN, including of the UNSC, but it has undertaken little concrete action in practice, including towards formulating a common position (Hill 2006). There is a clear gap between rhetoric and policy, between intentions and actions. In fact, it seems to have taken a 'back seat' (Laatikainen and Smith 2006: 19), leaving the front seats to the member states. The same goes for other regional groupings, so the AU could be seen as the exception to the rule. The question is whether one should not expect more from an actor that claims to be entitled to enhanced rights and privileges (see below).

Most EU member states, including France and the UK, support the proposal of the G-4. By contrast, Italy, Spain and Malta have joined the UfC movement – with Italy even acting as focal point. Both sides, however, have invoked the EU in their rhetoric and argued that their respective proposals would strengthen its international presence (Blavoukos and Bourantonis 2013). In reality, however, the lack of agreement has hampered the EU's credibility in promoting effective multilateralism, demonstrating that 'the EU's own machinery is far from being "effective"' (Ortega 2005: 13), but also progress in New York (Roos *et al.* 2008; Rufino 2005). The lack of urgency can be explained by the *status quo* benefitting the EU member states. The current distribution of seats favours these countries (see below), while the lack of progress gives them respite on closing ranks.[2] In fact, only one initiative can be mentioned in this regard. As part of the broader momentum on UN reform and following the adoption of the AU's common position on Annan's proposals (see above), the idea to present a similar EU position surfaced in the margins of the European Council meeting of 22 and 23 March 2005, also if no agreement would be reached on the reform of the UNSC and the use of force (Rufino 2005; Ginsberg and Penska 2012). Yet again, the European leaders were not able to move beyond rhetoric. When defining the EU's priorities at the Brussels European Council of 16 and 17 June 2005, they resorted to standard language. Masking dissent, they concluded that it was essential to achieve a balanced and ambitious outcome enabling the UN to be reformed so that it could respond more practically and effectively to the threats and challenges identified. Similar vague language had already been included in the EU's contribution to the High-Level Panel, and has been used ever since, in speeches and priorities lists, also now that the Lisbon Treaty is in force.

Likewise, the Lisbon Treaty did not change the fact that the EU member states have very different views on the reform of the UNSC, or that they see the membership of the UNSC as a national prerogative (see below). True, some EU member states have referred to the creation of an EU seat at the UNSC as a long-term goal of European integration, but a few of them have joined the European Parliament in advocating a permanent seat for the EU in the short run – the most notorious exception being Italy.[3] In fact, a detailed look at the different positions suggests that the introduction of regional seats does not seem to be on the cards at the moment. Tanin's inventory confirms that various members want a better representation of certain regions, though not by introducing collective seats, but rather by adapting the distribution of individual ones. His first mapping, which dates back from 2009, revealed that most UN members think that the principle of equitable geographical distribution should be exercised through 'existing structures' (United Nations General Assembly 2009: 13–18). For many delegations, regional seats are 'not feasible' because of the different character of the regional groupings and the differences in their working methods. Moreover, a wide number of delegations felt that the non-permanent UNSC members could not represent their respective regions, as they have a 'global accountability' and an obligation to 'the international community as a whole'.

The five facilitators mentioned above had reached a similar conclusion. Their report left many questions unanswered, but not that of regional representation. They recognized that there is a dual understanding of the notion 'regional representation', with some delegations seeing it as identical to the notion of equitable geographical representation and others understanding it as regional accountability (United Nations General Assembly President 2007: 14). Yet the introduction of regional seats was not considered an option because of the different nature of the regional groupings and the differences in their internal working procedures. Like Tanin, they found that the majority of the UN membership was still convinced that the principle of equitable geographic distribution should be exercised 'through the existing rules' and that seats for 'political organizations' would go against the UN's intergovernmental nature.

The continuing deadlock does not mean that there has been no improvement. However, if improvements were made, it was mainly in relation to working methods and this was not an unqualified success either. Some even write about 'revitalisation fatigue' (Swart 2008: 21). Numerous recommendations have been formulated, but few decisions have been taken. Moreover, even if decisions are taken, implementation continues to be lacking. True, a momentum was created in 2012, when Portugal chaired the *Informal Working Group on Documentation and Other Procedural Questions* (Security Council Report 2012). Together with the UK, for instance, who presided over the UNSC in March 2012, Portugal drafted a non-paper focusing on periodicity, conference resources, interactivity and the use of videoconferencing, following which those topics were discussed at ambassadorial level. But 2012 also had its downs. Most visibly, the S-5 (see above) decided to withdraw a draft resolution with 20 recommendations following pressure of the permanent members.

The leading role of the UK is no surprise. France and the UK are relatively open to reform, especially in comparison to the other permanent members. That open attitude can be seen as an attempt to justify their great power status in a world that is fundamentally different from six decades ago. The same has been said for their work ethic (Mahbubani 2004: 258–61). Indeed, both countries have been criticized for their permanent status, but practitioners tend to see them as the most active permanent members of the UNSC, even as the driving force ('particularly hard-working members'; Løj 2007: 33).

While there is no lack of literature on the reform of the UNSC, the same cannot be said about the UNGA. Surprisingly little attention has been paid to the fact that the working methods of the UNGA have also been subject of discussion, as well as to the revitalization of the UNGA more generally. Most authors discuss the UNGA only in passing and limit their analysis to the observation that the revitalization of the UNGA has a different connotation in North and South (Zifcak 2006). Most of the southern countries see the revitalization of the UNGA as a political matter. Arguing that the streamlining of working methods is only a means to an end and not the end itself, they ask for a reconsideration of the relationship with the UNSC as to strengthen the UNGA's central position in the UN system. By contrast, northern countries do not see the revitalization of the UNGA as a political question, but rather as a procedural or technical one. This group also includes the EU member states, which favour, for instance, the enhanced scheduling of meetings and debates, the introduction of electronic voting, better documentation management as well as timely translation. The following section explores the EU's answer to the external reform challenges in more detail. Concentrating on the Lisbon Treaty, it demonstrates that the demand and supply of reform are not equal.

Internal reform: the search for effective participation

The UNGA and UNSC can be seen as opposite ends of a continuum of EU representation and coordination (Bouchard and Drieskens 2013). The EU's practice at the UNGA is located towards the maximalist end; its functioning within the UNSC towards the minimalist one. As for representation, being UN members, all 28 EU member states have individual seats at the UNGA. In addition, the EU enjoys observer status. As of May 2011, this status includes new rights and privileges (see below). The picture is very different at the UNSC, where the EU's representation is de facto limited to a maximum of six member states. France and the UK have permanent seats; the others may obtain a two-year seat if elected by their respective electoral groupings. Being dispersed over three such groupings, the EU member states have three ponds to fish from. The older member states are part of Western Europe and Others Group (WEOG); the newer ones of the Eastern European Group (EEG).[4] There is one exception: Cyprus belongs to the Asia-Pacific Group. Whereas the African countries discuss their candidates within the framework of the AU, there is no EU coordination regarding candidacies, in Brussels or New York. A perceived lack of fit between the process of EU integration and the historically defined electoral groupings at the UN explains this, like the fact that a seat at the UNSC is still seen as a national prerogative. Moreover, as stated above, the status quo is beneficial from an EU point of view, even if the lack of coordination results in EU member states competing against each other and in UN members supporting non-EU candidates in protest against what they see as overrepresentation. In fact, the organization of coordination could even strengthen the latter argument.

Coordination, however, is often seen as the EU's *modus vivendi* in New York, particularly because more than 1,300 coordination meetings are organized on a yearly basis. This practice has resulted in a high overall degree of voting cohesion, notably at the UNGA, but also in the often-heard criticism that the EU is self-absorbed. Authors point at increasing levels of unity between the EU member states, except for security-related issues (Bouchard and Drieskens 2013).[5] However, percentages differ between studies because different calculation methods are used. Although some general trends can be noted, one should thus be careful with a direct comparison of findings. Also, most authors use the EU as reference point, raising the question if new steps of integration lead to increased unity. Few compare the EU's performance with other regional players. The exception is Rasch, who found that some regional organizations outperform the EU in terms of voting coherence even if their cooperation, coordination and representation at the UN is everything but comparable to the EU (Rasch 2008).

Equally important for our present purpose is that the EU's activities at the UNSC are less extensive than those at the UNGA. Granted, the new High Representative for Foreign Affairs and Security Policy is invited to the UNSC to present the EU's position in open debates – a task that is usually carried out by EUDEL (EU Delegation to the United Nations). But the representative rules that are included in the EU Treaty give the EU member states more leeway within this body, allowing them to defend the positions and interests of the EU without prejudice of their responsibilities under the UN Charter.[6] In practice, there is no systematic coordination between the (serving) EU member states, only systematic information-sharing with the non-serving ones. That said, the EU member states are the only UN members that are informed in such a manner because of their regional membership. In other words, when looking from an EU perspective, even from an UNGA one, the EU may seem absent at the UNSC, but looking from the latter's perspective it is rather present. This focus, yet also research on the EU at the UNSC more generally, remains limited. We explained elsewhere that studying the EU at the UNSC requires extensive fieldwork and process-tracing because the explanatory value of voting cohesion is limited (Drieskens 2012a). Looking then for alternative measurements, Blavoukos and Bourantonis analysed the EU member states' (co-)sponsorship of UNSC resolutions, as well as their financial contribution to peacekeeping. They concluded that EU's performance in the UNSC debate may be 'meager', but its contribution to the UNSC is 'by and large positive' (Blavoukos and Bourantonis 2011: 738–9). The question is then if and how that conclusion is affected by the introduction of the Lisbon Treaty.

In the post-Lisbon era, EU coordination at the UN is organized by the *EU Delegation to the United Nations* (EUDEL). Replacing the rotating Presidency for CFSP-related matters, EUDEL also delivers EU statements in plenary and commission meetings within the UNGA and represents the EU vis-à-vis external partners.[7] By replacing the rotating presidency with a more permanent structure, the Lisbon Treaty intends to increase the coherence and visibility of the EU's external representation. Granted, permanent presence may result in knowledge building and thus positively influence coordination. But the Lisbon Treaty only changed the actor that is responsible for organizing coordination between the EU member states, not the coordination practice as such or the variety in practice among the various UN settings. In fact, in terms of setting, the Lisbon Treaty explicitly defines its boundaries. Declaration 14 stipulates that the new provisions do not affect the responsibilities and powers of the member states in relation to their UNSC membership. It is not only this declaration and the fact that the role of the rotating presidency was rather developed at the UNGA that explain why the impact of the Lisbon Treaty has been the highest at the UNGA, but also the EU's quest for enhanced status. In what follows, we reconstruct the process that led to the adoption of the resolution granting the EU the representative rights that allowed Van Rompuy to address the UNGA's General Debate in September 2011.[8] This reconstruction shows that the EU was guided by the question 'who is representing the EU?' and prioritized messengers over messages and form over content, especially in the early stages.

Case study: the status saga

Episode 1

The EU rapidly targeted the UNGA as test case for introducing the new institutional arrangements for external representation that are included in the Lisbon Treaty. This setting was an obvious choice: the EU could build upon a solid basis as it already enjoyed observer status (see above). Reflection on the New York implementation of the Lisbon Treaty started under the Slovenian Presidency in spring 2008, but few initiatives were taken before the Irish referendum in late 2009. Following ratification, the EU embarked on a campaign to acquire additional rights for its new representatives. The wish list included privileges such as the right to speak in a timely manner, to circulate documents, to make proposals, to submit amendments, to raise points of order, to exercise the right of reply, and to be afforded adequate seating arrangements (United Nations General Assembly 2010b). The rights to challenge decisions of the presiding officer, to vote, or to put forward candidates, however, were not included. The EU wished for an UNGA resolution granting those rights to be adopted by consensus and more importantly, before the start of the 65th session. In EU circles it was argued that Herman Van Rompuy addressing the General Debate in September 2010 alongside other heads of state and government would be a strong symbol of the EU's newly defined identity as a global actor. Indeed, while text was submitted under the agenda item on 'Strengthening the United Nations system', claiming that,

> when an organisation for regional integration develops common external policies and establishes permanent structures for their conduct and representation, the General Assembly may benefit from the *effective participation* in its deliberations of that organisation's external representatives speaking on behalf of the organisation and its member States
>> (United Nations General Assembly 2010b; emphasis added),

the main focus was on the EU.

The EU's aspirations, however, were smashed to pieces on 14 September 2010, when the UNGA voted to postpone the debate on the EU's request following an intervention by the Caribbean Community (CARICOM). The latter claimed that more time was needed for consultation because the resolution would significantly change the working methods and the interaction among states (United Nations General Assembly 2010a). Likewise, the African Group and the small island states expressed their doubts about the EU's initiative. CARICOM's request to defer the vote was supported by 76 countries; 71 voted against and 26 abstained. More significantly, the countries that supported the adjournment or abstained included some of the EU's strongest allies like Canada, Australia and New Zealand.

With the vote on the EU's status being shelved, the EU decided not to speak at the General Debate that followed a few days later. It distributed a written statement saying that as an observer it could not participate 'under existing UN General Assembly practices' (European Union 2010). It appears that the team of Ashton rejected suggestions of resorting to the pre-Lisbon practice in which the EU member state holding the rotating presidency addressed the General Debate on behalf of the EU. The official explanation given by the EU at the time was that any efforts to enhance its status would have been in vain, though some have interpreted the EU's silence as a sign of protest.

Indeed, the EU felt that it had spared no effort to consult UN members, especially in the immediate run-up to the vote. Originally scheduled for 13 September 2010, the vote was postponed to allow for additional consultations and *démarches* in both Brussels and New York. Belgium, holding the seat of rotating EU presidency at the time, decided to use the 24-hour window of opportunity to suggest textual amendments. It hoped to answer the concerns of some Arab and African countries by opening the door for additional representative rights for other regional groupings, 'once they had reached the level of integration that would enable them to speak with one voice' (Belgian Presidency of the Council of the European Union 2010). Likewise, stronger language on the UN's intergovernmental nature and specifications on the choice of each regional organization for the modalities of its external representation were introduced to convince countries such as Argentina and Brazil and meet some of CARICOM's concerns.

The EU member states were well aware that success was not guaranteed when they tabled the amended draft one day later. CARICOM, without a doubt the most challenging interlocutor in the process, considered asking for an adjournment. Yet also the African Group had not yet reached a common position and the small island states wanted more time to study the EU proposal. Countries opposing further regionalization of the UN – Russia in particular – also had expressed their doubts. Nonetheless, the heads of mission of the EU member states decided to go ahead as this was their last chance during the 64th session, with the known result.

In hindsight, the following factors seem to have created a recipe for disaster: the *cavalier seul* ('going it alone') approach adopted by EUDEL (see above) and its small staff size; the limited support of the national capitals of the EU member states (and the ambivalent attitude of the UK in particular); a lack of negotiations on the resolution's text with external partners; the introduction of amendments at the very last minute; the EU's outspokenness in New York in the autumn (for instance, criticizing China's human rights record in the Third Committee); the elections in the UNSC (with Canada being candidate for a non-permanent seat); and the autonomous stance of some permanent representatives (notably the permanent representative of Jamaica). Furthermore, officials have pointed to more fundamental problems to explain the EU's failure. First, there was a clear gap between countries that hoped for a precedent (like African and Arab countries) and those that feared one (including the small island states, who feared a change in the balance of power, but also countries that oppose further regionalization). Second, certain UN members raised the question of reciprocity and perceived the EU as arrogant because it was asking without giving.[9]

Episode 2

The EU quickly concluded that it had encountered a procedural obstacle. Additional outreach was organized to break the local UN dynamics. A task force was established to coordinate and support the activities in New York, Brussels and third countries. Also the national capitals became more closely involved. In addition, the EU's wish list was rewritten to move the focus from the EU to the UN. The numbers speak for themselves: the first wish list mentioned the Lisbon Treaty five times in as many paragraphs, the revised list does not mention it any longer. The strategy paid off: a vast majority of the UN members approved the EU's revised wish list on 3 May 2011. The text was adopted with 180 votes in favour. Only two countries abstained; none voted against (see below).

The EU was granted the following rights in the sessions and the work of the UNGA and its committees and working groups, in international meetings and conferences convened under the auspices of the UNGA as well as in UN conferences: to be inscribed on the list of speakers with priority equivalent to that given to representatives of major groups; to participate in the General Debate, taking into account the practice for participating observers; to have its communications circulated directly and without intermediary, as documents of the UNGA meeting or conference; to make proposals and submit amendments; to raise points of order but not to challenge decisions of the presiding officer; and to exercise the right of reply (United Nations General Assembly 2011a).[10] The EU's representatives, who remain seated among the observers, do not have the right to vote or to put forward candidates. The amendments suggested by the Belgian Presidency (see above) were also included in the text, though after revision. As a result, regional organizations that enjoy observer status can now claim similar rights when their members 'have agreed arrangements that allow that organisation's representatives to speak on behalf of the organization and its member states' (United Nations General Assembly 2010b). The EU is thus no longer used as point of reference for upgrading the status of regional actors – unlike in the original version of the Belgian Presidency.

With 148 countries voting in favour, it is fair to say that the EU won a land-slide victory. Only Syria and Zimbabwe abstained; Azerbaijan, Ivory Coast, Kiribati, Libya, Nauru, Rwanda, Somalia, Sri Lanka, Vanuatu and Venezuela did not participate in the vote. In other words, the EU won over most UN members, but did not convince all of its aid beneficiaries. In fact, most EU member states were reticent to a consequential policy in which the power of the purse would be used, because of the danger that this could backfire. The EU tried nevertheless to address the Pacific islands' concerns over climate change and fisheries, announcing, for instance, new funding opportunities during a high-level conference in Vanuatu in early March 2011 within the framework of the *Joint EU–Pacific Initiative on Climate Change*. By contrast, the EU's consistent lobbying for CARICOM's support paid off: all its full and associate members voted in favour. While careful not to increase the sense of *démarche* fatigue, the EU intensified its efforts in April 2011 by having Van Rompuy, Ashton and Barroso enter the scene. Van Rompuy and Barroso wrote letters to the heads of state and government of the CARICOM countries. Likewise, Ashton sent a letter to the foreign ministries of all UN members and went to New York to force a breakthrough. The CARICOM countries changed their minds in the early hours of 3 May 2011; the African Group followed suit soon thereafter. However, when the EU entered the UNGA a few hours later, it was prepared for six different outcomes: adoption by consensus, adoption by vote, motion for adjournment, important questions, tabling of amendments, and request for a division of pro-posals and amendments. The second scenario soon became reality when Cuba, Iran, Nicaragua, Syria, Venezuela and Zimbabwe formulated an oral amendment regarding the right to reply, claiming that it would create a new category of observer by stealth. As 142 countries rejected the proposal, the way was open for the adoption of the EU's revised wish list.

CARICOM, however, once more spoiled the EU's mood by giving the res-olution a restrictive interpretation. Speaking on behalf of CARICOM, and echoing the position of hard-liners such as Jamaica, Saint Vincent and Saint Lucia, the Permanent Representative of the Bahamas stressed that the EU was only to enjoy the rights explicitly stated in the resolution (United Nations General Assembly 2011b). She stated that the EU will not be able to speak prior to any major group represented by a full state member, and that only the Pres-ident of the European Council and the High Representative for Foreign Affairs and Security Policy may represent the EU at the General Debate. Additionally, according to CARICOM, the EU is not allowed to make written proposals or amendments, or to put proposals and amendments to a vote. Its right of reply would be also more circumscribed than those for states. More generally, the rights and privileges granted to the EU would be the absolute maximum that a non-state can enjoy in the UN. Finally, CARICOM claimed that the conferral of representative rights to other regional groupings would not demand a certain level of integration or an integration process similar to the EU's. CARICOM's intervention prompted the Hungarian EU Presidency to state that the implemen-tation of the adopted resolution should be carried out 'precisely, according to text and respectful of the practice of the United Nations' and that there was no room for 'unilateral interpretations' (United Nations General Assembly 2011c).

The new arrangements allowed Van Rompuy to address the General Debate on 22 September on behalf of the EU without being an active head of state or government. Van Rompuy emphasized that the new arrangements would give the EU more continuity and coherence. Yet he was not the only European leader to address the audience that week and, interestingly, none of the seven EU member states that took the floor before him even mentioned the new institutional arrangements. Moreover, the focus of his address did not differ substantially from the speeches delivered by the EU presidency in pre-Lisbon era. As it required more than 15 long months to get the UNGA to grant Van Rompuy permission to stand on the podium on behalf of the EU, one may have wondered whether the EU's campaign to gain was worth the time and effort, and the disgruntled feelings from its UN partners.

Those partners seem to be mainly looking for a consistent and coherent message. A more permanent messenger does not result in a more credible international actor if the message is not persuading the audience. The implementation of the Lisbon Treaty may still be work in progress at the time of writing, but it is already clear that making real progress is difficult without moving from form to content. Moreover, the adoption of the resolution in May 2011 did not immediately end the status saga. The EU continued facing external and internal hurdles for quite some time. Again, CARICOM put most sand in the wheels. The most telling anecdote comes from the UNGA's Fifth Committee, which is responsible for administration and budgetary matters, where CARICOM did not want the EU to speak among major groups. Not knowing what else to do, the chairman decided the EU's faith by flipping a coin in the presence of the UN Secretary-General. The EU lost the coin toss and was banned to the back of the room. But also some of its own member states, and the UK in particular, decided to give a very strict interpretation to the new representative rights, as well as to the Lisbon Treaty more generally. Bickering started over the question *on whose behalf* the new EU representative may speak in the various UN bodies – the EU or the EU and its member states. Only in October 2011 was the issue settled, at least on paper, when Coreper adopted general arrangements on EU statements in multilateral organizations (Council of the European Union 2011). In other words, in the weeks and months after the status resolution was adopted, the EU's focus was still on the messenger.

Conclusion

A fair evaluation would recognize that it takes at least one diplomatic generation to measure the real impact of the Lisbon Treaty on the EU's functioning in international contexts. However, some first conclusions can be drawn from the status resolution experience, particularly in terms of reform. One could argue that the EU has contributed to the reform of the UNGA's functioning by opening the door for regional actors acquiring enhanced observer rights. However, by doing so, it seems to have given the wrong answer to the wrong question. Most UN members want a more inclusive form of multilateralism and question the membership of the UNSC. Importantly, the answer that they want to hear from the EU and its member states is not the enhancement of observer rights for regional actors in the UNGA. The EU's search for international status is not facilitated by its *have cake and eat it too* attitude to UN reform, but chances are small that it will break its silence on the reform of the UNSC in the near future. Ongoing differences of opinion between the member states, but also the blow that the EU has suffered when upgrading its status at the UNGA, explain this.

At the time of writing, the EU was still marching the path of externalizing internal reform, be it in a more discrete way (see Introduction). In December 2012, the Commission adopted an internal communication suggesting the status enhancement of the EU in various international settings, including in the UN context.[11] The settings were selected on the basis of four criteria (political importance of the organization, impact on the *acquis*, EU expertise and legal constraints) following a mapping exercise of the EU's status in international organizations, which was launched in January 2012.

Granted, improving the effectiveness of the EU's participation in multilateral settings can be seen as a stepping-stone towards effective multilateralism, but the same goes for enhancing the effectiveness of those settings. A better balance between internal and external reform would demonstrate that the EU not only speaks about enhancing the effectiveness of multilateralism, but acts accordingly and consistently. By further closing the gap between rhetoric and reality, and taking a more constructive attitude on the reform of the UNSC, the EU could show that is as serious about strengthening the UN system as it is about strengthening its own position therein.

Notes

1 Amending the UN Charter requires a two-thirds majority in the UNGA, including the support of the five permanent members of the UNSC.
2 Kissack writes that the reform of the UNSC creates a 'lose-win' situation between the EU and the UN, with the former losing and the latter winning (Kissack 2010: 170). Importantly, however, he leaves the door open for a 'win-win' scenario, since 'gains in efficacy, legitimacy and authority yielded by a more equitable membership far outweigh the costs of decreased representation'.
3 The European Parliament sees an EU seat at the UNSC as a long-term foreign policy goal. The European Parliament is the only EU institution that has expressed this view in a number of documents, even if also the European Commission has given a maximalist interpretation to the representative rules included in article 34 of the EU Treaty (see below). More generally, regional seats are particularly popular with countries that know a permanent seat of their own is wishful thinking, as is the case for Italy and Spain, but also in some academic circles.
4 Two non-permanent seats are allocated to the WEOG; only one to the EEG.
5 Some have looked into the presidency statements to measure the EU's effectiveness at the UNGA (Adriaenssen 2008; Hosli *et al.* 2010). Also their conclusion is one of success: the number of countries supporting the EU's interventions has gradually increased, encompassing not only EU member states, but also candidate and other countries.

6 See article 34 of the Treaty on European Union, as well as Chapter 8 of this volume.
7 The unit merges the former Commission Delegation to the UN and the former New York Liaison Office of the General Secretariat. The former was established in 1974, when the European Economic Community was granted observer status, and upgraded the information office that had been operational since 1964. The latter was created in 1994, following the entry into force of the Maastricht Treaty. Its main tasks included assisting the rotating presidency, providing a link with Brussels and representing the EU as part of the troika. During the first 15 months of operation, the unit's main focus was on the enhancement of the EU's status at the UNGA (see below). For a more detailed discussion on the new delegations more generally, see Drieskens 2012b.
8 The process is reconstructed on the basis of both formal and informal documents and correspondence, as well as conversations with ten officials involved, both in Brussels and New York.
9 It should have been no surprise that the UN membership was not willing to accept the EU's wishes without reservation, especially not for scholars who have followed the EU at the Peacebuilding Commission (PBC). The EU saw its representation within that body as a test case for the implementation of what would become the Lisbon Treaty at the UN in New York. The EU requested a double invitation – one for the EU and one for the EC – causing the Non-Aligned Movement to ask for similar representative rights for the Organisation of Islamic Countries. As a result, the EU's representation at the PBC was under discussion for most of the first session. Also important, the EU had to ensure the US that it was not entering the UNSC through the backdoor and that the arrangements for the PBC would not apply to other settings.
10 The UN Secretary-General clarified the scope of the adopted text in June 2001 by way of a note (United Nations Secretary General 2011). The note underlines that the text does not apply to the other principal organs or to their subsidiary organs. Also, it is without prejudice to any privileges of participation that have been or may be conferred upon the EU by them. In addition, the note specifies the modalities for the operationalization of the various rights and privileges obtained. For instance, it states that EU representatives will be invited to participate in the General Debate after the members, the Holy See and Palestine, and that their right of reply is restricted to one intervention per item.
11 See also Chapter 7 on the International Atomic Energy Agency.

References

Adriaenssen, P. (2008) 'Rapprochement between the EU and the UN: history and balance of intersecting political cultures', *European Foreign Affairs Review*, 13(1): 53–72.
Annan, K. (2005) 'In larger freedom: decision time at the UN', *Foreign Affairs*, 84(3): 63–74.
Barber, T. (2010) 'Ashton under fire at EU confirmation hearing', *Financial Times.* Online. Available www.ft.com/intl/cms/s/0/3f05759c-fede-11de-a677-00144feab49a.html#axzz2Rk6CQRQm (accessed 28 April 2013).
Belgian Presidency of the Council of the European Union (2010) *A/64/L.67 – possible amendments* (informal draft distributed to the UN membership), 13 September 2010.
Biscop, S. and Drieskens, E. (2006) 'Effective multilateralism and collective security: empowering the UN', in K.V. Laatikainen and K.E. Smith (eds) *The European Union at the United Nations: intersecting multilateralisms*, Basingstoke: Palgrave Macmillan, pp. 115–32.
Blavoukos, S. and Bourantonis, D. (2011) 'The EU's performance in the United Nations Security Council', *Journal of European Integration*, 33(6): 731–42.

Blavoukos, S. and Bourantonis, D. (2013) 'The UN Security Council Reform Debate', in K.E. Jørgensen and K.V. Laatikainen (eds) *Routledge Handbook on the European Union and international institutions: performance, policy, power*, London: Routledge, pp. 128–40.

Bouchard, C. and Drieskens, E. (2013) 'The European Union in UN Politics', in K.E. Jørgensen and K.V. Laatikainen (eds) *Routledge Handbook on the European Union and international institutions: performance, policy power*, London: Routledge, pp. 115–27.

Bourantonis, D. (2005) *The history and politics of UN security reform*, London: Routledge.

Council of the European Union (2011) *EU Statements in multilateral organisations – General arrangements* (15901/11), 24 October 2011.

Die Welt (2003) *Solana: Einheit Iraks muss erhalten bleiben*. Online. Available www.welt.de/print-welt/article519787/Solana-Einheit-Iraks-muss-erhalten-bleiben.html (accessed 28 April 2013).

Drieskens, E. (2012a) 'Measuring regional actorness at the UN Security Council: the EU as a paragon of complexity', in F. Baert, P. De Lombarde and T. Felício (eds) *The United Nations and the regions: Third World Report on regional integration*, New York: Springer-Verlag, pp. 59–70.

Drieskens, E. (2012b) 'What's in a name? Challenges to the creation of EU delegations', *The Hague Journal of Diplomacy*, 7(1): 51–64.

European Council (2003) *A secure Europe in a better world: European Security Strategy*, Brussels, 12 December 2003.

European Council (2008) *Providing security in a changing world: report on the implementation of the European Security Strategy*, (S407/08), Brussels, 11 December 2008.

European Union (2010) *Contribution of the European Union on the occasion of the General Debate of the 65th UN General Assembly* (EUUN10–085EN), 29 September 2010.

Ginsberg, R. and Penska, S. (2012) *The European Union in global security: the politics of impact*, London: Palgrave.

Hill, C. (2006) 'The European powers in the Security Council: differing interests, differing arenas', in K. Laatikainen and K. Smith (eds) *Intersecting multilateralisms: the European Union and the United Nations*, Houndmills: Palgrave Macmillan, pp. 49–69.

Hosli, M., van Kampen, E., Meijerink, F. and Tennis, K. 'Voting cohesion in the United Nations General Assembly: the case of the European Union', paper presented at the ECPR Fifth Pan-European Conference, Porto, June 2010.

Karns, M. and Mingst, K. (2009) *International organizations: the politics and process of global governance*, 2nd edn, Boulder: Lynne Rienner Publishers.

Kissack, R. (2010) *Pursuing effective multilateralism: the European Union, international organisations and the politics of decision making*, Houndmills: Palgrave Macmillan.

Laatikainen, K. and Smith, K.E. (2006) 'The European Union at the United Nations: leader, partner or failure?', in K. Laatikainen and K. Smith (eds) *Intersecting multilateralisms: the European Union and the United Nations*, Houndmills: Palgrave Macmillan, pp. 27–46.

Løj, E.M. (2007) 'Denmark's membership of the UN Security Council: what came out of it?', in N. Hvidt and H. Mouritz (eds) *Danish Foreign Policy Yearbook 2007*, Copenhagen: Danish Institute for International Studies, pp. 31–50.

Luck, E.C. (2005) 'How not to reform the United Nations', *Global Governance*, 11(4): 407–14.

Luck, E.C. (2006) 'Principal organs', in T.G. Weiss and S. Daws (eds) *The Oxford handbook on the United Nations*, Oxford: Oxford University Press: pp. 653–74.

Mahbubani, K. (2004) 'The permanent and elected council members', in D.M. Malone (ed.) *The UN Security Council: from the Cold War to the 21st century*, Boulder: Lynne Rienner, pp. 253–66.

Ortega, M. (2005) 'Introduction', in M. Ortega (ed.) *The European Union and the United Nations: partners in effective multilateralism*, Paris: European Institute for Security Studies.

Rasch, M. (2008) *The European Union at the United Nations: the functioning and coherence of EU-representation in a state-centric environment*, Leiden: BRILL.

Roos, U., Francke, U. and Hellman, G. (2008) 'Beyond deadlock: how Europe can contribute to UN reform', *The International Spectator*, 43(1): 43–55.

Rufino, F. (2005) *EU praises Annan's UN reform plan*. EU Observer. Online. Available http://euobserver.com/foreign/18735 (accessed 28 April 2013).

Security Council Report (2012) *Working methods* (November 2012 Monthly Forecast). Online. Available www.securitycouncilreport.org/monthly-forecast/2012–11/working_methods.php (accessed 28 April 2013).

Swart, L. (2008) 'Revitalization of the General Assembly', in Center for UN Reform Education (ed.) *Managing Change at the United Nations*, New York: Center for UN Reform Education, pp. 21–35.

Tanin, Z. (2011) 'Revision 3', in Center for UN Reform (ed.) *Compilation SC reform February 2011*. Online. Available www.centerforunreform.org/node/435 (accessed 28 April 2013).

United Nations General Assembly (2009) *Note by the President of the General Assembly* (A/63/960), 10 September 2009.

United Nations General Assembly (2010a) *Closing sixty-fourth session, General Assembly President urges concrete actions to ensure body's objectives are met, decisions respected, authority reinforced* (GA/10983), 14 September 2010.

United Nations General Assembly (2010b) *Participation of the European Union in the work of the United Nations* (A/64/L.67), 31 August 2010.

United Nations General Assembly (2011a) *Participation of the European Union in the work of the United Nations* (A/RES/65/276), 3 May 2011.

United Nations General Assembly (2011b) *General Assembly, in recorded vote, adopts resolution granting European Union right of reply, ability to present oral amendments* (GA/11079), 3 May 2011.

United Nations General Assembly (2011c) *88th Plenary meeting* (A/65/PV.88), 3 May 2011.

United Nations General Assembly President (2007) *Report of the facilitators to the President of the General Assembly on the consultations regarding 'The question of equitable representation and increase in the membership of the Security Council and other matters related to the Security Council'*, 19 April 2007. Online. Available www.un.org/ga/president/61/letters/SC-reform-Facil-report-20-April-07.pdf (accessed 28 April 2013)

United Nations Secretary General (2005) *In larger freedom: towards development, security and human rights for all. Report of the Secretary-General* (A/59/2005), 21 March 2005.

United Nations Secretary General (2011) *Participation of the European Union in the work of the United Nations. Note by the Secretary-General* (A/65/856), 1 June 2011.

United Nations Secretary-General's High-level Panel on Threats, Challenges and Change (2004) *A more secure world: our shared responsibility* (A/59/565), 2 December 2004.

Zifcak, S. (2006) 'United Nations reform: heading North or South?' *Global Change, Peace & Security*, 18(3): 135–52.

3 The EU's role in creating a more effective WHO[1]

Louise G. van Schaik and Samantha Battams

Introduction

This chapter considers discussions on the reform of the World Health Organization (WHO) and the role of the EU and its member states (hereafter the EU)
within them. The WHO is a specialized UN agency established in 1948. Based
in Geneva, it is one of the oldest UN bodies with a clear functional focus on the
international aspects of health (Lee 2009; Brown and Cueto 2011). It stands out
from other entities addressing international health matters (such as the World
Bank, OECD (Organisation for Economic Co-operation and Development),
Council of Europe, Gates Foundation and Global Fund) because of its central
role in combating infectious diseases and treaty making powers, as well as its
global membership.

The WHO's 194 members give political guidance to the organization through
the annual World Health Assembly (WHA) meetings that take place in May and
through an Executive Board (EB) that meets twice a year and consists of a sub-
set of 34 members. The WHO is unique because of its strongly decentralized
structure with six regional offices that operate in a relatively autonomous way
and spend most of the organization's budget.[2]

For a number of years, the WHO has been plagued by severe financial difficulties, criticism of its decentralized structure, accusations of being overly susceptible to private sector interests and its authority being undermined by a
plethora of other actors engaging in global health. However, having a strong
multilateral agency for health seems all the more important given the health
challenges confronting today's world. Globalization of trade, population expansion, migration, increased movement across state borders, climate change,
increased access to and use of some medicines (and poor accessibility of others)
and over-consumption of unhealthy foods have aggravated cross-border health
risks. These include an increased risk for pandemics, bioterror, outbreaks of new
diseases spreading from animals to humans, a steep rise in non-communicable
diseases, and resistance to antibiotics. In addition, communicable diseases such
as HIV/AIDS continue to affect and destabilize societies in developing countries. The need for better governance of global health, and the importance of
'other sectors' to health (such as trade) have been recognized, for instance in the

Trade Related aspects of International Property rights (TRIPS) agreement and Doha Declaration which ensured flexibility of TRIPS in order to promote access to affordable medicines.

Since the 1990s, development assistance for health more than tripled (Ravishankar *et al.* (2009) looked at figures up to 2007). The majority of these funds were channelled through new donors, the most important being The Global Fund and the Bill and Melinda Gates Foundation (the Gates Foundation). This development has raised important questions, not only about effectiveness, but also about a potential risk of bias towards certain topics and diseases like HIV/AIDS. In fact, it questioned the WHO's ability to act as the directing and coordinating authority on global health, as its Constitution stipulates, and impelled it into carrying out development-related activities. This in turn increased pressure on its other tasks, such as technical assistance, norm setting and ethical questions. Also, it reduced its capacity to work on new health threats and emerging topics, such as the viability of health systems in ageing societies.

WHO members, and particularly those states who contributed most to its finances, increasingly felt out of control with regard to the WHO's activities, and in 2010 a reform process was initiated by the Director-General Margaret Chan in response to their concerns. This chapter looks into the EU's role within this debate by analysing its positions and influence. Given that effective multilateralism is a central objective of EU foreign policy, one could expect the EU member states to come to the defence of a multilateral institution with regulatory powers to effectively tackle cross-border health issues, not only for financial reasons – combined, the EU and its member states are the largest financial donor of the WHO – but also for strategic reasons. Indeed, even if the European Security Strategy does not refer to the WHO as such, it does describe disease as a cause of untold suffering that gives rise to pressing security concerns. In fact, it considers AIDS one of the most devastating pandemics in human history, contributing to the breakdown of societies, and new diseases as potential global threats. Likewise, the Implementation Report of 2008 stipulates that threats to public health, and particularly pandemics, undermine development.

Exploring the fit between internal and external reform, this chapter analyses the EU's position and actions in the debate on WHO reform and explores whether it is in better shape due to its own internal reforms, notably the Lisbon Treaty. It concludes that the EU did come to the defence of the organization, but in a rather technical manner and without much success on key issues. As a result, WHO is not a success story in terms of the EU promoting effective multilateralism in practice.

External reform: the WHO under siege

The global health landscape has become increasingly crowded with players, partly because commercial interests in global health are on the rise. The WHO is perceived to be 'under siege' by private organizations and groups with their own interests (Szlezák *et al.* 2010; Sridhar 2012; Clift 2013). Subsequently, there have been emerging complaints about WHO's lack of transparency and account-ability, its high degree of fragmentation due to semi-autonomously operating regional offices and susceptibility to private interests.

After a rather intense debate on the 'decline of the WHO' in the 1990s, the organization recovered some of its strength at the end of this period under the leadership of Gro Harlem Brundtland, but inherent shortcomings in its structure and financing were never effectively addressed (Clift 2013). In 2008 an informal debate emerged on the need for a fundamental overhaul of the organization, resulting in the launch of an official debate on financing in 2010. This debate started as a result of problems regarding the financial situation and triggered a broader debate on WHO reform. In 2012, this resulted in the adoption of three reform objectives at the World Health Assembly: (1) review of core functions, (2) greater coherence in global health; and (3) an organization that is effective, efficient, responsive, objective, transparent and accountable.

At the EB-meeting of January 2013, a high-level implementation plan on the reform was presented, and at the WHA of May 2013 a new General Programme of Work for the period 2014–20 was adopted. This programme will set out the future political priorities for the organization. It is accompanied by a biannual budget, but large parts of this funding are still to be raised, making it in fact an 'aspirational budget' which does not guide priority setting due to allocation of funds. A so-called 'financing dialogue' is to subsequently ensure that voluntary pledges are made in line with politically set priorities.

In general, the debates and negotiations on WHO reform can be characterized as a struggle between the WHO members and the WHO secretariat, with the former striving to increase their control over what the organization does. Large funders of the organization, such as the US, several EU states, Switzerland, Canada, Japan, Norway and a few others are keen to strengthen the efficiency of the organization, to strengthen its role in setting regulations and standards for global health, are open to discuss more extensive stakeholder involvement and less keen on WHO engaging in development assistance for health. The emerging economies and other developing countries point to the role of the WHO in pro-moting health equity. Countries such as Brazil and Thailand are keen to under-line the need for the WHO to operate independently from (pharmaceutical) industry interests, and engage more in development assistance for health, for instance through a strengthening of WHO country offices. That being said, the debate cannot fully be characterized as a traditional North-South debate. For instance, emerging economies have some interests that are quite different from the least developed countries, which can be explained by their emerging health issues more closely resembling those of the Western countries. Moreover, not all WHO members contributed evenly or as actively as each other during the debate, raising some doubts about their true commitment to (reforming) the WHO.

In addition, NGOs, industry and other stakeholders, such a health researchers, influence the reform debate. They are keen to underline the usefulness of an upgraded involvement for stakeholders in WHO policy-making processes. For instance, the Democratising Global Health Coalition refers to good practices for stakeholder involvement at other international organizations, such as the Food and Agricultural Organization (FAO), comparing these favourably to WHO practices (Battams 2012a). Large donors such as the Gates Foundation, the Rockefeller Foundation, GAVI and The Global Fund have remained relatively quiet, but many of the NGOs in this field are funded by the Gates Foundation.

The general positioning of the EU and EU member states in the reform debate

The EU has engaged cautiously in the debate on WHO reform. At the start of the debate in 2008 there were no common positions of the EU and its member states on the question of reform. Coordination in this area is voluntary for the EU member states, since they are not obliged to operate with a single voice on health topics where no EU legislation (*acquis communautaire*) exists. Nevertheless, the EU member states considered it advantageous to operate in concert; consequently EU positions exist today on nearly all reform topics, despite the substantial time taken to decide upon these positions and the fact that they subsequently became rather detailed and complex (sometimes even too sophisticated for others to understand). Reform of the WHO appears to be one of the unspoken priorities of the EU since it has a strong interest (as a major donor) in its funding being well managed (see above).

In general, a strong global health policy is lacking at EU level. This is related to the fact that health is a topic where the EU's involvement is sensitive, although an increasing amount of EU legislation exists. It is seen by representatives of EU member states as a topic of national competence and action (see on this issue also van Schaik 2011). It is true that the EU adopted Council Conclusions on Global Health in 2010 (EU Council 2010), but this document is very much focused on the link between health and development cooperation objectives. It states that the EU and its member states will endeavour to speak with a stronger and more coherent voice at the global level on global health initiatives, in dialogue with third countries. It also calls for a shift from earmarked funding to assessed funding for the general WHO budget. In addition, it encourages the EU member states to support 'an increased leadership of WHO at global, regional and country level, its normative and guidance functions addressing global health challenges as well as in technical support to health systems governance and health policy, given its global mandate'.

Some EU member states have their own strategies on global health and/or WHO specifically, but most of them have no clear statements regarding the direction the organization should take. As with other EU foreign policy questions more generally, the UK, Germany and – in this case to a lesser extent – France, are taking the lead in the internal discussions, together with a few other member states. Sweden, for instance, is rather active and devised a specific strategy for WHO matters (Sweden 2011). It criticizes the WHO's internal efficiency and priorities, but comes to the defence of WHO playing a leading role in norm setting. Sweden refers to weak budget control systems, a mismatch between resources and targets of specific programmes and the existence of two parallel governance mechanisms: the official governing bodies and the financers of voluntary contributions (Sweden 2011: 4). Finland and the Netherlands are also referred to as being active contributors to the WHO reform debate (and notably have *health attachés* based in Geneva), like some other countries during their EU presidencies (e.g. Ireland). The UK accepts a considerable involvement of non-state actors when it comes to financing WHO activities, but argues that distinctions should be made clearer with regard to who pays for what. Its House of Lords was quite influential in pushing for WHO reform as it came out as a key recommendation of a 2008 inquiry into the contribution of intergovernmental organizations in controlling diseases (UK House of Lords 2008). A call for reform was subsequently enshrined in the UK's strategy *Health is Global* (UK 2008). France is generally concerned about the visibility of the WHO, the legitimacy of its governance processes and the effectiveness of decision-making. It emphasizes the central role of WHO member states in terms of formal decision-making authority.

By contrast, Germany takes a middle-ground position by supporting the idea of a greater involvement of non-state actors, but argues that agendas should always be set by states and not by big private donors. Germany is considered to be very active in the reform debate. At every possible moment it has emphasized the need to increase the transparency and financial accountability of the WHO and has made several operational suggestions for doing so. It promotes the strengthening of the WHO within the overall global health landscape, is very critical about it operating as a development agency and strongly propagates the centrality of the WHO as a leader in setting global health standards. After the Executive Board meeting of 2013, Germany together with a few other EU member states asked the EU presidency to organize a strategy meeting for member states, the EU delegation and Commission staff on WHO reform, specifically to strengthen the EU's positioning and diplomatic outreach on the issue. In short, if there is such a thing as the EU seeking to operationalize effective multilateralism in the WHO context, Germany could be considered its main advocate since it truly propagates a stronger WHO.

EU position on specific issues of the reform debate

This section analyses the EU's common positions on points of contention emerging throughout the WHO reform debate. These include: lack of priority setting; the alleged inefficiency of its decentralized structure; financial difficulties; possible conflicts of interest when engaging with the private sector; its relationship with other international actors encroaching upon its remit; and whether WHO should engage in health-related development cooperation activities.

Financial difficulties and priority setting

In the past, the WHO was largely financed by assessed contributions provided by its membership, related to their population and GDP. These contributions were frozen in 1982 after US opposition to WHO's essential drugs policy and the code for the marketing of breast milk substitutes (Legge 2012). This has led to a situation where the WHO relies on the voluntary contributions of member states, and other WHO sponsors largely determine the organization's priorities, through funding tied to specific projects or programmes. Voluntary contributions now make up most of the organization's budget (about 75 per cent) and most of these funds are earmarked. Nearly half of the funding is said to come from non-state donors. This has diverted the WHO's focus from its core functions and created incentives for other actors to compete for functions falling within WHO's remit.

The EU has developed a common position on the importance of the WHO's normative and global mandate, and the need for clear processes on priority-setting linked to resources. One problem is that regular budget contributions tend to come from ministries of health, whereas voluntary contributions are typically from ministries of foreign affairs or development agencies and private and inter-governmental bodies, who tend to have specific funding objectives (Clift 2013: 33). On top of this, it is difficult for most EU states to maintain their level of funding to the WHO, as they face severe budget cuts due to the economic and financial crisis, and funding for international governance and development assistance is not politically popular in home countries during such a crisis. As a result, pressure has increased to tie funds to national priorities.

Nevertheless, as an overarching objective the EU aims to move away from earmarked towards general budget funding for WHO (EU Council 2010), despite it being realized that some funding will continue to be earmarked. At the 2012 WHA, Germany's representative argued that the WHA should explore ways to better steer funding provided by individual donors, and that perhaps there is a need to earmark funds to very precise priorities, but first clear priorities need to be defined by the WHA. Furthermore, major parts of the earmarked funds (about 18 per cent of voluntary contributions) are provided by other UN agencies, who implement their specific goals through the WHO. Due to their specific missions they have to earmark funds and the same is often the case for foundations who are also major contributors to voluntary contributions (Battams 2012a).

The EU has thus emphasized the need for more transparency and account-ability with regard to funding. At the same time it is realized that, given the large share of voluntary contributions, it cannot demand that the WHO membership decide upon budget allocation. This also limits possibilities to ensure resources will flow to EU priorities. As a result, the focus of the EU was very much on administrative methods and criteria for disbursement of funds, instead of on WHO thematic priority issues. Eventually, in the reform debate it was decided to strengthen the Programme Budget and Administration Committee with regard to financial oversight and evaluation of programmes. Another decision was to reduce the number of resolutions to increase the level of debate at WHAs where political priorities can be discussed (Clift 2013: 47). The EU was said to be influential in generating this outcome.

The alleged inefficiency of the WHO's decentralized structure

The WHO is unique in having a strongly decentralized structure. Its six regions operate relatively autonomously with regional directors, regional committee meetings and most of the regular budget channelled through the regional offices. In addition, many country and sub-regional WHO offices are charged with delivering specific health programmes. All these entities compete with WHO headquarters for funding and often doubling up of work occurs. According to Legge (2012), the degree of WHO decentralization fragments the organization, jeopardizes programme coherence and weakens accountability. This viewpoint confirms a report of the UN Joint Inspection Unit (JIU) of 1993 which identified in the WHO's structure serious and complex problems of a constitutional, political, managerial and programmatic nature. However, the JIU's recommendations, one of which was to end the election of regional directors by the membership, were not adopted by the WHO membership (Clift 2013: 8).

The EU has called for an update of the JIU evaluation and argues that 'a highly decentralised organisation such as WHO can only be accountable and work in a truly transparent, efficient and effective manner once clear rules are established that govern the interaction between the global and regional structures' (EU Statement 2011). It furthermore argued that 'when discussing priority setting the role and function of WHO regions as well as the question of coherence and alignment of the Organisation as a whole should also be taken into consideration' (EU Statement 2012). According to the UK House of Lords (2008), a fundamental overhaul of the relationship between headquarters and regions, and a review of procedures by which regional directors are appointed, is long overdue. A strong headquarters with considerable know-how, and an adequate support structure for negotiating agreements and following-up and monitoring their implementation, is generally in line with the EU's objective of strengthening the international norm-setting role of the WHO.

At the same time, the EU appears to be quite comfortable with its majority position in 'WHO EURO', which in addition to the 28 EU member states consists of 25 other states on the European continent. Resolutions of WHO EURO give the EU an extra lever of influence in general WHO debates, despite this having caused some anxiety with Russia and Turkey, who are less happy about the EU dominance in WHO EURO (cf. Battams and van Schaik, forthcoming). Another reason for the EU not to overly criticize the WHO regional structure is a realization that changing it will be difficult, if not impossible.

Modest changes were agreed to. Regional committee chairs will now routinely report to the EB and the selection procedure for regional directors has been revised in line with those for the WHO Director-General (Clift 2013). Another outcome of the reform is enhanced delegation of authority to country offices. It is difficult to see how this matches the EU's objective of strengthening headquarters; in reality, the EU was said to be rather quiet on the issue. It was thus not very influential in addressing the flaws stemming from the regional set-up of the WHO. Nevertheless, it did obtain agreement on an update to the

JIU report, despite initial reluctance to this by the WHO Secretariat and – to a lesser extent – the US and Canada (who seemed to fear the JIU would be dominated by the views of developing countries). This report is due for the WHA of May 2013.

Accusations about private sector interests dominating

During the 2009 H1N1 swine flu pandemic, it was argued that representatives of the pharmaceutical industry responsible for the development of vaccines influenced WHO decision-making. In 2010, the Strasbourg-based Council of Europe's Parliamentary Assembly adopted a report and resolution in which grave shortcomings in the transparency of WHO decision-making on the pandemic were highlighted and concerns were expressed about the influence of the pharmaceutical industry (CoE 2010). Although not an EU body, but rather an intergovernmental organization for human rights, the parliamentarians voting in favour of the resolution came in large part from EU member states. Previously, in 2007, Indonesia refused to share samples of the H5N1 virus with the WHO before obtaining the guarantee that, once WHO had shared them with pharmaceutical producers, the resulting medicine would be made available at a reasonable cost.

Despite the criticism by the Council of Europe on WHO being overly-susceptible to industry interests in the field of communicable diseases, the EU in general sides with the US and Switzerland in advocating for the need of enhanced private sector involvement. Such involvement may lead to the WHO having better access to private industry know-how. The EU has also propagated the need for proper enforcement of intellectual property rights. It has been said that the US and the EU are advocating through regional trade agreements the extension of patent terms and donor exclusivity, which increase the cost of drugs (Battams 2012a).

However, in the reform debate, some EU countries (e.g. France) have also emphasized the need for the WHO to be more cautious with regard to its contacts with the private sector. The authority of the EU on stakeholder involvement appears to partly derive from the experience and practice of the European Commission in dealing with NGOs and the private sector, but the EU has been cautious about advocating its own practices too strongly, let alone to 'preach' certain models (Battams *et al.* 2012). It has emphasized the need for more transparency by establishing stakeholder registers and by increasing the use of declarations of interest when consulting experts.

The debate on accommodating the private sector and civil society in WHO governance is still ongoing, following the WHA rejecting a proposal for a so-called World Health Forum, out of fear of this giving civil society (including private industry) a formal role in WHO deliberations. The intergovernmental nature of WHO decision making, based on interest-free evidence, was pointed out as a principle to guide the relationship with non-state actors (Clift 2013). In particular, emerging economies such as Brazil and India have been critical about the degree of industry involvement in the organization's day-to-day operations. As a result, the EU and other Western countries did not manage to get their experience in working more pro-actively with the private sector and NGOs enshrined into the WHO's policy-making practices.

Stakeholder management, competition with other actors and the WHO's authority

As noted, according to its Constitution (article 2a), the WHO should 'act as the directing and coordinating authority of international health work', but in practice this can be called into question. Many international organizations engage in health activities, including the World Bank and other UN agencies. Health is also a topic on the agenda of the OECD, the Council of Europe and the EU. Various initiatives were established in addition to the WHO, such as GAVI, UNAIDS and The Global Fund. Moreover, the General Assembly of the UN has tackled the issue of HIV/AIDS and more recently discussed the rapid spread of non-communicable diseases (NCDs, e.g. cardio-vascular disease, cancer, mental health). On top of this, under the auspices of WHO a number of partnerships were established, such as the Stop TB (tuberculosis) Partnership and the Global Outbreak and Response Network, which operate rather autonomously. Recently, the NCD alliance, a global alliance of over 2,000 NGO member organizations, has advocated for a 'stand-alone' platform to tackle NCDs where the WHO would be just one player in partnership with others, rather than the lead agency (Battams 2012b). All these entities are said to illustrate the weakness of WHO and to question its ability to act as the coordinating and directing organization for international health issues.

The EU has not been very vocal on the issue of competition with other entities active in the field of global health. This was partially related to a WHO input paper on the matter being made available just a few days before the EB-meeting of January 2013, undermining the EU's ability to coordinate a common position. The EU's silence can also be explained by much of the funding to these newer entities being provided by EU states and the EU budget. For instance, several EU states and the European Commission are major donors to The Global Fund. Germany and others asked for a postponement of the debate to the next EB-meeting in May. This was agreed to and the EU now seems to be more firm in pushing for a stronger lead for the WHO within the overall global health landscape, with a clear focus on its standard-setting role, for instance in the area of NCDs.

The development assistance for health function of WHO versus its other priorities

Since the late 1990s, the WHO has increasingly aimed to bring health to the core of the development agenda. According to the EU, the WHO should not act as a 'development agency' due to the potential for overlap with the work of other agencies (Battams *et al.* 2012). This is despite the EU Council Conclusions on global health of 2010 focusing mainly on the development aspects of global health policy and specifically their emphasis on the development-related Millennium Development Goals (MDGs). It also contradicts the practice of voluntary funds of EU states being earmarked specifically for development assistance for health. Many of them, as well as the European Commission, use the WHO for implementing health programmes in developing countries.

Nevertheless, the EU considers that norm setting, rather than development, should be WHO's central task. Other joint EU priority areas for WHO's work include non-communicable diseases and continued attention to health security, e.g. pandemics and other health threats. In addition, EU states have specific wish-lists for WHO's work. For instance, Sweden (2011) is concerned that WHO's authority on tuberculosis and malaria has been called into question, and that it lacks capacity to focus on new global health threats such as resistance to antibiotics. Together with other EU member states, such as the Netherlands, Denmark and Finland, it highlights the importance of promoting sexual and reproductive health and rights. Other EU member states, such as Poland, Ireland and Malta take a rather different position on reproductive health, linked to beliefs inspired by the Catholic faith regarding abortion and homosexuality. Due to such national preferences and divergences, it is difficult for the EU to come up with a consolidated list with a few priorities for WHO's work. This hampers its ability to be effective in debates on political and spending priorities of the assessed contributions, for instance with regard to these being relocated from the regional to the headquarters level.

Overall assessment on WHO reform thus far and the EU's contribution to it

Within the current reform debate, the past shortcomings of WHO governance and activities have been highlighted, but many have not yet been addressed. According to Clift (2013), it is unclear whether reform efforts will be sufficient to enable the organization to fulfil its full potential. It proved difficult to effectively address many of the shortcomings in a previous reform effort undertaken in the 1990s, and it is well-known that organizational reform occurs in incremental steps rather than through sweeping reform processes. Nevertheless, the current failure to be more radical may hamper the full reinstatement of the WHO to its coordinating and directing authority for global health. This would undermine the viability of one of the oldest UN agencies and thereby also the EU's goal of effective multilateralism.

Throughout the reform process, the EU's stance on many issues has often been rather technical. Efforts undertaken to achieve specific EU objectives have not led to strong outcomes. The EU's focus on management reform has led to changes that are likely to strengthen the WHO, but strategic decisions with regard to involvement of stakeholders, priorities and the decentralized structure were either averted or taken in a different direction to EU preferences. Clear EU positions on the direction and priorities of WHO activities in the field of global health are still lacking. EU member states have rather different views, priorities and do not see the necessity of establishing a joint position on this matter, resulting in problems of credibility and criticisms about a divided EU.

The next section will analyse to what extent this might have been due to the EU's capacity being undermined by its internal struggles over EU coordination and external representation, its rather unclear status within the international governance system and coherence problems between health and foreign policy actors working on global health. All of these factors appear stronger than before, as a result of the implementation of new provisions of the Lisbon Treaty, and may therefore further jeopardize the EU's ability to strengthen the WHO in line with its striving towards effective multilateralism.

A more effective EU at WHO in the post-Lisbon era?

The Lisbon Treaty provisions would pave the way for a more coherent and consolidated role for the EU in multilateral *fora*, including the WHO. Following the establishment of the High Representative of the Union for Foreign Affairs and Security Policy, assisted by the newly created European External Action Service (EEAS), the EU is supposed to develop stronger representation and coordinated action in external affairs. For global health affairs, the EEAS works with the EU presidency and European Commission with the latter two actors driving the content of EU positions. The EU delegation to the UN in Geneva, part of the EEAS, represents the EU at working level on most WHO topics and receives instructions from Commission services as well. In fact, the two people working on global health issues receive most of their input from the Commission's DG for Health and Consumers (SANCO). Nevertheless, they are not as 'Commission-steered' as their colleagues from the EU delegation to the WTO, which in fact has been split from the rest of the delegation (see below).

Within the WHO's governance bodies the EU currently has only observer status, whilst EU member states are members of the organization. Nevertheless, the EU, for the vast majority of agenda topics, represents a unified voice and has at least one EU member state on the EB and at the WHA representing the EU position (normally the country holding the rotating presidency of the EU or closest in line to becoming so). In addition, in the European region, WHO EURO, the EU position is now brought forward by a single voice, which according to some observers has made it even more obvious that the EU is able to dominate policy debates within this regional branch of WHO (given its majority in terms of membership).

Article 168 of the Treaty on the Functioning of the European Union outlines the EU's role in public health, and states that 'the Union and the member states shall foster cooperation with third countries and the competent international organisations in the sphere of public health'. The Communication of the European Commission on the 'EU's role in global health' (EC 2010) recognizes challenges in global health governance, the importance of strong leadership and the need to coordinate the broad range of global health actors. It recommends a unified position for the EU on global health when dealing with UN agencies (EC 2010). The EU member states welcomed its suggestions in the Council Conclusions (EU 2010), but were somewhat cautious in formulating the role of the EU. In fact, this was formulated in the following way: 'Without prejudice to the respective competencies, the EU and its member states will endeavour to speak with a stronger and coherent voice at the global level and in a dialogue with third countries and global health initiatives' (EU Council 2010).

The above already illustrates that the matter of EU coordination on global health matters is sensitive for EU member states. In general, they consider health to largely be a topic of national competence and this would also entail a more modest role for the EU externally. In particular, the UK has been keen to underline national rights for external representation, a leading role for the country holding the rotating presidency (in cases where common EU positions exist) and EU statements to be made on behalf of EU member states (and insists that they not be made only on behalf of the EU). Other EU member states, such as Sweden and the Netherlands, supported its position, also because they were afraid of a weak EU voice on topics where agreement was unlikely to be reached within the EU (e.g. on sexual and reproductive health and rights). After the entry into force of the Lisbon Treaty, this resulted in a clash between the EU delegation to the UN in Geneva, who claimed a leading role in EU coordination and external representation, and the EU member states (see also van Schaik 2011).

Now the dust has settled down and the relationship between the EU member states and the EU delegation in Geneva has improved, with more clarity on which WHO topics the EU delegation can lead the EU's external representation, and on what other topics a coordinated position is more voluntary. Even though the EU delegation is now in charge of organizing the EU coordination meetings, preparation of a position is often still done by the EU presidency or jointly. EU member states still closely monitor that the EU delegation does not step out of its mandate. The sensitive relationship is a continuing source of frustration, and third countries and civil society do not always understand who is in charge of representing the EU.

Another sensitive topic is the extent to which foreign policy actors, including the new actors of the EU, should become involved in global health issues, possibly to the detriment of health policy experts from line ministries. In Geneva, the number of specific 'health attachés' is sometimes limited (especially in smaller embassies/missions) and many diplomats working on WHO matters are in fact foreign policy rather than health experts, employed by their foreign affairs department, and working on a range of international topics including health. WHO topics being labelled as foreign policy may mean not only the involvement of different people, but also of different EU decision-making procedures being followed and possibly different viewpoints being taken into account. This issue of 'multiple roles' is explained below, where another tricky issue, or rather 'elephant in the room', is discussed, the question of a possible upgraded status of the EU at the WHO. The issue is not openly discussed, but appears something in the back of the minds of many involved.

Between health and foreign policy

The initial EU member states' sensitivity toward the involvement of the newly established EU foreign policy actor, the EEAS and its EU delegation was also related to a split between the EU 'health track' on the one hand and the 'foreign policy track' on the other hand. The EU delegation in Geneva is considered a transformed version of the former Commission Delegation and also still viewed by member states as such (Battams *et al.* 2012). The people working on health issues are also seconded from the European Commission and likely to return there after having served in Geneva. EU member states believe that the Commission has its own preferences and interests, which tend to centre around economic and trade interests, rather than public health objectives (van Schaik 2011). This image was reinforced by the EU delegation to the WTO being placed under even more direct control of the Commission, to the detriment of potential EEAS influence on international trade matters. Health experts and policy-makers of EU member states feared a greater degree of influence over their positions within WHO debates by 'Brussels', aside from any concerns about foreign policy and development specialists having a greater say. Even though the number of health policy experts ('health attachés') with a background in national health policy may be limited, they are keen to underline the necessity of this expertise in international debates. For instance, they did not consider the Council Conclusions on Global Health adopted by development and foreign ministers a fully-fledged global health strategy and feel little commitment to it.

Over time, it became clear that member states could avoid an undesirable take-over of external representation by the EU delegation on all topics and that the involvement of the EEAS headquarters in Brussels on WHO affairs was rather limited. The multilateral affairs department of the EEAS appeared overburdened and not interested in dealing with the many technical health issues on WHO's agenda. This relieved fears of an unwarranted take-over of global health policy by foreign policy specialists. Nevertheless, this may also explain why the EU foreign policy objective of effective multilateralism is not referred to in EU official positions on WHO reform or other global health debates.

The question of the EU's status at WHO

Through a resolution adopted in May 2011, the EU obtained speaking rights at the UNGA (see Chapter 2 of this volume). The EU could seek an upgraded status at the WHO by seeking enhanced rights in line with this UNGA resolution, or through membership of the EU at the WHO. The question of the EU's status is somewhat related to the WHO reform debate, since it also covers questions regarding the relationship with non-state actors and the EU. Despite the EU being quite a different creature than a traditional intergovernmental organization or NGO, the possibility of upgrading their involvement in WHO governance may also open up opportunities for an upgraded EU status. This line of reasoning seems to be in the back of the mind of the EU delegation in Geneva and

European Commission in Brussels, the traditional advocates of an upgraded EU status. In an EU statement on WHO reform (EU Statement 2011), reference is made to the need to think about proper involvement and participation of regional economic integration organizations – the category of entities through which the EU normally operates within international governance structures – to which the EU is de facto the only participant. However, if the EU delegation and/or Commission really strive to upgrade the EU's status at WHO, it is uncertain whether EU member states would support this given the sensitivity of the EU's competence on health matters. Neither is the rest of WHO's membership likely to support an upgraded EU status, as indicated by earlier remarks about the EU's role within WHO (Battams *et al.* 2012; cf. van Schaik 2013: 149–50) and recent opposition to an upgraded EU status in other international bodies, such as the United Nations General Assembly (UNGA) (see Chapter 2).

Within the UNGA, the resolution has already resulted in the EU being represented directly in a High-Level meeting on the Prevention and Control of Non-communicable Diseases in 2011, where an EU statement was made by (former) EU Health Commissioner John Dalli. The process through which the UNGA resolution was eventually adopted was extremely difficult and now the debate on its extension to other parts of the UN family proves cumbersome as well. Many non-EU states may see an attempt by the EU to upgrade its status as merely a way to increase the influence and demands of individual EU member states. They argue an EU seat would require EU member states giving up their seats and votes in return for an upgraded role, which would in turn be inconceivable for many of them. There is also confusion about how to place the EU within the international system and particularly with regard to global health issues, especially when EU member states still take rather different national positions (e.g. sexual and reproductive rights). The need for separate EU involvement is also not always understood and accepted. Last but not least, an upgrade of the EU's status, particularly to enable EU membership of the WHO, would most likely require amending the WHO's Constitution. This would be a tremendous challenge, particularly when taking into account that previous changes took more than seven years on average to agree upon. This makes an upgrade of the EU's status at WHO very unlikely in the short term.

Conclusion

This chapter has discussed the EU's positioning in the debate on reforming the WHO (external reform) and changes to the EU's functioning following from the implementation of the Lisbon Treaty (internal reform). The EU has emerged as quite an active player in the debate on WHO reform, but its focus on the topic was rather technical. A (high-level) political commitment to strengthen the WHO as the undisputed directing and coordinating entity on global health is lacking. As a result of the efforts of several EU member states, most of them considerable funding contributors to the organization, modest progress was made in strengthening WHO transparency and accountability mechanisms. However, there is no guarantee that the WHO will become more proactive and stronger in international norm-setting processes for global health, an EU aim commensurate with its strive for effective multilateralism. Inherent shortcomings in WHO's functioning, resulting from its fragmented structure, its relationship to and competition with other international actors operating in the field of health and the (unclear) involvement of civil society (and industry) in its governance processes were insufficiently addressed. Often WHO acts or is expected to act as a partner with other international agencies, rather than a 'lead agency' in the governance of global health issues (e.g. NCDs).

The Lisbon Treaty did not empower the EU as a global health actor, but rather increased tensions between representatives of the European Commission and EU delegation, on the one hand, and representatives of EU member states, on the other. The EU's authority to engage in global health matters is sensitive, with EU member states considering health to be primarily a national prerogative. Issues regarding the EU's status at the WHO, and a greater coherence between EU foreign policy aspirations and the external dimension of national health policies, remain unresolved and most representatives of EU member states prefer them to remain under the carpet.

The EU's official striving for effective multilateralism does not mean much to EU member states working at the WHO level. Nevertheless, they are interested in the WHO, and in global health problems more generally. By propagating many practical and rather technical proposals, various representatives of EU states and institutions have worked hard to improve the WHO's operational functioning, so far with some modest successes, but without any radical changes and progress in the governance of global health. Implicitly, therefore, it could be argued that the EU in fact did try to operationalize the EU's striving for effective multilateralism by propagating its views on improving the WHO's functioning. However, a strong position on key issues, such as WHO priorities or its regional structure, were lacking and (health experts of) EU member states only seem to feel bound to develop a common EU approach when it suits them, which overall leads to the EU punching below its weight in the struggle over WHO reform.

Notes

1 The authors would like to thank Roland Driece, Edith Drieskens, Björn Kümmel, Remco van de Pas and Seriana van den Berg for their input and comments on earlier drafts.
2 The regions are: Africa (AFRO), the Americas (AMRO), the Eastern Mediterranean (EMRO), Europe (EURO), the Western Pacific (WPRO) and Southeast Asia (SEARO).

References

Battams, S. (2012a) 'The social determinants of health and civil society engagement in the WHO reform and beyond: negotiations at the 65th World Health Assembly', *Health Diplomacy Monitor*, Special Issue 65th World Health Assembly, 3(4): 9–12.

Battams, S. (2012b) 'Commitment to a target on non-communicable disease mortality: the role of NGO advocacy', *Health Diplomacy Monitor*, Special Issue 65th World Health Assembly, 3(4):18–20.

Battams, S. and van Schaik, L.G. (forthcoming) 'The European Union as a global health actor: a critical view', in I. Kickbusch and T. Emmerling (eds) *The European Union as a global health actor*, Singapore: World Scientific.

Battams, S., van Schaik, L. and Van der Pas, R. (2012) 'The European Union's voice and influence on global health and the reform of the World Health Organisation: the role of diplomacy', paper presented at the European Union in International Affairs III Conference, Brussels, May 2012.

Brown, T.M. and Cueto, M. (2011) 'The World Health Organization and the world of health', in R. Parker and M. Sommer (eds) *Routledge handbook of global public health*, London and New York: Routledge.

Clift, C. (2013) *The role of the World Health Organization in the international system*, London: Chatham House.

CoE (2010) *The handling of the H1N1 pandemic: more transparency needed. Report of the Parliamentary Assembly of the Council of Europe*, Strasbourg: Council of Europe.

EC (2010) *EU's role in global health: communication*. Brussels: European Commission.

Emmerling, T. and Heydemann, J. (2012) *The EU as an actor in Global Health Diplomacy. Textbook on global health diplomacy*, New York: Springer.

EU Council (2010) *Council conclusions on the EU role in global health*, Brussels: Council of the European Union.

EU Statement (2011) *First comments of the European Union and its 27 member states to the three concept papers on the reform of the World Health Organization*. Submitted by the Republic of Poland.

EU Statement (2012) *WHO reform: priority setting*, Geneva, 17 January 2012.

Lee, K. (2009) *The World Health Organization*, London and New York: Routledge.

Legge, D. (2012) 'Future of WHO hangs in the balance', *British Medical Journal*, 345:e6877.

Ravishankar, N., Gubbins, P., Cooley, R.J., Leach-Kemon, K., Michaud, C.M., Jamison, D.J. and Murray, C.J.L. (2009) 'Financing of global health: tracking development assistance for health from 1990 to 2007', *Lancet*, 373: 2113–24.

Sridhar, D. (2012) 'Who sets the global health research agenda? The challenge of multi-bi financing', *PLoS Medicine*, 9(9).

Sweden (2011) *Sweden's strategy for WHO 2011–2015*, Swedish Ministry of Health and Social Affairs, Regeringskansliet, S2011/3711/EIS.

Szlezák, N.A., Bloom, B.R., Jamison, D.T., Keusch, G.T., Michaed, C.M., Moon, S. and Clark, W.C. (2010) 'The global health system: actors, norms, and expectations in transition', *PLoS Medicine*, 7(1).

UK (2008) *Health is global: a UK government strategy 2008–2013*, London: HM Government.

UK House of Lords (2008) *Diseases know no frontiers. First report of session 2007–2008*, House of Lords Select Committee on Intergovernmental Organisations.

van Schaik, L.G. (2011) 'The EU's performance in the World Health Organization: internal cramps after the "Lisbon cure"', *European Integration*, 33(6): 699–713.

van Schaik, L.G. (2013) *EU effectiveness and unity in multilateral negotiations: more than the sum of its parts?*, Basingstoke and New York: Palgrave Macmillan.

4 The role of the EU in the reform of the FAO

Bridge builder or structural engineer?

Robert Kissack

Introduction

This chapter analyses the role of the European Union in the reform process of the Food and Agriculture Organization (FAO), one of the UN specialized agencies. The FAO was founded in 1945 and its mandate spans issues from food production and distribution, including ensuring food security, adequate nutrition and the prevention of hunger, through rural development and improvements to agricultural productivity. Since the establishment of the Millennium Development Goals (MDGs) in 2000, the FAO has played a central role in achieving the part of the first goal, namely halving the proportion of people suffering from extreme hunger. However, while the MDGs gave much needed coherence to the multitude of individual development goals across the UN system and UN members, specific programmes intended to realize these goals remained fragmented and incoherent. In response to this, the UN Secretary General presented the findings of a High-level Panel on UN system-wide coherence to the 60th session of the UN General Assembly, in a report titled 'Delivering as One' (UN 2006). A key recommendation of the report was the need to streamline UN operations in each country under a single UN office, rather than replicate the fragmented structure of the separate UN agencies. For a variety of reasons that are elaborated on below, the FAO embarked on a reform process in November 2004, when the members of the FAO's executive Council agreed to a comprehensive external audit with a view to major structural reform. While some elements of reform continue, January 2012 is taken in this chapter to mark the end of the substantial reform phase, when Jose Graziano de Silva of Brazil took up office as FAO Director-General, ending Jacques Diouf's 18 years tenure of the position. The chapter builds on previous work on the reform process, in Kissack (2010: 87–94).

The European Union's (EU) response to FAO reform was to publish its strategic vision for the organization, drawing on its commitment to effective multilateralism and the UN's 'Delivering as One' report, stating that 'today's challenges need a multilateral framework based on a strong UN system. Within that system, FAO has a specific role to play' (EU 2007a: 1). More specifically, the Council of the European Union stated in June 2007 (EU 2007b) that effective multilateralism, with a strong UN at its heart, is a central element of the EU's external action. The EU envisages FAO to be the key partner in the UN system for all its member countries in the field of its mandate.

The importance of the FAO is also indirectly acknowledged in the European Security Strategy, which notes that '45 million die every year from hunger and malnutrition' (EU 2003: 2). In the context of this book, this constitutes a seren-dipitous 'natural experiment' regarding UN reform that took place during the period before and after the signing of the Lisbon Treaty, providing an oppor-tunity to assess what impact (if any) the Lisbon Treaty had on the EU's capacity to influence the FAO's reform process. As such, it promises to be a highly insightful case study into the internal and external dimensions of the pursuit of effective multilateralism.

The EU has had a unique relationship with the FAO since 1991, when the European Community became a member of the FAO alongside its member states, as a result of changes to the FAO constitution that created the category of member organization. Specific rules (outlined in Section D of the *General Rules of the Organization*, FAO 2013) clarify when the Commission delegates (today the European External Action Service – EEAS) speak for the EU, and when EU member states speak in their capacity as FAO members, based on evaluating the division of competencies inside the EU and how they correspond to particular FAO agenda items. As a member organization, the EU is prevented from carry-ing out a number of tasks, including voting on the budget and participating in Programme, Financial, and Legal and Constitutional Affairs committees, as well as its representatives holding elected positions. The Lisbon Treaty's impact on EU–FAO relations has been less significant than in other international organiza-tions, insofar as the European Community's formal membership of the FAO has made granting an international legal personality to the EU, and right of the EEAS to speak on issues of exclusive *and* shared competence, as much an issue of continuity as of change. While the transition has in no way been completely smooth (the UK has sought the continued presence of the Presidency alongside the EEAS delegation representing the EU), the basic legal structure is in place in the FAO for the EEAS to take on the duties outlined in the Lisbon Treaty. Beyond Rome, the *modus operandi* of EU representation in the FAO has been of interest to other EEAS missions seeking to represent the Union in different UN agencies. To this end, the FAO case is simultaneously highly relevant in terms of illustrating the impact of the effective multilateralism on an external reform programme, and of limited wider applicability due to European Community membership pre-dating both the 2003 European Security Strategy and the com-pletion of the Lisbon Treaty.

The chapter proceeds in four sections. The first presents a brief overview and theoretical framing of the question of FAO reform, and the role of the EU within it. The second section sketches the major parts of the actual reform process, identifying the contribution made by the EU and EU member states, constituting the external environment in which effective multilateralism was pursued.

The third section analyses intra-EU coordination and EU representation geared towards pursuing effective multilateralism and identifies the impact of the Lisbon Treaty on the changing behaviour of the EU during the reform process. The final section concludes by weighing up the internal and external dimensions of reform, gauging to what extent they have been congruent, and if not, why. It is argued that the EU played a significant role in facilitating FAO reform and EU member state actors were instrumental during the reform process. For a number of institutional and political reasons, the EU was not highly visible as a leader, and the success of the FAO reform process may in part explain the reluctance of some EU member states to hand EU representation over to the EEAS.

External reform: the case of the FAO

When the FAO Council agreed in November 2004 to launch an Independent External Evaluation (IEE) of the FAO (FAO 2005a: 1), the organization was widely perceived as being unfit for purpose, having developed into a caricature of bureaucratic mismanagement, donor dissatisfaction and lacking strategic direction. Indeed, the IEE report noted this by saying the 'FAO is in a serious state of crisis which imperils the future of the Organization' (FAO 2007a: 9). There were several separate, but interrelated factors that systematically weakened the FAO over a period from the mid-1990s to mid-2000s. First, the organization's membership was sharply divided between a minority of donor states and the majority of middle- and low-income states. EU member states contribute 38.8 per cent of the annual FAO budget, and together with the other OECD members contribute 86.8 per cent (FAO 2011).[1] While such cleavages are relatively common in universal multilateral organizations, the dissatisfaction of the major donors was focused on the secretariat too, and in particular the management style of the incumbent Director-General, Jacques Diouf. In a survey of permanent representatives of the members to the FAO, the IEE-reported two commonly held opinions were that 'the Director-General is insufficiently communicative and is lacking in responsiveness to members' and that 'the Director-General and Secretariat are not sufficiently accountable to the Governing Bodies' (FAO 2007a: 180). Donors bemoaned the failure of the FAO to fulfil its mandate, while simultaneously reducing funding. Without doubt, these donor states bear some of the blame for the decline of the organization. However, their defence of their actions raises a third factor, namely the (mis)management of the FAO. Our conversations with diplomats[2] from a number of EU and non-EU donor states to the FAO reveal a widely held view that the Director-General remained in his position for 18 years thanks to his ability to canvass support from developing states, through strategic appointments and the dispersal of FAO resources.

> Put crudely, a significant number of OECD countries, including some of the largest contributors to the regular budget, consider that their interests and voice are not given adequate attention by the Organization and that the G77

uses its overwhelming voting power in favour of actions (including those promoted by the Director-General), which they believe will increase FAO support in their countries.

(FAO 2007a: 181)

Three elements stand out as the crucial determinants of the FAO's crisis. The first was the entrenched positions of the 'payers' (major donors) and the 'sayers' (the majority of members) that fuelled an atmosphere of distrust and suspicion. The second was a decade of declining funding coupled with a poor financial management within the organization. The third was the breakdown of the working relationship between major donors and senior FAO management, which was most apparent in the FAO governing bodies that were rendered ineffective and unable to take important decisions about the direction of the organization. In short, these elements conspired to create a perfect storm for institutional decline.

Having sketched out the context in which reform was needed, let us turn to consider why states fund and participate in the governance of multilateral organizations like the FAO. Leaving aside realist arguments that international institutions are built on power relations, both in terms of serving the interests of great powers and enforcing compliance with institutional rules through coercive measures, there remain two plausible explanations in the literature. The first is that states cooperate through international institutions because it serves their interests, and the second is that states participate in international institutions because they are perceived as being legitimate. Keohane argues that cooperation between states takes place under the shadow of discord and is a mechanism for reconciling different preferences (Keohane 2005: 51–4). Neoliberal institutionalism defends the expectation that states cooperate based on expected absolute gains, in contrast to the narrower conditions of achieving relative gains preferred by structural realists (Grieco 1988). In both cases interests are assumed to be fixed prior to entering into cooperative agreements, but this need not be the case. Cooperation between states in institutions can lead to revisions of state interests as a result of learning either from other states or from 'experts' recognized for their scientific and technical knowledge (Haas 1989, 1992). Whether interests and preferences are assumed to be constant or changeable, states participate in international organizations to receive benefits and make cooperation with other actors more stable and predictable.

An alternative explanation for why states participate in international organizations is because they are perceived as legitimate, either in terms of how decisions are reached (input legitimacy) or in terms of the efficiency of actions taken (output legitimacy) (Keohane 2006). Keohane argues that international organizations can never stake their claims to legitimacy based on the efficiency of their outputs, given the frequency with which they are slow to be enacted, and compromised in scope and purpose as a result of political bargaining. Thus, only input legitimacy remains, and Keohane questions the resilience of this form of legitimacy in an age where greater democratic accountability is demanded of the institutions of global governance, but intergovernmental organizations do not preoccupy themselves with the democratic standards of the members. Legitimacy can also be seen in relation to the prevailing distribution of power in the international system. As Thompson (2006) has argued, international organizations serve powerful states by providing legitimacy for their foreign policy goals (as well as lowering the costs of action). Ikenberry (2001) has made a similar argument on a grander scale by comparing the institutional design of different constitutional settlements engineered by great powers 'after victory' across time. Finally, participation in international organizations can be seen through a sociological lens, when legitimate behaviour is determined by norms and practices perpetuated over time (cf. Finnemore and Sikkink 1998; Hurd 1999; Clark 2003).

How can the issue of FAO reform be framed through these theoretical lenses? There are some common interests that many, if not all FAO members share, such as achieving the first Millennium Development Goal to 'halve, between 1990 and 2015, the proportion of people who suffer from hunger' (UN MDG, without year). Related to this is the FAO's response to the world food crisis of 2008 and the broader question of food security. The centrality of the FAO in finding solutions to these problems is unquestionable, but its capacity to act prior to reform was questionable, given its reputation as an 'unwilling and/or unreliable partner' (FAO 2007a: 41). There are also many issues where FAO members' interests diverge (for example on the production and use of bio-fuels and genetically modified crops) and here members seek endorsement of their policies by using the credibility of the organization as a source of independent scientific authority. This chapter focuses only on the fracture lines emerging between states over the issue of institutional reform. From the perspective of output legitimacy, and one championed by the EU (EU 2007a), reform was needed to improve the delivery of the core objectives of the organization, namely promoting agricultural development, improving food security and nutrition, and protecting global food and agricultural resources. From the perspective of input legitimacy, the need for reform was less clear. The majority of FAO members from the developing world, caucused through the G77, saw reform as a Trojan horse for implementing neo-liberal policies pushed upon them by a minority of donor countries. To complicate matters further, the distrust noted above between donors and senior FAO secretariat weakened the capacity of the organization's staff to perform the role of an epistemic community capable of shaping the reform issue in a neutral manner.[3]

The puzzle to be addressed is to explain why reform took place, and why was it comprehensive, rapidly executed and founded on consensus between all members. As noted above, many of the factors that we would expect to make reform unlikely are found in the FAO case, *inter alia* a universal organization with a high degree of heterogeneity between members, a highly politicized agenda and a low level of trust between members. A review of similar empirical cases points to an expectation of long drawn-out negotiations, such as in the Doha Development Round negotiations in the WTO (Kissack 2011). FAO reform took place contrary to expectations. The examination of the internal and external dimensions of effective multilateralism in the case of FAO reform hinges on two sets of questions. First, how well did the EU integrate into the reform process? Who represented the EU (European Commission/EEAS, presidency, or member states), and why? Did the EU have a clear set of goals for the negotiation process, and did it achieve them? The second set of questions relate to the role played by the EU as a catalyst for undertaking reform in the first place. What role did the EU play in initiating the reform process? Did it help break the impasse between donor states from the EU and the OECD and the majority of middle- and low-income states, and if so, how? In what ways did the EU facilitate the participation of all FAO members in the reform process? These questions refer to the structural environment in which the EU engages and pursues its goals. To this end, while the EU saw itself as a 'bridge-builder' within the negotiations between the G77 and the US and its allies, a more useful role is as a 'structural engineer' that has the capacity to change the FAO-level negotiating environment. In short, the analysis is not only of the role of the EU during the reform negotiations, but also of the role of the EU in making the reform negotiations possible in the first place. As shall be argued, the EU played a significant role in making negotiations possible, as well as being involved during the adoption of the reform programme through the diplomats of the member states.

Why was FAO reform needed? The external dimension of effective multilateralism

Such was the chronic state of decline that in November 2004 the FAO's executive Council accepted a proposal to commission an Independent External Evaluation (IEE) of the organization. Composed of seven individuals with expertise and knowledge either of international organizations in general or the FAO in particular, they began work in April 2006 and presented their report containing 117 recommendations to the FAO biennial conference in November 2007. The IEE opens with a stark assessment of the FAO: '[t]he Organization is today in a financial and programme crisis that imperils the Organization's future in delivering essential services to the world' (FAO 2007a: 3). The core message of the report was 'Reform with Growth', by which they advocated a renewal of the FAO through reform *and* increased resources, making a demand on every constituent of the FAO – developed states, developing states and the Secretariat itself. The proposed mechanism for reform was for all states to agree an Immediate Action Plan (IPA) detailing their shared commitment to four core tasks; 'a new Strategic Framework, investing in governance, institutional culture change and reform of administrative and management systems, and restructuring for effectiveness and efficiency in both headquarters and the field' (FAO 2007a: 5).

Before commencing with reform negotiations, the budget for 2008–9 had to be agreed. Since budgets are adopted by simple majority, the major donors rely on the good will of the majority of states that are beneficiaries of funds to reach a mutually acceptable agreement. The IEE recognized the potential hindrance agreeing the new budget could be.

How can the membership reach agreement and shared ownership ... of reform with growth? Some FAO members will incline towards 'financial growth first as the minimum requirement for reform'. Others wish to see 'major and sustained reform before financial growth'. The IEE concludes that if these two incompatible formulations persist, the decline of the Organization will continue and indeed accelerate.... Should the transformative reforms needed by the FAO not occur, the mutual trust required for 'reform with growth' would quickly erode.

(FAO 2007a: 4)

The IEE's warning of impasse on the budget proved accurate. In November 2007, G77 members (led by Brazil) pushed for a 21 per cent increase in the budget, against the wishes of all OECD members. Under the leadership of the Portuguese Presidency, the EU agreed a budget rise of 13.3 per cent, considerably higher than the 9–10 per cent the US and Canada had informally signalled they would be willing to accept, and breaking solidarity within the group of major donors. It was seen by non-EU OECD members (and a number of large EU member states) as a missed opportunity to drive a bargain with the G77 over solid commitments on reform in return for increased funding. Such was the level of dissatisfaction with EU's handling of the negotiations, four states voted against the budget and two abstained, a rare public demonstration of frustration over the budget.[4]

Seen from the perspective of January 2008, when the FAO membership was supposed to sit down and begin negotiating an Immediate Plan of Action (IPA) that would turn the IEE report into a resuscitation device for a moribund organization, the EU-brokered budget deal looked like another example of EU weakness. Rather than holding out for a stronger commitment from the G77 on change, the Portuguese EU Presidency buckled under pressure from the adroit Brazilian leadership of the G77. Diplomats from EU member states indicate that the Lusophone connection did not go unnoticed, and were concerned about the implications for relations between the EU and non-EU major donors. In defence of the Presidency, the agreement reached represented a compromise between the two intractable positions identified by the IEE. It also meant that the G77 entered the IPA discussions feeling buoyant, while a number of major donors (including the US) were resigned to seeing the IEE recommendations watered down in another example of the tyranny of the majority. A preliminary appraisal of the role the EU played in instigating FAO reform was that it facilitated the presence of the G77 at the IPA discussion, at the potential cost of failing to secure sufficient guarantees about the direction and degree of the reform to be undertaken.

An appraisal made five years later leads to different conclusions. The outcome of the negotiations over the IPA that lasted the whole of 2008 was the acceptance of a plan of action that largely resembled the proposals of the IEE in full, albeit with an appreciation of the need for gradual change in some areas. Agreement was reached on monitoring the reform process in order to ensure there was no slippage in the implementation by the Secretariat. Given the formally close working relationship between the Director-General and leading G77 members, slippage at this point might have been expected if the reform process had been merely a case of the major donors driving a harder bargain (or the G77 accepting concessions in return for the budgetary increases), as it provided an opportunity for the G77 or Secretariat to renege on any deals made. Significant changes include the election of Graziano de Silva in January 2012 to the position of Director-General under a strict limit of two four-year terms, replacing the incumbent of 18 years, Jacques Diouf (who agreed not to seek re-election), and an integrated work and programme budget has been adopted, allocating funds according to specific target goals rather than allowing departments to decide how to spend their budget. The position of the UN in the FAO seems to have gone from a lame duck to a leader, both in terms of the depth of reform, and the speed with which it was achieved. The 2011 budget negotiations demonstrate how far reform has come, where there was unanimous approval for a nominal zero growth budget.[5] Such an outcome would have been unimaginable in 2007, regardless of the global recession focusing all states on fiscal austerity. How was the impasse ended, how did so much of the IEE report get implemented, and how has the momentum of reform remained?

The key to answering these questions is to look in detail at the structure of the negotiations drafting the Immediate Plan of Action. As stipulated under Article IV §5 of the FAO Constitution, a Committee of the Conference (CoC) was established and divided into three working groups focusing on specific parts of the reform process.[6] The purpose of the design was to prevent 'grand bargains' being constructed across a wide range of issues, and instead follow a pragmatic approach to resolving specific questions of reform on a micro-level. Participation in working groups demanded a high level of commitment with regard to the frequency of meetings, and for that reason only one state (the US) had the diplomatic resources at its disposal to participate in all tracks and therefore keep abreast of the overall direction. The chairperson and vice-chairperson of each working group were from either an OECD country or a G77 country, and all three OECD representatives were European diplomats (from the UK, Italy and Austria). Meetings between the chairpersons, vice-chairpersons and senior FAO staff provided the only oversight of the entire process, and as will be discussed below, the EU attempted to capitalize on its triple representation through its member states directly involved in these coordination meetings when preparing common positions in Brussels and Rome. The working group structure had a number of positive externalities for the reform process, aside from minimizing log-rolling and other bargaining techniques in complex negotiations. The frequency of meetings fostered a collegial atmosphere between diplomats from donor states and those from G77 countries, allowing reform to be understood as a tool for improving the delivery of core services, and thus increasing the output legitimacy of the FAO. The arrival at consensus also increased the legitimacy of the reform process, with the shared ownership of the IPA.

The EU's role in facilitating the reform process can now be clearly articulated. The budget deal brokered in November 2007, which at the time appeared to be a sign of EU weakened vis-à-vis the demands of the G77, was the first step in breaking the impasse between the major donor states and developing countries. The EU Presidency, negotiating on behalf of all OECD members, agreed a deal with the G77 that the US, Canada and Japan would not have otherwise accepted (Britain and Germany, among others, were also unhappy). Immediately afterwards, when CoC working group meetings began in January 2008, the significance of the concessions made to developing states was not apparent, with donors entering negotiations with low expectations of reform. However, the structure of the negotiations played a significant role in ensuring the recommendations of the IEE were carried over into the IPA. Piecemeal agreements over specific items of reform in the three working groups helped to depoliticize the concept of macro-level reform, explaining how specific changes could benefit donor states, developing states, the organization itself, and the FAO's commitment to 'Delivering as One' goals established at the UN system level. The EU and its member states were also extremely important in helping to finance the reform process. In order to put the IPA into practice, a multi-million dollar annual voluntary contribution fund was set up ($21.8 million in 2009, $39.6 million in 2010–11, $39.5 million in 2012–13) to finance reform (FAO 2008a: 48, 2010: 6–8). By way of an example, 80 per cent of the initial round of pledges came from either EU member states ($5.8 million) or the European Community ($1.4 million), out of a total of $9 million (FAO 2010: 9). Finally, the strategic positioning of three EU member state diplomats as chairperson or vice-chairpersons provided the EU with an opportunity to 'parallel process' negotiations in the three groups and exert influence over their direction where necessary. This process is discussed in the next section. In summary, demand for reform came mostly from major donors, and most significant in terms of international organization reform was the decision to employ external evaluators to suggest a way forward. The IEE recommendations were closest to the preferences of the major donors, favouring maximal reform, and furthest from those of the Secretariat. The success of the reform process was due to the year-long negotiations preparing the IPA, which re-established a sense of trust among diplomats, and gave room for an unbiased appraisal of IEE reform proposals based on merit and utility.

The impact of the Lisbon Treaty on EU participation in FAO reform: the internal dimension of effective multilateralism

Recent scholarly interest in the impact of the Lisbon Treaty on the EU's coordination, representation and participation in the UN system has focused on the 2011 UNGA resolution (A65/276) allowing the EU, as a regional organization, to assume many (but not all) of the rights a member enjoys in the plenary sessions of the General Assembly (Emerson and Wouters, 2010; see Chapter 2 of this volume). Larger surveys of the EU across the whole UN system have attempted to systematically classify types of representation and identify best-practice models that could be applied more widely, and many have noted the heavily institutionalized EU representation in the FAO (Balfour *et al.* 2011; Comelli and

Matarazzo 2011; Palacio *et al.* 2011). As noted in Pedersen (2006), the European Community has been a member of the FAO since 1991, when a change in the FAO Constitution permitted the membership of regional economic integration organizations (REIOs) as member organizations.[7] Prior to the Lisbon Treaty, the European Commission spoke on behalf of the European Community on matters of exclusive competence, and the presidency on areas of shared competence (augmented by the member states speaking individually). In advance of all FAO meetings, the European Commission submitted to the FAO Secretariat details of legal competencies related to agenda items, identifying who would speak on what issues. Preparations for this took place both in Brussels, at the Coordination Working Party (FAO) in DG Agriculture and Fisheries, and in Rome. With 20 years of institutionalization, the coordination procedures between member states in the FAO should provide sufficient capabilities to effectively participate in the reform process, as well as a strong foundation for the post-Lisbon enhanced status of the EU and EEAS representation.

The three working groups charged with drafting parts of the IPA were instrumental in the ultimate success of the reform process. The chairpersons and vice-chairpersons of these groups played a significant role, facilitating informal networking between working group members and also being privileged with an oversight of the whole reform process. Diplomats and FAO Secretariat staff assert that individuals were chosen on personal merit, not nationality, and thus too much cannot be inferred from the strategic positioning of three EU diplomats in the process (British chairperson of WG1, Italian vice-chairperson of WG2 and Austrian as vice-chairperson of WG3). These candidates were drawn from a shortlist prepared by the OECD members at a meeting in Rome on 14 December 2007, intended to install one OECD nominee and one G77 nominee in tandem to serve each working group. In earlier work on the reform process I argued that these individuals with privileged global knowledge of reform negotiations could, if coordinated through established EU institutions, provide a unique opportunity to shape FAO reform (Kissack 2010). This would take place through policy entrepreneurship directing negotiating in working groups, informed by their collaborative oversight of the entire process. It was argued that the EU was uniquely placed to take advantage of 'parallel processing'. Evidence supporting this comes from the Coordination Working Party (FAO) meeting in Brussels in December 2007, which identified

> the need to have a representative of an EU Member State as coordinator for each WG but also for all three together.... Each EU coordinator would have to present immediate reporting on every meeting of each WG, and also a short analysis document on each of the main topics. *The information would be then transmitted by the General Secretariat of the Council.*
>
> (EU 2007c: 3, emphasis added)

Throughout 2008, there were updates on the progress of the working group meetings in AGRI-FAO Coordination Working Party meetings in Brussels (EU

2008a–e). The early meetings included instructions on how to coordinate member states' positions. The UK representative, Vic Heard, chairperson of Working Group 1 'appealed to EU delegations to repeat in the meetings their support for the need on prioritisation, so that the FAO secretariat takes adequate notice when writing its new strategy on the basis of views expressed in the WG' (EU 2008b: 1). In the meetings in April, May and June (EU 2008c–e) the reporting process focused more on what had happened rather than strategizing new coordinated actions. Later in 2008 the Coordination Working Party (FAO) became more concerned with the content of the IPA report, and preparations for the November conference. The EU, through its member states, was well integrated into the structure of the reform process. It capitalized on its comparative advantage of having multiple seats through its 27 members to occupy a number of positions that would not have been possible by a single sovereign state.

So how influential was the EU? Quite interestingly, diplomats with first-hand experience of negotiations do not seem to have the impression of a particularly coordinated EU. They point to the personal qualities of the EU member state diplomats who served as chairs as being significant to their appointment, and to their success in the role. Moreover, it does not seem to have been the case that any state or group of states was able to control the reform process. How, if at all, can this be reconciled with the documental evidence of Brussels coordination? One way to reconcile the two is by seeing EU objectives within the recommendations of the IEE report. In June 2007, three months before the IEE report was presented to the FAO, the EU set out strategic vision for the future of the FAO (EU 2007a). It identifies four core issue areas for reform: '(i) a clear strategy and plan owned by the FAO membership; (ii) prioritisation of objectives; (iii) allocation of financial resources according to a clear strategy and plan; and (iv) a multidisciplinary approach and inter-agency cooperation as soon as possible' (EU 2007a: 4). There were ten additional topics that the EU saw as being essential to reform that elaborated these points. All of these goals were realizable through closely following the IEE 117-point recommendations. The first, common ownership, was promoted through universal participation in the working group structure; the prioritization of goals was stressed by Mr Heard in his reports back to the Coordination Working party (FAO) in Brussels (EU 2008b). The third is realized through integrated work and budget programmes, and was seen by many diplomats as one of the biggest successes of the reform process, and the last, inter-agency cooperation, was stressed through numerous references to 'One UN' recommendations in the 'Delivering as One' report (UN 2006). Given the closeness of fit between what the EU set out as its overall strategic aims, and what the IEE proposed as the necessary reforms of the FAO, the best strategy for FAO reform according to EU preferences was to ensure FAO reform followed IEE recommendations. The path of least resistance towards achieving the EU's broadly specified aims was to facilitate adherence to the 117-point plan. Strategically, this meant less 'EU' and more 'IEE', in terms of profile, authorship and ownership.

The Immediate Plan of Action was one year underway when the Lisbon Treaty finally came into law on 1 December 2009. To what extent did the Lisbon Treaty impact on the reform process? As has been explained, the most significant work, in terms of 'structural engineering', took place during 2008 in the three working groups that fundamentally altered the negotiating environment and created a common shared view of a reformed FAO that could serve all members. The role of EU member state diplomats has been mapped out, pointing out the significance of the EU's representation through the member states. Even if the Lisbon Treaty had become law sooner, it would have made little difference in this case because member organizations are prevented from participating in budget issues (FAO Constitution Article XVIII §6, FAO 2013), and the majority of post-IPA implementation is in the Finance and Programme committees (FAO 2009), in neither of which member organizations are allowed to participate. As the FAO reform process has moved closer to completion, the impact of the Lisbon Treaty becomes more evident in the daily working of the organization, whereby the EEAS is supposed to represent the EU in issues of shared and exclusive competency. As a number of authors have pointed out, the Rome office of the EEAS (formerly the European Commission delegation) was understaffed during 2011 and relied on presidency teams to augment its capacity. This burden sharing was intended to be no more than a stopgap measure until the Rome office was fully staffed. The rotating presidency 'only temporarily and on behalf of the HR [High Representative], could continue exercising said representation in those areas and eventualities [of intergovernmental competence] where the figures are not yet fully active' (Palacio *et al.* 2011: 10). As Comelli and Matarazzo comment, while post-Lisbon the EU delegation should speak on all issues, be they exclusive or shared competencies, '[s]ince relevant national interests are at stake, in particular in the field of agriculture, MS are very jealous of their role and reluctant to accept the growing coordination role played by the EU delegation in Rome' (Comelli and Matarazzo 2011: 9). At meetings, the EEAS and Presidency diplomats sit together as the EU permanent representation to the FAO, and in every meeting 'indicate whether the competence belongs to the MS or to the EU, and this determines who is entitled to speak' (Comelli and Matarazzo 2011: 9). This 'solution' to the dispute has become known as 'one nameplate and two microphones' and has been most heavily insisted upon by the UK.

The reason why there was reluctance to hand representation over to the EEAS given by Comelli and Matarazzo is that intergovernmental preferences linger, due to the importance of agricultural policy. Although this is plausible, a couple of other explanations may be more persuasive. The first is that EU representation by the EEAS in the FAO is regarded as the thin end of the wedge of Lisbon Treaty implementation. Resistance in Rome is needed to prevent the established practices being exported into other UN organizations. While sharing an intergovernmental perspective, the national interests at stake are concerned with the bigger picture of EU member state/EEAS divisions of labour across the wider UN system. The second is that the reform process created an enhanced working relationship between EU member states and the wider FAO membership. A 'honeymoon period' of socialization between diplomats involved in IPA negotiations created an environment more open to cooperation, where key elements of multilateralism such as diffuse reciprocity and expectations about long-term gains were abundant. Since EEAS diplomats were not involved in the reform process, they are unable to capitalize on the 'cooperation dividend' paid by the reform process, and member state diplomats (who were instrumental in achieving that) are reluctant to be marginalized. As diplomatic staff from FAO members are rotated away from Rome, the dividend will likely wane and EU member states will be less unwilling to see EEAS staff represent the EU. In short, despite the fact that *a priori* one would expect the EU representation by the EEAS in the FAO to be highly developed as a result of the EU's institutionalized relationship with the organization dating back 20 years, there are theoretically grounded reasons to expect the new operating procedures to take longer to become established. It has been argued that some of the resistance to an internal reform is a product of the success of external reform in the FAO, and the role of EU member state diplomats in it.

Conclusion

Identifying the role of the EU within the FAO reform process is a complicated task. Using the framework of this edited volume, the external and internal dimensions of effective multilateralism have been presented. It was argued that the external dimension – FAO reform – dictated structural conditions in which the EU (and all other actors) operated, but during certain periods of the reform process the EU and its member states had influence over those conditions. For example, the EU presidency was instrumental in facilitating the 2007 budget agreement, and EU member state diplomats played a significant role in the transformation of negotiations during the drafting of the IPA, from one that began with mutual suspicion and ended in a clear sense of common ownership. Given that the EU's identified goals for reform closely matched the proposals of the IEE report, EU interests were best served in seeing the IEE proposals carried over into the IPA as closely as possible. Thus the EU, while swimming with the current of IEE reform, worked towards a maximal acceptance of the IEE report in the IPA. To this end, the long-established formal institutions of coordination between EU member states, both in Rome and Brussels, served as a useful platform from which to exert influence on the working groups. While there is documental evidence of this taking place in the first months of 2008, it is interesting to note that the recollections of EU and non-EU diplomats involved in the reform process did not perceive any state or group of states directly influencing the process. Paradoxically, the apparent absence of a strong EU push towards reform is a likely contributor to the overall success of the process, given that the purpose of the external evaluation was to overcome the FAO's divided membership. A vocal EU would have defeated the purpose of the reform process.

With regard to the internal dimension, the FAO stood out among UN special-ized agencies as the one where the implementation of Lisbon Treaty reforms *should* have gone most smoothly. The European Community had been a member organization since 1991, and the FAO had amended its constitution and rules accordingly. The agenda of the FAO spans exclusive and shared competencies, leading to the expectation that the EEAS would assume the role of the European Commission delegation in exclusive competency policy areas, and replace the presidency in shared competency issues, taking advantage of the existing AGRI-FAO coordination structure in Brussels, and the network of mission coordination in Rome. As has been shown, the roll out of Lisbon reform was not so straight-forward. The presidency remained a presence in EU representation, initially as a transitional measure while the Rome office of the EEAS recruited more staff, but later some member states, led by the UK, were reluctant to concede voice to the EEAS. Intergovernmental theory that points to the continued prioritization of national interests over European ones is a plausible reason for this continued lag in implementing the Lisbon treaty provisions in the field of external representa-tion. Another possible explanation is the success of the FAO reform process itself. The creation of a highly socialized group of diplomats with a common mission to reform the FAO, coupled with the fact that EU member state diplo-mats were centrally involved in creating and sustaining this group, leads us to ask why those same diplomats would want to take a back seat behind an EEAS mission that was not involved in the FAO reform process. The cooperation divi-dend yielded from the sustained negotiations on the IPA and the follow-up pro-gramme is less easily utilized by the EU *qua* EU. As diplomats involved in reform move on, and the dividend wanes, the acceptance of the EEAS will increase. The shadow of the successful FAO reform process will not hang over the implementation of the Lisbon Treaty in Rome forever, but it has made make the first years more complicated than expected.

Notes

1 The analysis in this chapter is based on a division between the major donors to the FAO and the remaining states, which are referred to as 'middle and low income', 'developing', or 'G77'. The 'major donors' are the 34 members of the OECD (21 of which are EU member states – Bulgaria, Cyprus, Latvia, Lithuania, Malta and Romania remain outside) that have relatively similar interests for the organization with regard to reform and negotiate budget issues collectively. Elsewhere in the literature, and in dis-cussions with practitioners, the term 'Geneva Group' is used, referring to the 14 leading UN donors which each pay 1 per cent or more to the UN budget. In the FAO there are currently 15 states that meet this definition.
2 This chapter draws on nine semi-structured interviews with EU and non-EU OECD diplomats to the FAO, EC and FAO staff on 15–16 January 2009, 14–15 January 2010, and 21 January 2012 in Rome. All interviews were held under the Chatham House rule, hence their identities cannot be revealed.
3 In 2005 the Director-General presented his own vision of FAO reform (FAO 2005b), which he conceded would be implemented alongside the independent reform process demanded by members.

4 Canada, Japan, Switzerland and the US voted against the budget, while Australia and South Korea abstained. The biennial budget rose from $765.7 million to $867.6 million (FAO 2007b).
5 This means that the cash value of the budget remains the same (i.e. $1 for $1), which in reality is a decreased budget once inflation is taken into account.
6 WG1: Priorities and Programmes of the Organization; WG2 Governance Reform; WG3: Reform of Systems, Programming and Budgeting Cultural Change, and Organizational Restructuring.
7 REIOs are defined in Article XIV §3b of the FAO Constitution as those 'which their Member States have transferred competence over matters within the purview of the conventions, agreements, supplementary conventions and agreements, including the power to enter into treaties in respect thereto' (FAO 2013: 15).

References

Balfour, R., Corthaut, T., Wouters, J., Emerson, M., Kaczynski P.-M. and Renard, T. (2011) *Upgrading the EU's role as global actor: institutions, law and the restructuring of European diplomacy*, Brussels: CEPS.

Clark, I. (2003) 'Legitimacy in a global order', *Review of International Studies*, 29(1): 75–95.

Comelli, M. and Matarazzo, R. (2011) *Rehashed Commission delegations or real embassies? EU delegations post-Lisbon*, IAI Working Paper 11–23, Rome: Istituto Affari Internazionali.

Emerson, M. and Wouters, J. (2010) *The EU's diplomatic debacle at the UN*, CEPS Policy Paper 1, October 2010.

EU (2003) *A secure Europe in a better world: European Security Strategy*, Brussels, 12 December 2003.

EU (2007a) *EU Strategic vision of the future of the Food and Agriculture Organisation of the United Nations (FAO) 8 June 2007*, (FAO-COORD 2007–022 REV 6), Brussels: Council of the European Union.

EU (2007b) *Conclusions of the Council of the European Union and of the representatives of the governments of the Member States of the European Union meeting within the Council of the Food and Agriculture Organisation of the United Nations (FAO) – 15 June 2007*, (10251/07 COR 1) Brussels: General Secretariat of the Council.

EU (2007c) *Report of the Coordination Working Party (FAO) – Brussels, 18 December 2007*, (16738/07), Brussels: General Secretariat of the Council.

EU (2008a) *Report of the Coordination Working Party (FAO) – Brussels, 13 February 2008*, (6642/08), Brussels: General Secretariat of the Council.

EU (2008b) *Report of the Coordination Working Party (FAO) – Brussels, 12 March 2008*, (7371/08), Brussels: General Secretariat of the Council.

EU (2008c) *Report of the Coordination Working Party (FAO) – Brussels, 16 April 2008*, (8599/08), Brussels: General Secretariat of the Council.

EU (2008d) *Report of the Coordination Working Party (FAO) – Brussels, 23 May 2008*, (9894/08), Brussels: General Secretariat of the Council.

EU (2008e) *Report of the Coordination Working Party (FAO) – Brussels, 17 June 2008*, (10515/08), Brussels: General Secretariat of the Council.

FAO (2005a) *Independent external evaluation of the FAO*, (C 2005/17), Rome: FAO.

FAO (2005b) *FAO reform: a vision for the 21st century*, (C 2005/INF/19), Rome: FAO.

FAO (2007a) *FAO: the challenge of renewal, report of the Independent External*

Evaluation of the Food and Agriculture Organization of the United Nations (FAO), (C 2007/7 A.1-Rev.1), Rome: FAO.

FAO (2007b) *FAO conference approves biennium budget of FAO*, Food and Agriculture Organization of the United Nations. Online. Available www.fao.org/newsroom/en/news/2007/1000715/index.html (accessed 8 February 2012).

FAO (2008a) *Report of the Conference Committee on follow-up to the Independent External Evaluation of FAO (CoC-IEE): Immediate Plan of Action*, (C 2008/4), Rome: FAO.

FAO (2008b) *Adoption of the Immediate Plan of Action (IPA) for FAO renewal (2009–2011). Draft Resolution*, (C 2008/LIM/3). Rome: FAO.

FAO (2009) *Implementation of the IPA regarding reform of the programming, budgeting and results-based monitoring system*, (Resolution No. 10/2009), Rome: FAO.

FAO (2010) *Finance Committee (135th Session 25–29 October 2010.) Immediate Plan of Action: financial plan 2010–11 and estimated financial requirements 2012–13*, (FC 135/7), Rome: FAO.

FAO (2011) *Scale of contributions 2012–2013 (Draft resolution)*, (C 2011/LIM/7), Rome: FAO.

FAO (2013) *Basic texts of the Food and Agriculture Organization of the United Nations*, Rome: FAO.

Finnemore, M. and Sikkink, K. (1998) 'International norm dynamics and political change', *International Organisation*, 52(4): 887–917.

Grieco, J.M. (1988) 'Anarchy and the limits of cooperation: a realist critique of the newest liberal institutionalism', *International Organization*, 42(3): 485–507.

Haas, E.B. (1989) *When knowledge is power: three models of change in international organizations*, Berkeley: University of California Press.

Haas, P. (1992) 'Introduction: epistemic communities and international policy coordination', *International Organization*, 46(1): 1–35.

Hurd, I. (1999) 'Legitimacy and authority in international politics', *International Organization*, 53(2): 379–408.

Ikenberry, G.J. (2001) *After victory: institutions, strategic restraint, and the rebuilding of order after major wars*, Princeton, NJ: Princeton University Press.

Keohane, R.O. (2005) *After hegemony: cooperation and discord in the world political economy*, Princeton, NJ: Princeton University Press.

Keohane, R.O. (2006) 'The contingent legitimacy of multilateralism', in E. Newman, R. Thakur and J. Tirman (eds) *Multilateralism under challenge? Power, international order, and structural change*, Tokyo: United Nations University Press, pp. 56–76.

Kissack, R. (2010) *Pursuing effective multilateralism: the European Union, international organisations and the politics of decision making*, London: Palgrave.

Kissack, R. (2011) 'Crisis situations and consensus seeking: adaptive decision making in the FAO and applying its lessons to the reform of the WTO', in T. Cottier and M. Elsig (eds) *Governing the World Trade Organization: past, present and beyond Doha*, Cambridge: Cambridge University Press, pp. 241–62.

Palacio, V., de la Rocha, V., Escario, J.L. and Ruiz, D. (2011) *The EU as a global actor: its evolving role in multilateral organizations*, Brussels: European Parliament.

Pedersen, J.M. (2006) 'FAO-EU cooperation: an ever stronger partnership', in J. Wouters, F. Hoffmeister and T. Ruys (eds) *The United Nations and the European Union: an ever closer partnership*, The Hague: T.M.C. Asser Press, pp. 63–91.

Thompson, A. (2006) 'Coercion through IOs: the Security Council and the logic of information transmission', *International Organization*, 60(1): 1–4.

UN (2006) 'Delivering as One: Report of the Secretary General's High-Level Panel', New York: United Nations. Online. Available www.un.org/events/panel/resources/pdfs/HLP-SWC-FinalReport.pdf (accessed 6 December 2012).

UN MDG (without year) *We can end powerty 2015. Millenium Development Goals.* The United Nations. Online. Available www.un.org/millenniumgoals/poverty.shtml (accessed 29 October 2012).

5 The EU and multilateralism in the environmental field

UNEP reform and external representation in environmental negotiations

Tom Delreux

Introduction

This chapter assesses the EU's commitment to effective multilateralism in the field of environmental governance. Internally, the EU's environmental policies encompass by far the most far-reaching multilateral environmental regulatory framework in the world. This is also reflected in the EU's position at the external level. The EU is generally known as one of the strongest supporters of strict environmental policies at the multilateral level. The EU's adherence to multilateralism is thus very apparent in the environmental domain, as the EU considers multilateral cooperation and governance structures at the multilateral level as the most appropriate ways to tackle global environmental problems, such as global warming or the loss of biodiversity. The EU not only assumes that the environmental dimension of these challenges is most appropriately addressed at the multilateral level, but it also declared that these challenges have a strong security dimension requiring multilateral cooperation. Indeed, the environment takes a prominent place in the EU documents that are the main points of departure of the approach taken by this volume, the ESS and its Implementation Report. In 2008, the European Council confirmed for instance that multilateralism is essential in dealing with the security consequences of climate change: 'The EU cannot do this alone. International co-operation, with the UN and regional organisations, will be essential' (European Council 2008: 6).

In the area of environmental governance, the EU's commitment to effective multilateralism is illustrated by a couple of observations: the EU is a party to more than 60 multilateral environmental agreements (MEAs), it usually takes one of the most reformist positions in international environmental negotiations, it basically aims to upload its environmental regulatory framework to the global level, and it sees for itself a leadership role in global environmental governance. This leadership role has, nonetheless, been badly damaged in recent years, undermining the EU's multilateral aspirations. The 2009 Copenhagen climate change conference, which was considered – in the words of the then Swedish European Council President Frederik Reinfeldt – 'a disaster for the EU', is of course illustrative in this regard. However, three points qualify this negative evaluation of the EU's recent performance in international environmental affairs. First, the EU seems to have found a new bridge-building and coalition-making role in the Cancún (2010), Durban (2011) and Doha (2012) climate change conferences. Second, it needs to be noted that the EU's failing leadership attempts in climate negotiations not only relate to intra-EU reasons, such as diverging positions between member states or controversies on the issue of external representation, but also – and particularly – to the constellation of the international negotiation set-up, which is based on consensus rules, where the countries with the most conservative positions, such as China and the US, dominate the game. Third, the EU's declining role in climate change negotiations is not to be automatically extrapolated to international negotiations on other environmental issues, where the EU continues to be an important actor. In other words, EU external environmental policy is more than merely climate change policies.

The EU has been confronted with two major institutional reform debates in the last decade in the area of external environmental policy. The first institutional reform debate is an external one, namely discussions at the international level on upgrading the United Nations Environment Programme (UNEP). UNEP is the Nairobi-based UN programme that coordinates a broad range of UN environmental activities and that should function as a 'catalyser' of global environmental policies (Vogler and Stephan 2007). It was created by the 1972 Stockholm Conference as a programme of the UN. The latter is important because in the UN structure, 'programmes' are less independent than 'specialized agencies', such as the FAO or the WHO. Programmes are, for instance, not financed through the regular UN budget but through voluntary contributions of members. Since the very establishment of UNEP, several proposals to strengthen the international environmental governance framework have been on the table (see Bauer and Biermann 2005). They all start from the observation that the current system of international environmental governance is not sufficiently adequate to deal with complex environmental challenges we are facing today and that 'effective multilateralism' is far from being realized global environmental governance (on the effectiveness and performance of UNEP, see Andresen and Rosendal 2009; Ivanova 2009, 2010). Indeed, the globe faces increasing environmental problems, but the institutions to cope with them are unsatisfactory. Indications for this finding include the non-compliance problems that several MEAs are facing, the fuzziness of the distribution of work between various international environmental regimes, and UNEP's resources and status that are considered insufficient to fulfil its role as coordinator and catalyser of global environmental policies. The EU has been among the strongest supporters of strengthening the global environmental governance framework.

The second institutional reform that affected the EU as international environmental actor took place inside the EU, namely the entry into force of the Lisbon Treaty in December 2009. One of the political rationales behind the Lisbon Treaty was reinforcing the international actorness of the EU, for instance by streamlining its external representation. How the EU should be represented in multilateral environmental negotiations was intensely debated in the EU in 2010.

Inter-institutional tensions, mainly between the Commission and the Council, initially weakened the EU as negotiator in environmental negotiations. Yet the adoption of so-called 'practical arrangements' calmed down these tensions and essentially resulted in a situation in which the pre-Lisbon *status quo* was largely retained.

Following the analytical framework of this volume, this chapter is structured as follows. The second section analyses the position, contribution and effectiveness of the EU with regard to the external reform debate, focusing on the talks on upgrading UNEP and on the more recent negotiations in (the run-up to) the 2012 Rio+20 UN Conference on Sustainable Development, where the institutional framework for sustainable development was one of the two main themes. Then the third section delves deeper into the internal reform question, demonstrating how the post-Lisbon era has affected the EU's external representation in international environmental negotiations. Many environmental negotiations that take place under the UN umbrella do not occur in UNEP, but in Conferences of the Parties (COPs) to UN Conventions. This section specifically analyses the EU's external representation in two such cases, both dating from the second half of 2010: the EU's representation in the 10th Conference of the Parties (COP10) to the Convention on Biological Diversity (CBD) in Nagoya (18–29 October 2010) and the 16th Conference of the Parties (COP16) to the United Nations Framework Convention on Climate Change (UNFCCC) in Cancún (29 November–10 December 2010). These analyses are placed in their broader context of inter-institutional tensions in the EU, also leading to difficulties in other environmental negotiations, such as those on a new mercury treaty. Finally, the fourth section presents some conclusions on the EU's contribution to effective multilateralism in the environmental area. The empirical data presented in the paper are based on a range of interviews with officials who were closely involved in the EU decision-making processes with regard to biodiversity, climate change, UNEP and Rio+20 talks,[1] as well as on the study of semi-confidential documents that were used in these processes.

External reform: upgrading UNEP

The EU has been – and still is – among the most fervent supporters of strengthening the role of UNEP in global environmental governance. The EU is one of the strongest advocates of UNEP, with the EU, Germany, Sweden and the UK being among UNEP's largest contributors (ENDS Europe 2013). However, the preference constellation at the international level was not favourable for the EU, as it was the only main actor – together with some usual suspects like Switzerland or Norway – with a firm reformist position. The reluctance of the G77 and countries like the US and China to genuinely strengthen the institutional framework for international environmental governance has been a constant throughout the 2000s (Vogler and Stephan 2007). The limited financial support from many industrialized countries – in terms of voluntary contributions to the Programme – is illustrative in this regard. The US, for instance, on average contributed 15 per cent of UNEP's budget since the mid-1990s, whereas it would be expected to pay 22 per cent if contributions were 'assessed' (and thus obligatory) rather than voluntary (Ivanova 2010). Both the preference constellation at the international level and the political will to reinforce UNEP as it can be derived from the financial contributions demonstrate that the EU was relatively isolated at the international level, as it did not find natural allies there in the debate on upgrading UNEP. As mentioned, reform options have been discussed for more than a decade, but because the scope of this volume is limited to the period 2003–13, the focus of this section is on the EU's position on UNEP reform since the early 2000s.

The EU has always had a preference for strengthening the global authority on environmental governance by upgrading UNEP to a specialized agency for the environment in the UN framework. This specialized agency has been conceptually referred to in many different ways – United Nations Environment Agency, International Environmental Agency, World Environment Organization, Global Environmental Organization – but the most commonly used name is United Nations Environmental Organization (UNEO) (Biermann 2007). Irrespective of its specific name, the EU envisaged such an UNEO as a specialized agency in line with article 57 of the UN Charter. No other major player at the international scene supported the EU's demand for granting UNEP an agency status. The reason behind the EU preference to upgrade UNEP from a programme to a specialized agency was double. First, in the UN framework, specialized agencies have more autonomy vis-à-vis the UNGA and/or Economic and Social Council (ECOSOC) than other bodies like programmes and funds. Second, whereas programmes have to count on voluntary financial contributions, agencies rely on stable and predictable funding based on mandatory contributions (so-called 'assessed contributions') from UN members. Both an increased autonomy and a stronger financial basis of a specialized agency (the UNEO) are considered to allow for more effectively addressing global environmental challenges than it is the case with a programme (UNEP). The EU has repeatedly used these arguments in the debates on UNEP reform that took place since the beginning of the 2000s.

Although there is a general consensus in the EU that the role of UNEP should be upgraded, two minor divergences can be identified between the member states in the Council on this external reform debate, but these have never prevented the EU from finding a common position on the issue. On the one hand, upgrading UNEP's status has clearly been more important to some member states than to others. France is certainly one of the member states that presented itself as one of the strongest promoters of a far-reaching upgrade, with President Chirac strongly campaigning for a genuine 'World Environmental Organization' in the early 2000s. Germany also has been a strong advocate of an upgrade. On the other hand, the traditional dichotomy in the UN between countries emphasizing purely environmental concerns and other countries putting these discussions in the broader perspective of sustainable development is also reflected in the EU. Sustainable development is a broader concept than merely the environment, since it includes not only an environmental dimension but also a social and an economic one. Countries like the Netherlands and the UK are typically member states stressing the broader sustainable development perspective in these discussions, whereas France and Germany traditionally more frequently draw the environmental card. The debate between environment and sustainable development clearly came to the forefront in the run-up to the Rio+20 conference in 2010 (see further).

In 2001, UNEP's Governing Council established an 'Open-Ended Intergovernmental Group of Ministers or their Representatives on International Environmental Governance', which had to evaluate the institutional weaknesses of international environmental governance. One year later, in February 2002, the recommendations of that Intergovernmental Group of Ministers were adopted by the Seventh Special Session of UNEP's Governing Council. These recommendations, the so-called 'Cartagena Package', were aimed at reinforcing the UN structure with regard to environmental matters (Ivanova 2012). The Cartagena Package had five components: a strengthened role for UNEP's Global Ministerial Environment Forum to give real guidance to the UN system on environmental matters; a reinforced financial situation for UNEP; improved coordination and coherence between existing MEAs; capacity building for developing countries; and enhanced cooperation across the UN system (Earth Negotiation Bulletin 2002). A few months later, these recommendations were confirmed at the level of heads of state and government at the World Summit on Sustainable Development in Johannesburg. However, implementing the Cartagena Package was largely unsuccessful, maybe with the exception of the capacity building component.

In the run-up to the 2005 UN Millennium Review Summit, the European Council confirmed the EU position on the upgrade of UNEP to a UN agency, stating that

> The European Council supports the Secretary-General's urgent appeal for a more integrated international environmental governance structure, based on existing institutions. In this perspective, and given the environmental challenges associated with development, the EU proposes that the high-level meeting in September 2005 initiate a process, as part of UN reform, which will lead to negotiations on the establishment of a UN agency for the environment, based on UNEP, with a revised and strengthened mandate, supported by stable, adequate and predictable financial contributions and operating on an equal footing with other UN specialised agencies.
>
> (European Council 2005: paragraph 39)

In September 2005, world leaders at the UN Millennium Review Summit agreed to 'explore the possibility of a more coherent institutional framework' for addressing environmental challenges (UNGA 2005: paragraph 169). However, this exploration process, consisting of informal UNGA consultations in New York in the period 2006–8, did not result in a consensus. Therefore, the co-chairs of that New York-led process asked the Nairobi-based UNEP Governing Council to re-dynamize the discussions. The February 2009 UNEP Governing Council decided to establish a 'Consultative Group on International Environmental Governance' of ministers or high-level representatives, comprising two to four governments from each UN region, while remaining open to other interested governments (Earth Negotiation Bulletin 2009). From the EU side, the governments of Belgium, Italy, Spain, France and Germany participated in this Consultative Group. In November 2010, these talks resulted in the so-called 'Nairobi–Helsinki outcome' (UNEP 2010).

Until the adoption of the Nairobi–Helsinki outcome, the debate on UNEP reform was primarily a debate in the environmental field. However, this debate expanded in the beginning of the 2010s when it became part of the broader discussions on sustainable development. In the preparatory talks for Rio+20 conference, which was the 20-year follow-up conference to the 1992 UN Conference on Environment and Development (UNCED, or 'Earth Summit') in June 2012, two main themes for this conference were identified: green economy in the context of sustainable development and poverty eradication (GESDPE); and the institutional framework for sustainable development (IFSD). That second theme indeed dealt with the institutional structure at the global level to coordinate sustainable development related discussions. The role of UNEP took a prominent place in these discussions, as a result of which it was removed from the environmental arena and put into a broader sustainable development perspective.

In January 2012, a first draft for a Rio+20 outcome document was tabled: the so-called 'zero draft' (UNCSD 2012). The zero draft contained two alternatives for reforming the role of UNEP in the institutional framework on sustainable development. The first option was to 'strengthen the capacity of UNEP to fulfil its mandate by establishing universal membership in its Governing Council and call for significantly increasing its financial base' (paragraph 51), whereas the second option was to

> establish a UN specialized agency for the environment with universal membership of its Governing Council, based on UNEP, with a revised and strengthened mandate, supported by stable, adequate and predictable financial contributions and operating on an equal footing with other UN specialized agencies.
>
> (paragraph 51alt)

In other words, the first option enhances UNEP without changing its status as a subsidiary body of the UNGA, while the latter transforms UNEP to a specialized agency. It is clear that paragraph 51alt reflected the EU position. The text even draws on EU language (Ivanova 2012), but the EU was fairly isolated in supporting paragraph 51alt.

The EU's position with regard to the IFSD theme of Rio+20 was decided in the Conclusions of the Environment Council of March 2012. Here, the Council reiterates its strong resolve to strengthen the environmental dimension of the IFSD and in this regard to upgrade UNEP into a specialized UN agency for the environment based in Nairobi with a revised and strengthened mandate and universal membership, supported by stable, adequate and predictable financial contributions and operating on an equal footing with other UN specialized agencies; calls for Rio+20 to decide on the process for taking forward the reform option agreed, including timeframes; and stresses the need for further efforts to enhance synergies between the Multilateral Environmental Agreements.

(Council of the European Union 2012a: paragraph 22)

It is clear that the EU preferred a Rio+20 outcome on IFSD consisting of a package of reform measures, of which the reinforcement of international environmental governance through an upgrade of UNEP to a specialized agency was a core element. This was also confirmed by the heads of state and government of the EU member states at their March 2012 European Council, where they concluded that Rio+20 'should contribute to a strengthened global institutional framework for sustainable development which should include the upgrading of UNEP to a specialised agency' (European Council 2012: paragraph 28).

At first sight, the outcome of Rio+20 – 'The Future We Want', in September 2012 endorsed by the UNGA – does not reflect the EU's preference, or at least not its pet topic of changing UNEP's status into a specialized agency. Paragraph 88 of the Rio+20 outcome document refers to 'strengthening the role of the United Nations Environment Programme', but without upgrading UNEP to a specialized agency (UNGA 2012a). Nonetheless, although UNEP remains a programme in the UN architecture, two major concerns of the EU are met. First, universal membership of UNEP's Governing Council will be established (paragraph 88/a). The first session of the Governing Council with universal membership was held in February 2013, where countries agreed to rename the Governing Council as the 'United Nations Environment Assembly of the UNEP' (UNEA). In March 2013, the General Assembly adopted a resolution formally changing the designation to UNEA (UNGA 2013). Second, the financing issue will also be tackled in the direction preferred by the EU: UNEP will get 'secure, stable, adequate and increased financial resources from the regular budget of the United Nations and voluntary contributions' (paragraph 88/b). Furthermore, other language in paragraphs 88/c to 88/h is considered to meet some of the EU's concerns with regard to the UNEP reform. The UNEP reform as politically agreed in Rio+20 was legally implemented by the UNGA in December 2012, which decided to 'strengthen and update' UNEP in the manner set out by the 'The Future We Want' outcome document (UNGA 2012b).

Examining the effectiveness of the EU in Rio+20 on the UNEP reform question, the conclusion seems to be that the formal label and status of a specialized agency are lost, but that a number of important issues that are maybe more important that the formal status, most notably the universal membership and a stronger financing, are achieved. If one just looks at the status question, the EU's effectiveness was low, but if one looks beyond the formality of the status, the effectiveness picture is likely to be more positive since Rio+20 opens the door for solving several concerns of importance to the EU. In short, agency status was not achieved, but the main reasons to have an agency were: universal membership and a stronger financial base.

The IFSD debates in Rio+20 not only dealt with the role and status of UNEP, which handles *environmental* issues, but also with the institutional framework in the UN coping with *sustainable development* topics. Since 1992, the Commission on Sustainable Development (CSD) is the UN body – formally a 'functional commission' under ECOSOC – that is to ensure the follow-up of the Earth Summit. The CSD is, however, often criticized for its ineffectiveness and its failure to further advance the sustainable development agenda, making it merely a 'talking shop' whose relevance was no longer recognized (Kaasa 2007: 107; Van den Brande 2012). Given the dissatisfaction about the CSD, it does not come as a surprise that reviewing the way sustainable development is institutionally dealt with in the UN was one of the two major themes of the Rio+20 conference. Rio+20 put an end to the CSD, as paragraph 84 of the 'The Future We Want' outcome document foresees in the establishment of a 'High Level Political Forum' (HLPF) that will replace the CSD (UNGA 2012a). The new HLPF should be operational at the beginning of the 68th session of the UNGA in autumn 2013. In the meantime, its relationship with the UNGA and/or ECOSOC still needs to be clarified since the Rio+20 outcome leaves the format and the organizational aspects to be determined by the UNGA.

This new institutional framework for sustainable development is in line with the EU's position on this issue, although the origin of the concept 'High-Level Political Forum' is not European (and it is not clear who came up with this name). The EU had become dissatisfied with the CSD and wanted an institutional framework that could give more political guidance and did not meet as frequently. Moreover, the EU aimed to guarantee an important role for stakeholders in the HLPF, which was also one of the characteristics of the CSD, and paragraph 84 of the Rio+20 outcome seems to confirm this. Finally, the Rio+20 outcome seems to include guarantees for meeting the European concerns about not creating a *CSD-bis*. The HLPF seems to meet these concerns, although the future practical functioning of the HLPF will demonstrate whether this new forum is more helpful in achieving effective multilateralism in the domain of sustainable development than the CSD. Hence, in its evaluation of the Rio+20 outcome, the Environment Council 'welcomes the agreement on the establishment of a High-Level Political Forum (HLPF) that will enhance the integration of the three dimensions of sustainable development in a holistic and cross-sectoral manner at all levels' (Council of the European Union 2012b: paragraph 17).

In the run-up to the formal establishment of the HLPF by the UNGA in autumn 2013, the EU still had to refine its position on the HLPF's relationship to UNGA and/or ECOSOC. Was the HLPF to be placed inside, alongside or under ECOSOC or rather be directly linked to the UNGA? Moreover, it was important for the EU that the HLPF would ensure a balanced integration of the three dimensions of sustainable development in order to avoid the HLPF overemphasizing the environmental dimension and developing into a parallel structure to UNEP.

Although some modest principled decisions on an improved functioning of UNEP and on a successor for the CSD were secured by the EU at Rio+20, the EU departed from Rio rather disillusioned. It had expected much more from this major conference and its effectiveness over the whole outcome package – and thus not only the IFSD issues – should be assessed as rather low. Back in Brussels, Environment Commissioner Janez Potočnik talked about 'the disappointment many have felt about the Rio+20 outcome', adding that 'together with my colleagues in the Commission, I have been clear that we would have wanted more' (European Commission 2012). Development Commissioner and chief EU negotiator Andris Piebalgs declared that 'we would have hoped for a more ambitious outcome', but he immediately added that he considered the agreement on the IFSD, and in particular the deal on strengthening UNEP, as 'a step forward' (Agence Europe 2012: 14).

It is clear that the EU in Rio did not manage in doing what it had successfully done half a year earlier at the climate negotiations in Durban (COP17 of the UNFCCC), namely playing the role of coalition builder and in that way restoring (or even redefining) its environmental leadership ambitions at the international level (see Pavese and Torney 2012; van Schaik 2012). A couple of reasons may explain its limited effectiveness at Rio+20. First, the EU had almost no allies in its call to upgrade UNEP to a specialized agency and it had been persisting on this point for too long. Second, the Brazilian presidency of the conference wanted to have a deal before heads of state and governments arrived in Rio in order to avoid a deadlock at the political level. Following that strategy, the Brazilians had put pressure on the EU to abandon its (untenable) UNEP position, leaving the EU yet more isolated on that point. Third, as already mentioned, the preference constellation at the international level was very unfavourable for the EU, with a coalition of the US and the G77 – including countries like China, India and Brazil – that clearly opposed an ambitious outcome. The combination of these reasons meant that the EU was not able to play an influential role in Rio and to fulfil its effective multilateralism commitment.

Internal reform: external representation in environmental negotiations after Lisbon

Shifting our focus from the external reform debate on UNEP and the broader institutional framework for sustainable development to the internal reform debate, this section examines how the entry into force of the Lisbon Treaty affected the way the EU is represented in multilateral environmental negotiations that take place in the UN framework.

As far as the day-to-day EU representation at UNEP is concerned, the EU Delegation in Nairobi is the main actor. The Delegation is responsible for the EU's bilateral relations with Kenya and Somalia, as well as for the relations with UNEP and the other UN programme that is headquartered in Nairobi, namely the UN Human Settlements Programme (UN-HABITAT). The role of the EU Delegation in representing the EU in UNEP's highest body – previously the Governing Council, since February 2013 the UNEA (see second section above) – is limited, since this is mainly carried out by those EU member states serving in the Governing Council/UNEA. Before the entry into force of the UNEP reform discussed earlier in this chapter, the Governing Council consisted of 58 countries (for four years elected by the UNGA). This meant that not all EU member states were members of the Governing Council. Today, the UNEA has universal membership and all EU member states are represented. However, even in the 'old' – non-universal – Governing Council, the EU always tried to present an internally coordinated EU position. The internal coordination on such an EU position takes predominantly place in Brussels (and not in Nairobi), in particular in the Council Working Party on International Environmental Issues/Global (WPIEI Global).

Rather than examining in detail how the EU is externally represented in UNEP, the current section analyses how the Lisbon Treaty affected the way the EU negotiated in conferences of two major UN Conventions: the Framework Convention on Climate Change (UNFCCC) and the Convention on Biological Diversity (CBD). This reflects the current state of play in global environmental governance that major UN-wide environmental negotiations do not take place within UNEP, but under the umbrella of existing UN conventions. This section therefore focuses on the external representation of the EU in the framework of two of these UN conventions.

As outlined in the Introduction to this volume, the Lisbon Treaty intended to increase the EU's international profile and performance, mainly by streamlining the EU's external representation. However, what the Lisbon Treaty does not do is provide a clear-cut answer to the representation question when shared competences are at stake. This is, for instance, the case for environmental issues. The Lisbon Treaty, just like its predecessors, only tackles the question of the EU part of shared competences and leaves it open to the member states to what extent and to whom they will delegate powers to a common negotiator for the issues that are still covered by national competences. As a consequence, from the Treaty perspective, the entirety of the EU representation, understood as 'the representation of the EU and its member states' in environmental negotiations leaves room for political interpretation. These grey zones came to the forefront in the environmental domain, particularly since the transition arrangements for the Lisbon Treaty, which were put into place to gradually implement the external relations provisions of the Lisbon Treaty during the course of 2010, were only applicable to the EU's external representation on those locations with EU delegations (i.e. capitals of third countries or headquarters of international organizations). These transition arrangements were, for instance, used in Nairobi (where UNEP is headquartered – see above) or in other UN locations that are discussed throughout this book. However, major international environmental conferences – like those on biodiversity and climate change analysed in this chapter – do not usually take place at such locations, which meant that even the transition arrangements did not apply to these cases.

The lack of clarity and immediate applicability of the Lisbon Treaty for determining the EU representation in environmental conferences, combined with the fact that the European Commission wanted to maximize its powers by claiming these grey zones, have led to inter-institutional battles in the EU, particularly between the Commission and the Council, on the issue of external representation in the environmental domain (see also Oberthür 2011; Delreux 2012). The Commission used the political rationale (or at least its interpretation thereof) behind the Lisbon Treaty that it should increase the coherence of the EU's external representation as an argument to claim a larger role for itself, even in cases where shared competences were at stake. This claim should be seen in the context of that time: the Lisbon Treaty formally entered into force in December 2009 and the first steps for its implementation were taken in the beginning of 2010. This is indeed exactly the period in which the EU was also confronted with one of the biggest disappointments in its external relations of the last decade: the climate change conference of Copenhagen (COP15, 7–18 December 2009).

The Copenhagen climate conference was clearly disillusioning for the EU (see also Chapter 11 in this volume). This had to do, first, with the fact that the EU had to accept a deal, the 'Copenhagen Accord', that was far below its expectations and ambitions. Second, not only the result of the negotiations was disappointing for the EU, but also the negotiation process as such, since the EU was indeed 'marginalized' at decisive moments in the COP (Curtin 2010: 1), when the emerging powers and the US struck a deal. Many observers relate this to the multiplicity of European leaders who wanted to play a role in these negotiations and thus to the lack of unity in the European representation (e.g. Emerson *et al.* 2011; Groen *et al.* 2012). Also European Commission President Barroso linked the EU's lack of effectiveness in Copenhagen to its lack of a coherent representation arrangement at the decisive moments. He declared in his 2010 State of the Union that 'Copenhagen showed that, while others did not match our ambition, we did not help ourselves by not speaking with one voice' (European Commission 2010). The Copenhagen experience – and the will not to make the same mistake again – 'provided additional fuel for Commission requests, after the entry into force of the Lisbon Treaty, to take over the external representation of the EU in the climate change regime' (Oberthür 2011: 668) and by extension in the entire environmental domain.

In the first months of 2010, the Commission indeed recommended full negotiation mandates to the Council for a large range of international environmental conferences. What was even more oppressive for the member states was that the Commission also proposed practical negotiation arrangements that left practically no room for the Council and its rotating presidency, which normally plays an important role in representing the EU in international environmental negotiations (Delreux 2011). Moreover, the Commission is said to have done so in a very dogmatic and assertive way, which generated a reaction among the member states taking the opposite stance (Corthaut and Van Eeckhoutte 2012).

The Commission's requests backfired and the member states reacted in an equally dogmatic way, wanting to prevent any point of that grey zone being occupied by the Commission. This all led to a complete standstill in the discussion of the EU's external representation in environmental affairs at the beginning of 2010.

The toughest inter-institutional battle between the Commission and the Council in the field of the external representation of the EU in international environmental affairs was certainly the debate on a negotiating mandate for the Commission in the negotiations for a treaty on mercury, which ultimately resulted in the signing of the Minamata Convention on Mercury in October 2013. It was not so much the fact that the Commission made recommendations for a mandate which led to highly tense institutional relations, but rather the scope of the proposed mandate (Delreux 2012: 214). Already in the summer of 2009 the Commission had recommended the Council to grant it a mandate so that the Commission would be the sole EU negotiator on all issues, as it was an international negotiation session touching upon exclusive EU competences (European Commission 2009, SEC (2009) 983 final; followed by other 'restricted', i.e. not public, Commission documents in which the Commission's request to be the sole negotiator for all issues was made even more strongly). The coherence argument – a single voice will make the EU more effective – substantiated the Commission's claim. The member states, which were definitely opposed to the competence claim by the Commission, prepared a counterproposal in which they made use of an innovation – and grey zone – of the Lisbon Treaty, namely the possibility of appointing a 'Union's negotiating team' (Article 218(3) TFEU). 'Restricted' Council documents show that the Council, building on this grey zone, proposed that the Commission and the rotating presidency would jointly form such a 'negotiating team'. A consequence of this option was that the presidency would also be able to negotiate issues falling under EU competences. The Commission interpreted this as a loss of the powers it had won many years ago (namely to be sole negotiator for issues falling under EU competences). This inter-institutional battle culminated in the Commission withdrawing its recommendation and leaving the EU without any negotiating mandate for the first Intergovernmental Negotiating Committee (INC) on the new mercury treaty in June 2010. This led to embarrassing situations at the international level in the INC, where the internal division in the EU was extremely clear to its external partners and where coherence seemed to be further away than ever.

These experiences shaped the context in which the EU had to prepare and conduct the first two major environmental conferences under the Lisbon regime: the biodiversity conference in Nagoya and the climate change conference in Cancún, both in the second half of 2010. Both conferences took place in a UN framework, as they are formally 'Conferences of the Parties' to a UN Convention, respectively the CBD and the UNFCCC. Examining the EU's representation in these two UN conferences, it becomes clear that the pre-Lisbon *status quo* has not been changed in one or another direction (such as giving a larger role to the Commission, or making use of the 'Union's negotiating team'). Changing the *status quo* was simply politically not feasible if the EU wanted to avoid a new mercury scenario – where its international actorness and effectiveness was largely put at risk – in much more visible and politicized negotiations like the biodiversity and climate change ones. This maintenance of the *status quo* reveals itself in two ways: the EU external representation in environmental affairs is still largely led by the rotating presidency of the Environment Council, and it is – particularly in climate change negotiations – characterized by a system of informal division of labour inside the EU. Let us have a deeper look into these two elements.

A first element of continuation is that the rotating presidency still plays an important role in the external representation of the EU on environmental matters (Delreux 2012). At the Nagoya biodiversity conference, the Presidency spoke for the EU for most of the issues. Only in the negotiations on the legally binding 'Nagoya Protocol' (on Access and Benefit Sharing) was the Commission the EU negotiator. According to the general interpretation of article 218 TFEU, negotiation mandates are only granted to the Commission if the outcome of the international negotiations is meant to be a legally binding treaty. The Commission indeed negotiated the Nagoya Protocol for the EU on the basis of a mandate that it received from the Council in 2009 (and which was renewed – and extended to incorporate the Nagoya conference – in the months before). The majority of 40 other issues – including a new strategic plan to stop the loss of biodiversity in the next ten years and a plan on resource mobilization – dealt with in Nagoya were negotiated by the then Belgian Presidency (Delreux and Criekemans 2012).

At the Cancún climate conference, the rotating Presidency also acted as EU negotiator. Since the Environment Council takes the central position in the EU's external climate policy-making, it is indeed traditionally the presidency of the Environment Council that directs the EU representation (van Schaik 2010). However, the role of the Commission was much stronger in the Cancún climate negotiations than it was in the Nagoya biodiversity talks. At a couple of meetings before the Cancún conference, e.g. at the informal Environment Council of Ghent (July 2010) or in a joint meeting with the European Parliament, Belgium's Minister Joke Schauvliege and European Climate Action Commissioner Connie Hedegaard had made clear they would speak with 'one voice' (European Parliament 2010). In the plenary meetings, the official speaking time allocated for the EU statement was properly divided in two separate time slots, one for the Presidency's Minister and the other for European Commissioner. However, during the final night of the negotiations, when the outcome of the COP was discussed in plenary before the decisions were adopted, the minister from the Presidency had de facto left the final negotiation work to the Commissioner. This may be indicative for an evolution that has taken place since the end of 2010 in the EU's representation arrangement in climate negotiations: the role of the Commission is increasing at the expense of the rotating presidency. This dynamic was confirmed one year later, at the 2011 Durban climate conference (COP17), suggesting that the balance may tip to the advantage of the Commission in the near

future at a cost to the presidency (and thus the Council) in the external representation in climate change negotiations. Arguing that the Commission took a
stronger stance in representing the EU in Durban in 2011 than in the climate
conferences before, de Jong and Schunz explain this by referring to the personality of the current Climate Action Commissioner, 'the charismatic former
Danish Minister Connie Hedegaard' (de Jong and Schunz 2012: 184).

The observation that a system of informal division of labour is still used by
the EU in the context of international climate negotiations is a second element of
continuation. A specific characteristic of the EU representation in climate change
negotiations is indeed that since 2004 the EU has used a system of 'lead negotiators' (Delreux and Van den Brande 2013). This is an informal system in the EU
that takes place under the umbrella of the rotating presidency. The negotiation
task is informally divided among a couple of negotiators, irrespective of their
national or institutional affiliation. They each negotiate on behalf of the EU for a
longer period than the six-monthly rotating presidency and for a particular set of
issues. Using such a system allows for sharing the burden of the negotiation task.
Moreover, in this way, the available expertise, know-how and experiences of
many actors are pooled and optimally made use of. Finally, this system guarantees continuity, since the representation of the EU does not change every six
months when a new member state enters the presidency seat. In Cancún, the EU
was represented by a lead negotiator coming from the Commission for all issues
related to the discussions on the second commitment period of the Kyoto
Protocol. In the negotiation sessions that dealt with a future all-encompassing
(i.e. with all UNFCCC parties, and not only the Kyoto countries) climate change
agreement, there were four EU lead negotiators, coming from the UK, Germany,
France and Poland (Delreux 2012).

A final point that needs to be considered to fully understand the impact of the
internal reform debate – and thus the Lisbon Treaty – on the external representation of the EU in international environmental negotiations, is the importance of
the so-called 'practical arrangements'. They prescribe, for instance, who is chairing the EU coordination meetings, from behind which nameplate the EU is
speaking, or which formulation the EU negotiator should use to introduce the
EU statement ('on behalf of the EU', 'on behalf of the EU and its member
states', etc.). The importance of these practical arrangements – which may at
first sight seem rather trivial – is that they allow the EU to apply rather pragmatic solutions in order to negotiate as effectively as possible, even in a context
that is characterized by strong inter-institutional tensions (see above). It is
important here to point at the different dynamics that may be present among the
generalist Brussels-based policy-makers (e.g. in Coreper) and the officials and
diplomats with an environment background who do the real negotiation work on
the floor (e.g. in Nagoya and Cancún). Whereas the Brussels-based policy-
making dynamic tends to handle the external representation questions rather
legally, the environmental negotiators prefer a more pragmatic approach allowing them to do their job. Indeed, they regularly emphasize that the reality of
international environmental negotiations does not always fit with the aspirations

and guidelines of the Brussels circuit and that the EU needs pragmatic and flexible negotiation arrangements in order to negotiate effectively.

The discussion about the nameplate as it occurred at the Nagoya biodiversity conference illustrates this point quite well (Delreux 2012: 219–20). From the beginning of 2010, in biodiversity negotiations the EU negotiator spoke from behind the EU flag, irrespective of whether he/she came from the Commission or the Presidency. It was the preference of the Belgian Presidency to continue this arrangement in Nagoya as well. However, during the first EU coordination meeting *sur place* (i.e. the Sunday before the start of the Nagoya meeting on Monday morning), a group of member states, led by the UK, opposed this system, arguing that they wanted the Belgian Presidency to speak from behind the Belgian nameplate, and not from behind the EU one. Given the extreme time pressure and the fact that the EU had to speak at the international level the next day, the Presidency then proposed an unseen and unprecedented ad hoc arrangement, which met the UK instructions: the Belgian and the EU nameplate were put together, everyone spoke from behind both nameplates, but through a single (European) microphone. Using this arrangement, which was described as 'unexplainable and hallucinatory, but a solution' by people from the Belgian Presidency but which did not provoke any significant reaction from the EU's negotiation partners, the EU was represented in the plenary meetings. Equally indicative, the negotiators in Nagoya have tried to hide this 'double nameplate, single microphone' arrangement as much as possible from the people in Brussels (and they took advantage of the time difference between Japan and Belgium). This way, the biodiversity negotiators aimed at preventing their ad hoc practical arrangements affecting the ongoing debate in Coreper on the practical arrangements that would be used in other environmental negotiations, most notably those on climate change in Cancún a few weeks later. Indeed, the practical arrangements for Cancún were, in contrast to those for Nagoya, determined in Coreper. They stipulated, among other things, that Commission and the Presidency would speak from behind the EU nameplate (which was new in climate change negotiations), but that this did not establish a precedent.

Conclusion

The preceding analysis has shown that in order to assess the EU's record in effective multilateralism in the environmental domain one needs to scratch the top layer of the empirical evidence and to look at the details that emerge then. This holds true for the impact of both the external and the internal reform debate on the EU's commitment to effective multilateralism. First, in the discussions of the reform of UNEP – later on incorporated into the broader debate on the institutional structure on sustainable development – the EU has *sensu stricto* not obtained what it strived for over more than a decade. UNEP will not be upgraded to a specialized agency and, with the new rules on UNEP being just adopted, it is unlikely that this will happen in the near future. However, a detailed examination of the decisions taken at the multilateral level reveals that many of the

European concerns about UNEP are addressed (most notably universal member-ship and a more stable financial basis), but that the 'big fish', the agency, has not been secured. Second, the internal reform debate clearly caused severe tensions inside the EU on the question of external representation in multilateral environ-mental negotiations. The environmental domain is certainly not an area where implementation of the Lisbon Treaty – and particularly its consequences for the EU's external representation – went smoothly. This is certainly not to deny that they have in some instances largely affected the negotiation behaviour, perform-ance and effectiveness of the EU internationally. However, and undoubtedly less visibly, systems of informal division of labour and ad hoc practical arrangements have been put in place to moderate, as far as possible, the negative effects of these internal reforms. Bringing the internal and the external reform debate together, it is clear that the negative impact of the internal reform debate on the EU's quest for external performance and effectiveness did not contribute to its striving for strengthening the global institutional framework and for making significant progress towards effective multilateralism in the environmental field.

Note

1 I interviewed eight national officials who were involved in the decision-making pro-cesses in the Council in the preparation of the EU position for the international negoti-ations on UNEP reform, the Rio+20 conference and the Nagoya and Cancún negotiations. The interviews took place between January 2011 and December 2012.

References

Agence Europe (2012) *Sustainable development: much ado about (virtually) nothing*, 26 June 2012, p. 14.

Andresen, S. and Rosendal, K. (2009) 'The role of the United Nations Environment Pro-gramme in the coordination of multilateral environmental agreements', in F. Biermann, B. Siebenhüner and A. Schreyögg (eds) *International organizations in global environ-mental governance*, Abingdon: Routledge, pp. 133–50.

Bauer, S. and Biermann, F. (2005) 'The debate on a World Environment Organization: an introduction', in F. Biermann and S. Bauer (eds) *A World Environment Organization. Solution or threat for effective international environmental governance?*, Aldershot: Ashgate, pp. 1–23.

Biermann, F. (2007) 'Reforming global environmental governance: from UNEP towards a world environment organization', in L. Swart and E. Perry (eds) *Global environ-mental governance: perspectives on the current debate*, New York: Center for UN Reform Education, pp. 103–23.

Corthaut, T. and Van Eeckhoutte, D. (2012) 'Legal aspects of EU participation in global environmental governance under the UN umbrella', in J. Wouters, H. Bruyninckx, S. Basu and S. Schunz (eds) *The European Union and multilateral governance: assessing EU participation in United Nations human rights and environmental fora*, Basingstoke: Palgrave Macmillan, pp. 145–70.

Council of the European Union (2012a) *Rio+20: pathways to a Sustainable Future – Council conclusions* (7514/12), 12 March 2012.

Council of the European Union (2012b) *Conclusions on Rio+20: outcome and follow-up to the UNCSD 2012 Summit* (15477/12), 25 October 2012.

Curtin, J. (2010) *The Copenhagen conference: how should the EU respond?* Dublin: Institute of International and European Affairs.

de Jong, S. and Schunz, S. (2012) 'Coherence in European Union external policy before and after the Lisbon Treaty: the cases of energy security and climate change', *European Foreign Affairs Review*, 17(2): 165–88.

Delreux, T. (2011) *The EU as international environmental negotiator*, Surrey: Ashgate.

Delreux, T. (2012) 'The rotating presidency and the EU's external representation in environmental affairs: the case of climate change and biodiversity negotiations', *Journal of Contemporary European Research*, 8(2): 210–27.

Delreux, T. and Criekemans, D. (2012) 'Environment, climate change and energy: inter-institutional compromises and international representation', in S. Van Hecke and P. Bursens (eds) *Readjusting the Council presidency: Belgian leadership in the EU*, Brussels: Academic & Scientific Publishers, pp. 169–87.

Delreux, T. and Van den Brande, K. (2013) 'Taking the lead: informal division of labour in the EU's external environmental policy-making', *Journal of European Public Policy*, 20(1): 113–31.

Earth Negotiation Bulletin (2002) 'Summary of the Seventh Special Session of the UNEP Governing Council, Third Global Ministerial Environmental Forum and Final Open-Ended Intergovernmental Group of Ministers or their Representatives on International Environmental Governance: 12–15 February 2002', *Earth Negotiation Bulletin*, 9(544).

Earth Negotiation Bulletin (2009) 'Summary of the 25th Session of the UNEP Governing Council/Global Ministerial Environment Forum: 16–20 February 2009', *Earth Negotiation Bulletin*, 16(78).

Emerson, M., Balfour, R., Corthaut, T., Wouters, J., Kaczynski, P. and Renard, T. (2011) *Upgrading the EU's role as global actor*, Brussels: Centre for European Policy Studies.

ENDS Europe (2013) *UN environmental body put on firmer foundations*, Environmental Data Services Europe daily newsmail, 9 January 2013.

European Commission (2009) *Recommendation from the Commission to the Council on the participation of the European Community in negotiations on a legally binding instrument on mercury further to Decision 25/5 of the Governing Council of the United Nations Environment Programme (UNEP)*, (SEC(2009) 983 final), 15 July 2009.

European Commission (2010) *State of the Union 2010*, (SPEECH/10/411), 7 September 2010.

European Commission (2012) *Rio+20: outcome and follow-up*, (SPEECH/12/551), 11 July 2012.

European Council (2005) *Presidency conclusions of the Brussels European Council (16 and 17 June 2005)*, (10255/1/05 REV 1), 16 and 17 June 2005.

European Council (2008) *Report on the implementation of the European Security Strategy: providing security in a changing world*, (S407/08), 11 December 2008.

European Council (2012) *Conclusions of the European Council (1/2 March 2012)*, (EUCO 4/2/12 REV 2), 1 and 2 March 2012.

European Parliament (2010) *Preparations for Cancún Climate Change Conference (29 November-10 December) (debate)*, (CRE 24/11/2010–14), 24 November 2010.

Groen, L., Niemann, A. and Oberthür, S. (2012) 'The EU as a global leader? The Copenhagen and Cancún UN climate change negotiations', *Journal of Contemporary European Research*, 8(2): 173–91.

Ivanova, M. (2009) 'UNEP as anchor organization for the global environment', in F. Biermann, B. Siebenhüner and A. Schreyögg (eds) *International organizations in global environmental governance*, Abingdon: Routledge, pp. 133–50.

Ivanova, M. (2010) 'UNEP in global environmental governance: design, leadership, location', *Global Environmental Politics*, 10(1): 30–59.

Ivanova, M. (2012) 'Institutional design and UNEP reform: historical insights on form, functioning and financing', *International Affairs*, 88(3): 565–84.

Kaasa, S. (2007) 'The UN Commission on Sustainable Development: which mechanisms explain its accomplishments?', *Global Environmental Politics*, 7(3): 107–29.

Oberthür, S. (2011) 'The European Union's performance in the international climate change regime', *Journal of European Integration*, 33(6): 667–82.

Pavese, C. and Torney, D. (2012) 'The contribution of the European Union to global climate change governance: explaining the conditions for EU actorness', *Revista Brasileira de Política Internacional*, 55: 125–43.

UNCSD (2012) *The future we want: zero draft of the outcome document*, 10 January 2012.

UNEP (2010) *Consultative Group of Ministers or High-level Representatives. Nairobi–Helsinki Outcome*, 23 November 2010.

UNGA (2005) *Resolution adopted by the General Assembly – 60/1. 2005 World Summit Outcome*, (A/RES/60/1), 24 October 2005.

UNGA (2012a) *Resolution adopted by the General Assembly – 66/288. The future we want*, (A/RES/66/288), 11 September 2012.

UNGA (2012b) *Resolution adopted by the General Assembly – 67/213. Report of the Governing Council of the United Nations Environment Programme on its twelfth special session and on the implementation of section IV.C, entitled 'Environmental pillar in the context of sustainable development', of the outcome document of the United Nations Conference on Sustainable Development*, (A/RES/67/213), 21 December 2012.

UNGA (2013) *Resolution adopted by the General Assembly – 67/251. Change of the designation of the Governing Council of the United Nations Environment Programme*, (A/RES/67/251), 13 March 2013.

Van den Brande, K. (2012) 'The European Union in the Commission on Sustainable Development', in J. Wouters, H. Bruyninckx, S. Basu and S. Schunz (eds) *The European Union and multilateral governance: assessing EU participation in United Nations human rights and environmental fora*, Basingstoke: Palgrave Macmillan, pp. 171–90.

van Schaik, L. (2010) 'The sustainability of the EU's model for climate diplomacy', in S. Oberthür and. M. Pallemaerts (eds) *The new climate politics of the European Union*, Brussels: VUB Press, pp. 251–80.

van Schaik, L. (2012) *The EU and the progressive alliance negotiating in Durban: saving the climate?*, London: Climate and Development Knowledge Network working paper 354.

Vogler, J. and Stephan, H. (2007) 'The European Union in global environmental governance: leadership in the making?', *International Environmental Agreements*, 7(4): 389–413.

6 Discreet effectiveness

The EU and the ICC

Laura Davis

Introduction

In July 2002, the Rome Statute of the International Criminal Court (ICC) came into force. The world's first permanent court to bring to justice the perpetrators of genocide, war crimes and crimes against humanity was established. The European Security Strategy notes that 'Large-scale aggression against any Member State is now improbable. Instead, Europe faces new threats which are more diverse, less visible and less predictable' (European Council 2003: 3). These threats include terrorism, the proliferation of weapons of mass destruction, regional conflicts, state failure and organized crime. The Rome Statute reflects the changing perception more generally of threat from inter-state conflict to transnational or intra-state armed conflict and terrorism (Slaughter and Burke-White 2002). It also articulates long-held beliefs in the protection of civilians and of individual, rather than state, responsibility for crimes committed against civilians (Schabas 2001). Unlike the International Criminal Tribunals for the former Yugoslavia and for Rwanda, the ICC is a permanent institution with – potentially – a global reach. A decade after the Rome Statute was signed, over 120 states – including all EU member states – are party to the Rome Statute system, 16 cases in seven situations have been brought before the Court and trials are underway.

The Court is a young institution – it handed down its first sentence in July 2012. The system established by the Rome Statute includes and goes beyond setting up the Court itself. It is

> one of the most complex international instruments ever negotiated, a sophisticated web of highly technical provisions drawn from comparative criminal law combined with a series of more political propositions that touch the very heart of State concerns with their own sovereignty.
>
> (Schabas 2001: 25)

When states ratify the Statute, they undertake to enact extensive implementing legislation that affects their domestic justice systems. The ICC is a court of last resort and responsibility to investigate and prosecute the crimes coming under its jurisdiction remains with states. It can only undertake cases that the state concerned is genuinely unable or unwilling to investigate and prosecute: this is known as the principle of complementarity. The Court relies on states to cooperate as it has no independent police force or means to execute arrest warrants, for example. The influence of the Court goes beyond the courtroom, however, as the threat of its engagement in a country – the 'shadow of the ICC' – may precipitate efforts to address impunity in that country, as it has in Kenya, for example (Sriram and Brown 2012) and some – such as the prosecutor – also claim a wider deterrent effect in other conflict zones (Bensouda 2012).

There have been initiatives to reform the Statute. For some states, the Court has developed too fast and reaches too far. The Bush Administration 'unsigned' the Rome Statute in 2002 and embarked on a campaign to undermine the Court through bilateral immunity agreements. After the prosecutor indicted President Al-Bashir of Sudan, a non-state party, in 2009, several African states sought – bilaterally and through the African Union – to curb the powers of the Court. In 2010, the Review Conference of the Rome Statute of the International Criminal Court in Kampala offered states parties the first opportunity to amend the Rome Statute since its entry into force. It reopened the question, carried over from the founding Rome conference in 1998, of extending the Court's jurisdiction to cover the crime of aggression. The proposed amendments were contentious as they affected a core aspect of the Court: its relationship with and independence from the UN Security Council. The main reform debates centre therefore on the level of independence the Court should enjoy from the UN Security Council.

The European Security Strategy places EU support for the ICC firmly in the context of effective multilateralism, and states that 'we have an interest in further developing existing institutions such as the World Trade Organisation and in supporting new ones such as the International Criminal Court' (European Council 2003: 10). This support is deepened in the implementation report on the European Security Strategy: 'The International Criminal Court should grow further in effectiveness' (European Council 2008: 12).

The Council does not, however, elaborate on how it understands 'effectiveness', and in the thorny debates on reforming the Rome Statute, member states hold divergent views on central issues. Effectiveness of the court cannot be only understood as amending the Rome Statute, however. Given the recent establishment and complexity of the Rome Statute system, effectiveness has to include setting up the system and making it work. In this chapter, I consider how the EU has contributed to reforming the ICC, in both the creation of a functioning Rome Statute system and through initiatives to amend the Statute. I consider how the EU has been represented in the formal bodies of the Court. I then assess the likely impact of the Lisbon reforms on effective EU support for the ICC and challenge the assumption that one EU voice in the Court would enable the EU to achieve its objective of a more effective ICC. I conclude that one EU voice in the formal bodies of the Court would bring little to the EU beyond visibility, but could seriously undermine the Court. The EU would better contribute to a more effective Court if it is discreet and focuses on putting its policies in support of the ICC into practice with third countries rather than attempting a show of unity in the Court's official bodies.

This chapter is empirical and I draw on policy documents, publications by expert organizations and media reports, as well as seven semi-structured interviews with officials from the European Commission and European External Action Service, a member of the European Parliament and a civil society expert, conducted by the author in December 2011 and January 2012. The interviews were held on condition of anonymity.

External reform: the EU's contribution to ICC reform

In 2002, Javier Solana wrote that 'the EU and the rest of Europe has been a leader in the process of setting up the International Criminal Court' (Solana 2002), a view endorsed by scholars (Groenleer and van Schaik 2007; Groenleer and Rijks 2009). The European Security Strategy places EU support to the ICC in the context of effective multilateralism, and the implementation report stresses that the EU supports a more effective Court. The Council does not indicate what it means by a more effective Court, which is the subject of intense debate. Given the relative youth of the ICC as an institution and the complexity of the Rome Statute system, reform of the ICC should be understood as including setting up the Rome Statute system and making it work as well as efforts to change it. In this section, I consider the EU's contribution to the development of the Rome Statute and subsequent initiatives to amend it.

EU contributions to reform

The EU was not represented at the Rome conference that created the Statute in 1998, and there was no EU common position on the ICC. Until late in the negotiating process the UK and France sided with the other permanent members of the UN Security Council, while the majority (EU13) joined the Like-Minded Group (LMG)[1] (Groenleer and Rijks 2009). A major area of division was the power of the UN Security Council over the Court. The permanent members – including the UK and France – originally wanted the Court to be subordinate to the Security Council, while the other EU member states, along with the rest of the LMG, supported an independent court. The permanent members also feared a politicized prosecutor. France proposed an amendment, which became the controversial Article 124, to allow a country to decline the court's jurisdiction over war crimes for seven years after the entry into force of the ICC. Once the proposal was agreed, France signed the Statute. Of the permanent members of the UN Security Council, only France and the UK have ratified the Rome Statute. Despite the hostility of China, Russia and the US to the Court, these states have not blocked the referral of either Darfur (Sudan) or Libya to the ICC, although a lack of agreement at the Security Council has, at the time of writing, prevented the referral of the situation in Syria.

Once the member states signed the Rome Statute, the EU developed a common position in which it committed to advancing universal support for the Statute, and the Agreement on Privileges and Immunities of the International

Criminal Court (Council of the European Union 2003). The Common Decision of 2003 was followed by an Action Plan to implement it in 2004; these were replaced by a new Decision and Action Plan in 2011 (Council of the European Union 2004, 2011a, 2011b). The EU has an extensive agreement on cooperation and assistance with the ICC (European Council 2006), which legally obliges the EU to cooperate with the Court, and is the first agreement to bind the EU and an international organization in this way (Groenleer and Rijks 2009). These policies are the basis of EU contributions to supporting the Rome Statute system, how they have been implemented is considered in more detail below.

The Rome scenario was largely repeated at the Kampala Review Conference in 2010 over the proposal to extend the jurisdiction of the Court to include the crime of aggression. At Rome, the Like-Minded Group, which included the majority of EU member states, did not have a unanimous view on whether or not the ICC should have jurisdiction over aggression (Schabas 2001: 16). By Kampala, the outstanding areas for negotiation were the jurisdictional filter – how and under what conditions the Court might pursue such crimes – and the procedure for entry into force. These latter aspects were the most significant as they went to the heart of the relationship between the UN Security Council and the Court. The debate over extending the Court's jurisdiction to cover the crime of aggression demonstrates the range of opinion on what an 'effective' Court would look like. Some of the strongest supporters of an effective Court did not believe that extending the Court's jurisdiction to include the crime of aggression was in the Court's interests. The Coalition for the International Criminal Court (CICC) did not take a position on the issue (Coalition for the International Criminal Court, undated), neither did Human Rights Watch, which also raised concern that extending the ICC's jurisdiction could hamper its credibility and effectiveness as a neutral arbiter of justice and compromise its ability to address the crimes of genocide, war crimes and crimes against humanity (Human Rights Watch 2010: 5). A more effective Court is not, therefore, necessarily one that may also prosecute the crime of aggression.

The EU did not have a common position in the run-up to the Kampala conference. Council conclusions in May 2010 'reiterate[d] the European Union's unwavering support to the Court' and considered the conference 'an important step in the consolidation of the ICC as an effective tool of the international community for bringing to justice those individuals bearing criminal responsibility for genocide, war crimes and crimes against humanity'. Although the Conclusions note the amendments to be discussed, they do not mention the content (Council of the European Union 2010). The divisions between the member states on the crime of aggression were clear: some member states such as Greece were strongly in favour of the extension, while the UK and France sided with other members of the UN Security Council as broadly against, unless there were changes to the jurisdictional filter (International Criminal Court 2010). All the EU member states – and even the US, which sent a large delegation and was active in the discussion on aggression – argued from a position of defending the existing system.

There have been attempts to limit the reach of the Court. In the US, the Bush Administration was hostile to the ICC and sought to undermine it, including by threatening to cut off military aid to countries that would not support bilateral immunity agreements and by forbidding US agencies from cooperating with the Court. But by the time of the Kampala conference the US position had changed. The US is probably no closer to ratifying the Statute and has not repealed the legislation preventing US cooperation with the Court, but Ambassador Rapp's statement at Kampala underlined American support for the Court's current prosecutions (Rapp 2010). The US was no longer the main threat to the integrity of the system. This role seemed to have been taken up rather by the African Union.

In 2009, the Court indicted President Al-Bashir of Sudan for war crimes and crimes against humanity, and charges of genocide were added in 2010. After the first indictment, the African Union, meeting in Sirte, Libya, passed a motion that recalled its demand that the UN Security Council suspend the prosecution of President Al-Bashir for one year, in accordance with Article 16 of the Rome Statute. The Sirte motion stated that 'the AU Member States shall not cooperate pursuant to the provisions of Article 98 of the Rome Statute of the ICC relating to immunities, for the arrest and surrender of President Omar El Bashir of The Sudan' (African Union 2009). The motion challenged the independence of the Court and the prosecutor and indicated that AU member states would prepare resolutions for the Kampala conference to curb the powers of these organs. After the Sirte motion, African ICC state parties led by Botswana and civil society organizations spoke out in support of the ICC. The South African government was strongly criticized for supporting the motion, not least by South African civil society. It then clarified its intention to honour its commitments as a state party to the ICC (du Plessis 2010: 15–17). Since the motion, President Al-Bashir has not been able to travel freely across the African continent, and the resolutions were not tabled at Kampala. Nonetheless, the incident underlined the importance of state party cooperation – and indeed the cooperation of regional organizations – for the functioning of the Court.

EU effectiveness

The EU member states were divided on the crime of aggression, so the EU played no role in that debate. It did, however, contribute to heading off AU opposition to the Court: the EU Special Representative (EUSR) to the AU has reportedly facilitated improved communication between the Court and AU and the EU funded an ICC–AU seminar on technical aspects of the ICC (General Secretariat of the Council 2010). The EU and the member states have remained visibly united in calling for President Al-Bashir's transfer to The Hague, and High Representative Ashton has made repeated statements in relation to his travel.

Away from the formal bodies, the EU has used a broad range of tools to further universality, complementarity and cooperation with the Court, in line with its agreements. Although the Czech Republic was able to join the EU without ratifying the Rome Statute, all member states and Croatia are now states parties to the Court. The EU itself is not a state party, and the EU institutions have a limited role in furthering support for the ICC within the EU. The Brussels-based ICC sub-area of the Public International Law Working Party (COJUR-ICC) has a coordinating role in meeting the objectives of universality, cooperation and complementarity within the EU (Council of the European Union 2011b), including preparations for the Kampala conference. COJUR-ICC is the main body working on the ICC, and remains largely unchanged by the Lisbon Treaty, to the extent that it remains, unusually, chaired by the presidency and not the EEAS. The EU focal point and the national focal points exchange information on member state progress, including on adopting and implementing legislation, which reportedly encourages progress. There is no EU delegation in The Hague as the Netherlands is a member state, although there are representations of the European Commission and Parliament. Member state diplomats and officials exchange information and coordinate in The Hague, often with EU officials. The extent to which this happens is often determined by the activism of the member states concerned. During the Belgian EU Presidency in 2010, for example, the Belgian Ambassador to the Netherlands was reportedly very proactive in coordinating EU member state engagements with the ICC as a way of complementing COJUR-ICC but these efforts faded with subsequent presidencies.

The Stockholm Programme outlines the EU's role in promoting cooperation with the ICC and other tribunals, including through the European Network of Contact Points (Council of the European Union 2009b). The EU institutions have reportedly also taken early steps to facilitate the prosecution of alleged perpetrators resident in the EU, such as when the French authorities arrested a suspect (who was subsequently released when Pre-Trial Chamber I declined to confirm the charges against him) in Paris in October 2010, acting on an ICC arrest warrant for charges of war crimes and crimes against humanity allegedly committed in DR Congo.

The EU institutions have an impressive range of instruments that can be used with third countries to promote universality, cooperation and complementarity, covering trade, aid and crisis management. The European Instrument for Democracy and Human Rights (EIDHR) provides direct financial support to the ICC (€2.5 million in 2000–6, €2 million in 2007–9) and indirectly (€14.4 million in 2000–6 and €3.9 million in 2007–9) which includes support to NGOs, such as the CICC which was crucial in the creation of the ICC and contribute to its effectiveness (EuropeAid 2007; European Commission 2009). Karel Kovanda, Deputy Director-General of RELEX, announced the Commission's plans for a 'complementarity toolkit' during the Kampala conference.

At the EU–Africa summit in Lisbon in 2007, African and European leaders declared that:

> Africa and the EU will work together to protect and promote the human rights of all people in Africa and Europe ... the partners agree that the

establishment and the effective functioning of the International Criminal Court constitute an important development for peace and international justice.

(Council of the European Union 2008: 24)

This reflects a previous, legally binding commitment made in 2005 in the revised Cotonou Agreement between the EU and 79 African, Caribbean and Pacific (ACP) countries to ratify and implement the Rome Statute, and 'fight against international crime in accordance with international law, giving due regard to the Rome Statute' (African, Caribbean and Pacific Group 2005). As a result of this article and the ICC warrant against President Al-Bashir, the government of Sudan chose not to ratify the revised Cotonou Agreement. Consequently, it cannot access aid worth around €300 million from the 10th European Development Fund (European Commission 2010).

The ICC clause from the Cotonou agreement is the 'standard' clause, to be adapted to other contexts. ICC clauses are used to promote universality and have been included in partnership and cooperation agreements, trade and development agreements and association agreements between the EU and Indonesia, South Korea, South Africa, Ukraine and Iraq (General Secretariat of the Council 2010: 12). ICC clauses are not 'essential' – they do not carry sanctions if they are broken and there is no standard follow-up or fixed timeframe for implementation – but the EU invests considerable time and effort in persuading the partner to accept the commitment, and in some cases, the ICC clause was reportedly among the last elements to be agreed.

The EU also pursues universality through *démarches* carried out by the EU delegations. The effectiveness of these measures, particularly when up against US hard power politics over bilateral immunity agreements, is challenged (Thomas 2012) but officials point to the fact that the institutions target countries close to ratification, as well as resistant states such as China, India, Russia and the US, demonstrating consistency. The accession of Japan to the system following intensive *démarches* is an example of success (Council of the European Union 2007: 10). Political dialogues – at the country and regional level – may also address the issue of the ICC.

Cooperation with the ICC is a priority of the European Neighbourhood Policy (ENP) (European Commission 2004: 13). The ENP action plans for Armenia, Azerbaijan, Egypt, Georgia, Jordan, Lebanon, Moldova and Ukraine include ICC clauses, and the EU's Strategy on Central Asia also includes the goal of ratifying and implementing the Rome Statute (Council of the European Union 2009a: 16–17). In 2011, however, the ENP was revised to reflect the EU's new priority of 'deep democracy' in the region, but there is no reference to the ICC in the new document (European Commission and High Representative 2011), despite calls from the Parliament that the High Representative include ratification of the Rome Statute (European Parliament 2011).

The Development Cooperation Instrument does not reference the ICC (European Parliament and Council 2006), neither does the 'Agenda for Change', which sets out the Commission's new development strategy in 2011. The latter, reflecting international trends in development aid,[2] asserts however that the EU will apply more conditionality, including on human rights grounds (European Commission 2011b).

The cooperation and assistance agreement between the EU and the ICC sets out the ways in which the EU institutions can support the Court, including by sharing information (including EU classified information), and cooperating with the prosecutor. The EU, upon the request of the ICC, shall also provide facilities and services, including 'support at field level' (European Council 2006). These commitments have important implications for EU delegations, EU special representatives (EUSRs) and Common Security and Defence Policy (CSDP) missions. The European Union guidelines on promoting compliance with international humanitarian law (IHL) state that 'collecting information which may be of use for the ICC or in other investigations of war crimes' could be included in relevant crisis management mandates (Council of the European Union 2005).

Seven situations – Central African Republic (CAR), Côte d'Ivoire, the Democratic Republic of Congo (DRC), Darfur/Sudan, Kenya, Libya and Uganda – are under investigation by the ICC. But although EUSRs are present in four of these (DRC, Libya, Sudan and Uganda), only the EUSR for Sudan is mandated to support the ICC's work. The guidelines on compliance with IHL include the possibility for CSDP missions to prevent or suppress violations of IHL or assist war crimes investigations (Council of the European Union 2005), but to date no CSDP mission has been mandated to support the work of the ICC. Looking beyond their mandates, the EUSR for the African Union reportedly facilitated improved communication between the Court and AU, and EU Satellite Centre has provided imagery relevant to the Darfur case (General Secretariat of the Council 2010).

Analysis of the Country Strategy Papers (CSPs) of the seven ICC situations shows that reference to the ICC or support for complementary measures is uneven. The CSP for the DRC includes as an indicator of success both the execution of ICC arrest warrants and the passage of implementing legislation and includes extensive rule of law and security sector reform measures to support complementarity (République Démocratique du Congo–Communauté Européenne 2007). In CAR, where the ICC referral pre-dates the CSP, there is no reference to the ICC in the CSP, or to related justice sector provisions (République Centrafricaine–Communauté Européenne 2007). The CSP for Uganda does not include complementary support to the justice and security sectors (Republic of Uganda–European Community 2008), the CSPs for Kenya and Côte d'Ivoire note the status of the Rome Statute and were finalized before investigations began (Republic of Kenya–European Community 2007; Communauté Européenne–République du Côte d'Ivoire 2007). Libya was not part of the European Neighbourhood Policy at the time its CSP was agreed in 2011 (European Commission 2011a). Since then, the war in Libya and the referral of the situation to the ICC by the UN Security Council render it out of date, but there was no reference to the ICC or to Libya's non-ratification of the Rome Statute in the document – a point picked up and protested by Members of the European Parliament (MEPs) at the time.

This analysis shows that the EU contributes more to the effectiveness of the Court away from the ICC's formal bodies, through its support for the universality, complementarity and cooperation in its relations with third countries. The EU was divided over the main reform issue – the crime of aggression – but is united in protecting the integrity of the Rome Statute. When the Statute has come under pressure, it has contributed to heading off opposition, most recently from the African Union. But although the EU has extensive external policies supporting a more effective Court and instruments from across the pre-Lisbon pillar system to implement them, it rarely puts all these policy provisions into practice. Support for the Court has been uneven across and within the different parts of the EU.

Internal reform: the EU's effectiveness in the ICC

The EU is not a state party to the Rome Statute, so it is not a member of the Assembly of States Parties (ASP), the managing oversight and legislative body of the ICC. The EU has observer status in the ASP and the EEAS fills this role. As observers do not have speaking rights, the presidency speaks for the EU in the ASP. The dominant discourse is to consider opportunity as broadly the chance to influence the ICC in formal, multilateral *fora* such as the Assembly of States Parties. The assumption that greater coherence leads to more effectiveness is prevalent (Thomas 2012). Michael Emerson *et al.* argue that the EU's 'observer status could be enhanced, either in formal terms, or at least through a more active participation in the conferences of the Assembly of [States] Parties' (Emerson *et al.* 2011: 92). In this section, I challenge the assumption that one EU voice in the ICC's formal bodies would make the EU or the ICC more effective.

EU contributions to reform in practice

The Council, Commission and Parliament were all represented, in addition to the member states, at the Kampala review conference in 2010. The EU presidency – Spain – delivered a statement on behalf of the EU in the High Level Opening Debate, which emphasized universal adherence to the Court and did not address the substance of the proposed amendments (Kingdom of Spain 2010). In the debate, 22 EU member states took the floor. Thirteen member states associated themselves with the EU presidency statement and eight (France, Poland, the Netherlands, Austria, Slovakia, Slovenia, Denmark and Portugal) did not (International Criminal Court 2010).[3] As international justice is a high priority for the Netherlands and Denmark, this suggests that neither state perhaps saw the EU as a player at the ICC.

The divisions between the member states on the crime of aggression were not the only division in evidence at Kampala. The European Parliament (EP) sent an ad hoc delegation to the conference. Prior to Kampala, Prosecutor Moreno-Ocampo attended a joint meeting of the EP's Foreign Affairs and Development Committees and the Subcommittee on Human Rights (DROI) and DROI held an exchange of views with ICC President Song. The Parliament passed a detailed resolution that, in contrast to the Council conclusions, expressed robust support for extending ICC jurisdiction to cover aggression using the existing mechanisms within the Rome Statute and resisted a stronger role for the UN Security Council (European Parliament 2010b). This resolution gave the MEPs 'a clear political mandate on the main issues to be discussed' (European Parliament 2010a). Delegation leader Richard Howitt MEP commented 'as Parliamentarians … it is our duty to speak out at this conference, to give guidance and leadership to the EU member states and to all UN member states on the crucial issues being debated here' (Howitt 2010). Member states did not agree: the MEPs participated in one of the daily coordination meetings but participants recalled 'unpleasant internal exchange' between the parliamentary delegation and the presidency as to who had the right to speak for EU citizens, and what to say on their behalf. The interventions by the MEPs apparently led to some confusion as to who represented what and whom, anger from member states and from the states parties criticized by MEPs, and praise from civil society organizations supportive of the MEPs' human rights perspective. This underscored an important aspect of the *sui generis* nature of the EU – its parliament – and the unclear role of parliamentarians in delegations. Indeed, the MEPs concluded that their role in international delegations needs further clarification (European Parliament 2010a).

As EU member states support the integrity of the Rome Statute, there is no obvious need for one EU voice in ASP. Where there are major amendments related to the Security Council, the EU does not reach a common position. As EU member states already coordinate their positions through the EU, further coordination could risk a lowest-common-denominator approach on issues such as the budget, possibly curtailing the contributions of activist member states like the Netherlands or Denmark, or might not be worth the effort required to arrive at a common position. EU member states in ASP can and do build alliances with a range of like-minded non-EU ASP members – greater intra-EU coordination should not come at the price of these alliances.

A single EU voice in the official bodies of the ICC would not necessarily strengthen the Court. The EU prides itself on its support to the system. This image is reinforced by the little research available on the EU and the ICC, which considers the role of the EU and its member states and/or in comparison to the US (Groenleer and van Schaik 2007; Groenleer and Rijks 2009; Thomas 2012). Comparison between EU support and that of African states or other regional groupings has not yet received scholarly attention. As a result, the discourse on the role of the EU and its member states in supporting the ICC risks focusing too much attention on the EU's role and overshadowing the contributions of other actors. The Like-Minded Group at Rome was a geographically mixed group in which EU members and future members were not the majority. In the Americas, the Mercado Común del Sur (MERCOSUR) and the Caribbean Community (CARICOM) are, for example, both supportive of the Court, as is Brazil, the emerging power. The commitment to the ICC in the EU–Africa strategy is the product of African as much as EU leaders. The Southern African Development Community (SADC) played an important role in the human rights agenda at the Rome conference (Schabas 2001; du Plessis 2010), and SADC member states adopted 'Principles of Consensus and Negotiations' ahead of the Rome conference (Maqungo 2000), in marked contrast to the EU.

This discourse also obscures the fact that, unlike for most other regional groupings, the chances of the ICC opening an investigation in an EU member state is to all intents and purposes nil. The EU is free from violent conflict, EU member states are able to investigate and prosecute ICC crimes and their willingness must be assumed from their domestic, European and international commitments. This is not lost on the rest of the world. In Sub-Saharan Africa there is already a sense amongst some leaders that the Court targets Africans: 'The chairman of the AU Commission, Jean Ping, said they were not against the ICC, but felt that the court was "discriminatory" and targeted only officials from the African continent' (BBC 2011). EU officials may dismiss these criticisms, stating it is simply the reality of international law and while this is correct, legally speaking, it misses the important political significance of these perceptions.

It may be dangerous to introduce regional representation into ASP. The EU is supportive of an effective ICC, but there is no guarantee that other regional organizations would be, as moves within the AU to undermine the Court suggest. The AU's relationship with the ICC is critical for the success or failure of the Court: 33 of the 53 members of the African Union are states parties to the Rome Statute, all seven ICC situations are in AU member states and some AU members which are not ICC-states parties (e.g. Sudan) are vociferous opponents of the Court. These factors arguably make the AU a more important regional actor in the ICC than the EU, regardless of the latter's ability to project its support for the Court beyond its borders. As developments on the African continent suggest, it is far from certain that the African states in favour of the *status quo* at the ICC would win out within the AU if a regional position were required. In Asia, only nine states have ratified the Rome Statute, and key powers such as China and India remain hostile to the Court. Regional representation would achieve little for the EU other than a show of unity, but would risk scuppering the EU's objective of a more effective Court by squeezing out pro-ICC voices within other regional groupings.

The effects of EU reform

As I have shown, the EU's influence on the ICC – and on third countries – is arguably greater away from the formal ASP bodies. The analysis of EU instruments shows that the EU struggles to be consistent in implementing its policies towards third states. This is not to suggest that there must be a rigid, one-size-fits-all approach to enforcing ratification of the Rome Statute and its implementing legislation with all third countries, but putting policy into practice more consistently might strengthen the EU's contribution to the Court. The revised ENP, for example, includes no reference to the ICC in contrast to its predecessor and to the EU–Africa strategy. Some ENP action plans contained ICC clauses, but the 2011 plan for Libya did not. This geographic – or geopolitical – inconsistency could be interpreted as double standards, particularly in Sub-Saharan Africa.

The presidency continues to chair COJUR-ICC post-Lisbon, while most other working parties are chaired by the EEAS. Pre-Lisbon, officials within RELEX (Directorate-General for the External Relations), the Council Secretariat and AIDCO (EuropeAid Cooperation Office) were tasked with the ICC, in addition to other responsibilities. The individuals concerned worked well together across the structural divide. Broadly speaking, universality in the past fell more to DG RELEX/Council Secretariat and complementarity to DG Development. Post-Lisbon, the RELEX and Secretariat positions have now been merged into a single position in the EEAS (the focal point) and complementarity rests with DEVCO. Such divisions are artificial, however, as complementarity needs diplomatic as well as technical support, and *démarches* and the funding instruments remain within the remit of the Commission. This suggests that the Lisbon reforms have in reality changed little. The extent to which the structural division between the presidency, Council Secretariat and Commission will be replicated by the EEAS, presidency and Commission will depend on how the relationship particularly between the EEAS and Commission develops over time, as well as the working practice of the individuals in these positions.

Arguably the larger challenge for the EU is not, however, institutional arrangements but implementation – the decision to use the available instruments to further the cause of an effective Court. Other developments, such as the Strategy on Human Rights planned for 2014 and the newly-appointed EUSR for Human Rights, may lead to more consistent use of the tools, even if the ICC does not figure in his mandate (Council of the European Union 2012). The 'Agenda for Change' may also enable greater coherence in pursuing complementarity, even though it does not mention the ICC either (European Commission 2011b). The extent to which the external dimension of internal justice, freedom and security policies, such as the Stockholm programme, will be strengthened in the future, particularly in relation to the role of EU delegations abroad and CSDP missions remains to be seen. The Parliament may also play a stronger role in shaping future external relations, through insisting on ICC clauses in a wider range of agreements, for example.

Conclusion

The EU is committed to a more effective Court. It supports universality, complementarity and cooperation in its dealings with third countries through a wide range of aid, trade and crisis management tools. In some parts of the world, notably Africa, and through some instruments, the EU puts its policy of supporting an effective ICC into practice. It has contributed to heading off opposition to the Court from the African Union. Yet the potential of CFSP instruments such as EUSRs and CSDP missions has not been realized, and geographic inconsistency may lead to allegations of double standards.

The EU's internal reforms brought about by the Lisbon Treaty have, to date, made little change to the EU's contribution to a more effective ICC. Prior to the Lisbon reforms, officials worked across the structural pillar divide and EU engagement in support of the ICC was largely consistent across the pillars. The extent to which the structural division between the EC and Council are replicated by division between the EEAS and Commission will be influenced by the larger dynamics of that relationship, and the working practice of the few individuals concerned. If MEPs gain a stronger role in delegations to multilateral organizations in the future, this would be likely to lead to conflict between the Parliament's position on the ICC and those of member states, particularly France and the UK. The reform likely to have the greatest impact is the creation of EU delegations, which may take a stronger role in the future in engaging with the host governments on a range of ICC-related issues, from ratification of the Rome Statute to cooperation with active investigations and prosecutions. This, however, will depend on the extent to this potential is realized.

Other developments may have more impact than institutional change in addressing the main challenge for EU support to the Court to date, namely putting policy into practice. The Agenda for Change, the new EUSR for Human Rights and the planned Strategy on Human Rights may enable greater implementation of policies supporting the Court. The ICC is, however, strikingly absent from the EUSR's mandate, suggesting that the Court will be a low priority for his work and therefore possibly also in the planned Human Rights Strategy. The extent to which the external dimension of internal justice, freedom and security policies such as the Stockholm programme will be strengthened in the future, particularly in relation to the role of EU delegations abroad and CSDP missions remains to be seen. The Parliament may also play a stronger role in shaping future external relations – through insisting on ICC clauses in a wider range of agreements, for example.

In international *fora*, such as the ASP, the possibility for greater EU representation foreseen in the Lisbon Treaty has not been implemented and the EU continues to be represented by the presidency rather than the EEAS. Beyond a desire for visibility for the EU institutions, there is no clear need for one EU voice. EU member states are united in defence of the existing system, yet divide between the permanent members of the Security Council and the rest over proposals to amend significantly the Rome Statute. Even for more day-to-day business, representation by the EEAS may reduce the engagement of activist member states and lead to a lowest-common-denominator approach.

Introducing regional representation carries significant risks for the Court, however. The African Union is arguably more important than the EU for the Court's success or failure. Many African states, like Botswana, are staunch supporters of the Court but the continent is also home to vociferous opponents of the Court, like Sudan, and to states, like South Africa, which are critical of the Court in the wake of the Al-Bashir indictment. Introducing regional representation would reduce the ability of EU states to build alliances with like-minded states, and it would also likely squeeze out pro-ICC voices within the AU. This would be too high a price to pay for a show of EU unity.

The EU could make its support for a more effective International Criminal Court more effective in two ways. First, by putting its policies into practice in its relations with third countries. Second, by not pursuing representation in the Court's formal bodies where showing EU unity could come at too high a price for the Court. EU effectiveness in the Court is likely to be discreet.

Notes

1 The Like-Minded Group comprised geographically mixed states, including 13 then-EU members. Members of the LMG were committed to a set of principles, including independence of the Court from the Security Council, and were generally at odds with the positions held by the permanent members of the Security Council (including France and the UK) (Schabas 2001: 15).
2 See, for example, World Development Report 2011 (World Bank 2011).
3 The statement made by Hungary is not available.

References

African, Caribbean and Pacific Group of States and European Community Member States (2005) *Agreement amending the Partnership Agreement between the members of the African, Caribbean and Pacific Group of states, of the one part, and the European Community and its member states, of the other part, signed in Cotonou on 23 June 2000 – Final Act*, 22 December 2005.

African Union (2009) *Decision on the meeting of African States Parties to the Rome Statute of the International Criminal Court (ICC) Sirte, Libya.* (Assembly/AU/13 (XIII)), 3 July 2009.

BBC (2011) *Libya rebels welcome AU's 'Gaddafi-free' talks offer*, 2 July 2011, BBC News Africa. Online. Available www.bbc.co.uk/news/world-africa-14003786 (accessed 24 April 2013).

Bensouda, F. (2012) *The International Criminal Court: a new approach to International Relations*, 12 September 2012, Council on Foreign Relations. Online. Available www.cfr.org/international-criminal-courts-and-tribunals/international-criminal-court-new-approach-international-relations/p29351 (accessed 24 April 2013).

Coalition for the International Criminal Court (undated) Online. Available www.iccnow.org/?mod=aggression (accessed 27 November 2012).

Communauté Européenne–République du Côte d'Ivoire (2007) *Document de stratégie pays et programme national indicatif 2008–2013*, 4 June 2008. Online. Available http://ec.europa.eu/development/icenter/repository/scanned_ci_csp10_fr.pdf (accessed 29 May 2013).

Council of the European Union (2003) *Council Common Position 2003/444/CFSP on the International Criminal Court*, 16 June 2003.

Council of the European Union (2004) *Action Plan to follow-up on the Common Position on the International Criminal Court* (5742/04), 28 January 2004.

Council of the European Union (2005) *The European Union guidelines on promoting compliance with international humanitarian law (IHL)* (15246/05 III), 5 December 2005.

Council of the European Union (2007) *The European Union and the International Criminal Court.*

Council of the European Union (2008) *The Africa-European Union strategic partnership.* Online. Available www.consilium.europa.eu/uedocs/cms_data/librairie/PDF/EN_AFRICA_inter08.pdf (accessed 29 May 2013).

Council of the European Union (2009a) *The European Union and Central Asia: the new partnership in action.* Online. Available http://eeas.europa.eu/central_asia/docs/2010_strategy_eu_centralasia_en.pdf (accessed 29 May 2013).

Council of the European Union (2009b) *The Stockholm Programme: an open and secure Europe serving and protecting the citizens* (17024/09), 2 December 2009.

Council of the European Union (2010) *Council Conclusions on The Review Conference of the Rome Statute of the International Criminal Court*, 25 May 2010. Online. Available www.consilium.europa.eu/uedocs/cms_data/docs/pressdata/en/intm/114615.pdf (accessed 29 May 2013).

Council of the European Union (2011a) *Council Decision 2011/168/CFSP on the International Criminal Court and repealing Common Position 2003/444/CFSP*, 21 March 2011.

Council of the European Union (2011b) *Action Plan to follow up on the Decision on the International Criminal Court* (12080/11), 12 July 2011.

Council of the European Union (2012) *Council Decision 2012/440/CFSP appointing the European Union Special Representative for Human Rights*, 25 July 2012.

du Plessis, M. (2010) *The International Criminal Court that Africa wants*, Pretoria, South Africa: Insitute for Security Studies.

Emerson, M., Balfour, R., Corthaut, T., Wouters, J., Kaczynski, P.M. and Renard, T. (2011) *Upgrading the EU's role as global actor: institutions, law and the restructuring of European diplomacy*, Brussels: CEPS.

EuropeAid (2007) *EuropeAid EIDHR European Initiative for Democracy and Human Rights 2000–2006: promoting democracy and human rights worldwide*, 1 January 2007.

European Commission (2004) *European Neighbourhood policy strategy paper* (COM(2004) 373 final), 12 May 2004.

European Commission (2009) *The European Instrument for Democracy and Human Rights (EIDHR)*, Compendium, January 2007.

European Commission (2010) *Answer given by Commissioner De Gucht on behalf of the European Commission to a written question 4 February 2010.* Online. Available www.europarl.europa.eu/sides/getAllAnswers.do?reference=E-2009–6327&language=EN (accessed 24 April 2013).

European Commission (2011a) *European neighbourhood and partnership instrument Libya: strategy paper and national indicative programme 2011–2013.* Online. Available http://ec.europa.eu/world/enp/pdf/country/2011_enpi_csp_nip_libya_en.pdf (accessed 29 May 2013).

European Commission (2011b) *Increasing the impact of EU Development Policy: an agenda for change* (COM(2011) 637 final), Brussels.

European Commission and High Representative (2011) *Joint communication to the European Parliament and Council. 'Human rights and democracy at the heart of EU external action – towards a more effective approach'* (COM 211 (886)), Brussels.

European Council (2003) *A secure Europe in a better world: European security strategy*, 12 December 2003. Online. Available www.consilium.europa.eu/uedocs/cmsUpload/78367.pdf (accessed 29 May 2013).

European Council (2006) *Agreement between the International Criminal Court and the European Union on cooperation and assistance* (ICC-PRES/01–01–06).

European Council (2008) *Report on the implementation of the European Security Strategy – providing security in a changing world* (S407/08), 1 December 2008.

European Parliament (2010a) *Sub-Committee on Human Rights Committee on Development* Ad hoc *delegation to the review conference of the Rome Statute of the International Criminal Court. Final report.* Online. Available www.europarl.europa.eu/document/activities/cont/201108/20110810ATT24996/20110810ATT24996EN.pdf (accessed 29 May 2013).

European Parliament (2010b) *First Review Conference of the Rome Statute. European Parliament resolution of 19 May 2010 on the Review Conference on the Rome Statute of the International Criminal Court, in Kampala, Uganda* (P7_TA(2010)0185), 19 May 2010.

European Parliament (2011) *European Parliament resolution on the review of the European Neighbourhood Policy – Southern dimension (B7–0199/2011)*, 16 March 2011.

European Parliament and Council (2006) *Regulation of the European Parliament and of the Council of 18 December 2006 establishing a financing instrument for development cooperation.* (EC) No 1905/2006, 18 December 2006.

General Secretariat of the Council (2010) *The European Union and the International Criminal Court – May 2010*, Brussels: European Union.

Groenleer, M. and Rijks, D. (2009) 'The European Union and the International Criminal Court: the politics of international criminal justice', in K.E. Jørgensen (ed.) *The European Union and International Organizations*, London: Routledge, pp. 167–87.

Groenleer, M.L. and van Schaik, L.G. (2007) 'United we stand? The European Union's international actorness in the cases of the International Criminal Court and the Kyoto Protocol', *Journal of Common Market Studies*, 45(5): 969–98.

Howitt, R. (2010) *Press release – Communiqué de presse – 01.06.2010*, 1 June 2010.

Human Rights Watch (2010) *Making Kampala count: advancing the global fight against impunity at the ICC Review Conference*, New York: Human Rights Watch.

International Criminal Court (2010) Online. Available www.icc-cpi.int/Menus/ASP/ReviewConference/GENERAL+DEBATE+_+Review+Conference.htm (accessed 27 November 2012).

Kingdom of Spain (2010) *Declaración realizada en nombre de la Unión Europea en el debate general de la Conferencia de Revisión del Estatuto de Roma.* Europa. Online. Available http://consilium.europa.eu/uedocs/cmsUpload/DeclaracionES-en-nombre-de-la-UEkampalaES-EN-FR-final.pdf (accessed 27 November 2012).

Maqungo, S. (2000) 'The establishment of the International Criminal Court: SADC's participation in the negotiations', *African Security Review*, 9(1): 42–53.

Rapp, S.J. (2010) *Statement by Stephen J. Rapp, U.S. Ambassador-at-Large for War Crimes.* Online. Available www.icc-cpi.int/iccdocs/asp_docs/RC2010/Statements/ICC-RC-gendeba-USA-ENG.pdf (accessed 24 April 2013).

Republic of Kenya–European Community (2007) *Country Strategy Paper and Indicative Programme for the period 2008–2013.* Online. Available http://ec.europa.eu/development/icenter/repository/scanned_ke_csp10_en.pdf (accessed 29 May 2013).

Republic of Uganda–European Community (2008) *Country Strategy Paper and National Indicative Programme 2008–2013.* Online. Available http://ec.europa.eu/development/icenter/repository/scanned_ug_csp10_en.pdf (accessed 29 May 2013).

République Centrafricaine–Communauté Européenne (2007) *Document de stratégie pays et programme national indicatif 2008–2013*. Online. Available http://ec.europa.eu/development/icenter/repository/scanned_cf_csp10_fr.pdf (accessed 29 May 2013).

République Démocratique du Congo–Communauté Européenne (2007) *Document de stratégie pays et programme indicative national, 10e FED 2008–2013*. Online. Available http://ec.europa.eu/development/icenter/repository/scanned_cd_csp10_fr.pdf (accessed 29 May 2013).

Schabas, W.A. (2001) *An introduction to the International Criminal Court*, Cambridge: Cambridge University Press.

Slaughter, A.-M. and Burke-White, W. (2002) 'An international constitutional moment', *Harvard International Law Journal*, 43(1): 1–21.

Solana, J. (2002) 'International court signals a new era', *International Herald Tribune*, 11 April 2002.

Sriram, C.L. and Brown, S. (2012) 'Kenya in the shadow of the ICC: complementarity, gravity and impact', *International Criminal Law Review*, 12: 219–44.

Thomas, D.C. (2012) 'Still punching below its weight? Coherence and effectiveness in European Union foreign policy', *Journal of Common Market Studies*, 50(3): 457–74.

World Bank (2011) *World development report 2011: conflict, security and development*.

7 Effective multilateralism in the IAEA

Changing best practice

Johanne Grøndahl Glavind

Introduction

The EU Security Strategy identifies the proliferation of weapons of mass destruction as 'potentially the greatest threat to our security' (European Council 2003). Subsequently, the EU adopted the EU Strategy against the Proliferation of Weapons of Mass Destruction (further: WMD Strategy) with the aim to strengthen the international non-proliferation regime (Council of the European Union 2003). A key actor in this regime is the International Atomic Energy Agency (IAEA), which is an international organization based in Vienna promoting peaceful uses of nuclear energy. It is this Agency that is in the focus of the present chapter.

The IAEA was established in 1957 following US President Eisenhower's famous 'Atoms for Peace' address to the General Assembly of the United Nations on 8 December 1953. Though established as an autonomous organization independent of the UN, its treaty, the IAEA Statute, requires it to report to both the UN General Assembly and the UN Security Council. The IAEA is furthermore entrusted by the Non-Proliferation Treaty (NPT), adopted in 1968, to control the members' use of nuclear technology and to verify compliance with the provisions of NPT. The 'grand bargain' of this treaty is that while it promotes the peaceful use of nuclear energy for all, it prohibits non-nuclear-weapon states from developing nuclear weapons and obligates the five recognized nuclear-weapon states (Russia, China, US, UK and France) to disarm (Müller 2010).

The Agency, which is sometimes given the nickname 'the UN's nuclear watchdog', is probably best known in the general public for its inspections in states suspected of secretly developing nuclear weapons such as North Korea, Iran and Syria. However, verification is only a part of the IAEA's work. Safety of nuclear power plants is another important function, which has attracted increased attention after the Fukushima accident in March 2011. Technical assistance and cooperation in peaceful uses of nuclear energy is also an important part of the IAEA mandate and was in fact the original purpose of the establishment of the Agency in 1957.

In recent years, an old division between North and South has grown bigger. Critical voices are raised primarily from developing countries that the Agency fails to fulfil the part of technical assistance, and due to pressure from Western states mainly focuses on the so-called three Ss: security, safety and safeguards. Furthermore, many states from the South feel that the 'grand bargaining' of the NPT is being undermined by the nuclear-weapon states. Without seriously disarming themselves, they still demand that the other, non-nuclear-weapon states are subject to a strict verification regime. As a result, political tensions are rising in the IAEA, and more and more developing states are questioning the political mandate of the Agency. Yet, with increased threats from nuclear terrorism and nuclear proliferation, the IAEA is now more important than ever. In recent years, 58 IAEA members have announced that they are considering introducing nuclear power (Lundin 2012: 7). The Agency thus has a key role in ensuring that new power plants are both safe from accidents, secure from theft and proliferation and, most importantly, that they are not being used for military purposes.

The EU in the IAEA: effective multilateralism?

According to the WMD Strategy, the EU will make 'multilateralism more effective' by 'enhancing political, financial and technical support to verification regimes' (Council of the European Union 2003: 8). Although the IAEA is mentioned only in passing in this strategy, the IAEA is the non-proliferation organization that has received the most financial support from the CFSP-budget. In the period 2003–12 various EU institutions and instruments have allocated over €100 million to the IAEA. The question is whether the EU has been able to enhance its own effectiveness in the Agency as well as the Agency's effectiveness. Some are sceptical and argue that the EU's role in the WMD nonproliferation area at best is modest (Van Ham 2011); others are more optimistic and point to several areas where the EU influences the IAEA's policy (Grip 2011b; Lundin 2012). Furthermore, because EU member states' interests are divided on key areas such as nuclear weapons and disarmament (France and the UK are the only recognized nuclear-weapon states among the EU member states; other states like Denmark, Ireland and Sweden praise disarmament), the IAEA thus arguably poses a hard case for EU effectiveness.

While there is plenty of academic work on the EU's non-proliferation policy more broadly, not many case studies actually investigate the EU's role in various organizations targeting weapons of mass destruction (see, for example, Delaere and van Schaik 2012, for a case study on the EU at the Organization for the Prohibition of Chemical Weapons). Apart from an article by Lars-Erik Lundin (2012), the former head of the EU delegation to the IAEA, not much has been written about the relationship between the EU and the IAEA (see also Grip 2011b). This lack of interest may be due to a general perception of the IAEA as a technical rather than a political organization. Yet the IAEA is not only a highly technical organization, it is political as well. Its decision-making bodies, the Board of Governors and the General Conference, carry out important political work (Lundin 2012: 12) and it is thus very interesting to investigate the role of the EU in these bodies.

All EU member states are members of the IAEA. The EU as an organization in Vienna does not have formal status in the Agency, because the Lisbon Treaty is not yet fully implemented at the time of writing. However, the relationship is somewhat complicated by the European Atomic Energy Community (Euratom), a separate legal entity in EU sharing the same institutional bodies as the EU (Grip 2011a: 16). Euratom, which is represented locally by the EU delegation, has formal observer status in the Agency, including a standing invitation to the General Conference with the right to speak as an observer (Lundin 2012: 5). However, although the EU delegation formally represents Euratom in the IAEA, Euratom is a Luxembourg-based organization. All official statements from Euratom in the IAEA are made by members of the Commission or the EU delegation in Vienna rather than the rotating EU presidency, which delivers all other EU statements at the IAEA. The Lisbon Treaty did not change the relationship between the EU and the Euratom, which is still a separate legal entity within the EU. Thus to sum up, the EU is formally represented by the rotating presidency in the Agency, while the EU delegation representing the European External Action Service internally coordinates and chairs the cooperation between the EU member states and represents the EU informally in the IAEA.[1] As a result of the Lisbon Treaty, the mandate and resources of the EU delegation have been strengthened. The question of this study is whether this has improved not only the internal but also the external effectiveness of the Union in the IAEA, thereby fulfilling the goal of effective multilateralism.

The chapter consists of three sections. The first section begins by analysing the EU's policy towards reform questions of the IAEA before discussing the external effectiveness of the EU in the IAEA. The second section investigates the internal effectiveness of the EU, including the effects of the Lisbon Treaty. The chapter ends with a conclusion summarizing the main findings.[2]

External reform: making the IAEA more effective

Reform of the IAEA is not mentioned in any of the EU strategies or in the six Council decisions allocating funding to the Agency. In fact, the EU has not supported the two recent IAEA reform proposals, mainly because of political interests of both the Union and its member states.

The first reform proposal is a long-standing Iranian demand to reform the political structure of the Board of Governors (the Board and the General Conference are the two decision-making bodies in IAEA). In contrast to the General Conference, which includes representatives from all members, the Board of Governors only consists of 35 members, of whom the 13 most technologically advanced have permanent seats and 22 have rotating seats for two-year terms based on their regional groupings. Among the Board's important political tasks are making recommendations to the General Conferences regarding IAEA activities and budget; considering membership applications; approving safeguards agreements; and appointing the Director General of the IAEA – the latter with the approval of the General Conference.

According to Iran, the representation of the members in the Board is 'limited, unbalanced and inequitable' and the Board's 'mandate and composition' must be reconstructed (IAEA 2012a). The Iranian reform initiative is supported by a few states, primarily traditional Iranian allies such as Syria, Cuba and Venezuela, but it is rejected by the EU member states as well as most other Western states (IAEA 2012c). Although Iran might be right that the Board does not geographically represent the members equally and this may affect the legitimacy of its decisions, the current composition of the Board politically favours the EU. As is the case in other international organizations, the last enlargement of the EU increased its geographical representation in the IAEA. The Union is now represented in two regional groups in the Agency; the Western Group and the Eastern Group (see also Chapter 2). In other words, the current organizational structure of the Board is a political advantage for the EU, making it easier for it to affect the Board's decisions. The EU therefore has no desire to push for a political reform of the IAEA.

The second reform proposal regards the legal mandate of the IAEA Secretariat to enforce safety measures on the Agency's members. The EU member states are divided on this issue due to different interests. Following the accident at the Fukushima power plant in Japan in March 2011, the IAEA faced serious criticism for its handling of the disaster, which was claimed to be too slow and confusing. While acknowledging the Agency's responsibility, the General Director, Yukiya Amano, also defended the Agency pointing out that it does not have a legal mandate to enforce safety standards. Today, nuclear safety standards are voluntary and the IAEA has no legal right to control or enforce safety standards in members. Amano thus called for reforming the Agency's safety mandate, including the promotion of a new Action Plan that was adopted in September 2011 by the General Conference and the Board of Governors (Pomper 2012). However, due to pressure from the US and other great powers, Amano's proposal to change the legal mandate of the IAEA was not included. Hence, the Action Plan did not increase the powers of the Agency or bind members to any mandatory steps (Findley 2012: 18). It seems that the EU member states were divided on this issue. While many of the non-nuclear-energy states supported a legal enforcement mandate for the Agency, the nuclear-energy states maintained that nuclear safety is a sovereign matter. Consequently the EU did not support Amano's reform proposal. The two cases thus show that the EU is not prepared to support political and legal reforms of the IAEA that may affect the self-interests of either the Union or some of its member states, especially the European great powers.

The lack of European support for the reform proposals by no means implies that the Union does not support smaller reform initiatives that strengthen the Agency's work on non-proliferation and the three Ss mentioned above: security, safety and safeguards which, besides technical cooperation, are the core tasks of the IAEA. The strategy of effective multilateralism within IAEA is instead being pursued using financial, technical and political means.

The EU uses various financial instruments to support the IAEA.[3] Since 2003 these funds amounted to at least €100.7 million (see Table 7.1 for an overview

Table 7.1 The funding of EU instruments to the IAEA (2003–12)

EU Instrument	Aim of the Fund	Funding to IAEA
European Union Instrument for Nuclear Safety Cooperation[a]	Assistance to third countries in safe operations of peaceful nuclear activities	2009: €6.5 million 2010: €4.5 million 2012–13: €10.0 million Total of €21 million
European Union Instrument for Pre-accession Assistance[a]	Assistance to candidate countries in the areas of nuclear safety and security	Total of €21 million
European Union Instrument for Stability[b]	Mitigation of chemical, biological, radiological and nuclear risk	2011–12: Low-enriched uranium fuel bank: €20 million[1] 2011: New IAEA safeguards laboratory: €5 million[2] Total of €25 million
Common Foreign and Security Policy (Council decisions)[b]	Support for the Agency's nuclear security plan through its Office of Nuclear Security	IAEA activities on nuclear security and verification 2010: €9.966 million 2008: €7.703 million 2006: €6.995 million 2005: €3.914 million 2004: €3.329 million 2007: IAEA monitoring and verification activities in the DPRK: €1.780 million Total of €33.687 million
Total		€100.7 million

Sources: a IAEA 2011b; b Council of the European Union 2013.

Notes
a Another contribution (€5 million) is to be provided from the CFSP budget in 2013, depending on progress made between the IAEA and the host country for the bank, Kazakhstan (Council of the European Union 2013).
b Additional €5 million is to be provided in 2013 (Council of the European Union 2013).

of the EU funding). Two-fifths go to cooperation projects with the IAEA on nuclear safety and security in EU candidate countries as well as third countries, for example the Vinča Nuclear Decommissioning Programme, which supports the return of spent fuel from the Vinča research reactor in Serbia to Russia (IAEA 2011b). A quarter of the money comes from the Instrument for Stability and supports specific IAEA projects such as the low-enrichment fuel bank and a new IAEA safeguards laboratory. Finally, one-third of the money comes from the CFSP budget based on six Council decisions, five of which allocate funding to general IAEA activities on nuclear security and verification, and one specifically funds IAEA monitoring and verification activities in North Korea.

Compared to voluntary contributions by other regional or international organizations, the EU is by far the largest donor. For example, in terms of contributions to the Technical Cooperation Fund (TCF) as of December 2010, the total funds available from the EU Commission are worth almost US$12.5 million. The only other regional organizations funding the TCF are the Gulf Cooperation Council with almost US$0.5 million and the OPEC fund with almost US$20,000. Furthermore, the EU is the only regional organization providing in-kind support, e.g. experts to the Agency, with a worth of almost US$21,000 in 2010 (IAEA 2011a). Finally, the Nuclear Security Fund, another important IAEA instrument funding nuclear security projects, mainly relies on voluntary contributions. Besides funding from primarily Western states, the EU Commission is a major contributor as well (Findley 2012: 52).

In addition to funding from the EU institutions, the EU member states bilaterally fund the Agency. In 2012, the IAEA received approximately €104.6 million in national contributions by the EU member states and approximately €11.7 million in voluntary contributions from the member states to the TCF[4] (IAEA 2012b) (see Table 7.2). The largest single donor is the US, which in 2012 donated approximately €70 million in national contribution and approximately €7.8 million in voluntary contribution to the TCF (IAEA 2012b). Nevertheless, the total EU voluntary contributions from the institutional instruments and the member states are thus high in comparison to other voluntary contributions (Grip 2011b: 3). EU diplomats in Vienna explain that the aim of all this EU funding is not only to increase the EU's influence within the Agency, but more importantly to get things done. The substantial funding is thus a means to support projects that the EU finds especially important. If, for instance, the EU thinks it is important to eliminate all the accumulated, unstable spent fuel from nuclear reactors in Serbia, the IAEA is the easiest way to get it done.

The EU also uses technical measures to strengthen the IAEA's work. One central EU actor is the Joint Research Centres, the scientific and technical arm of the EU Commission. The Centres consist of seven scientific institutes located in five EU states.[5] They cooperate with the Agency in the field of nuclear safeguards and in the field of combating illicit trafficking of nuclear materials. Again, the EU here is a key player compared to other IAEA members and regional organizations. In the field of nuclear safeguards, the EU's so-called Cooperative Support Programme ranks second among the 21 IAEA members' support programmes in terms of number of active tasks (IAEA 2011b). Another central EU actor is Euratom, which cooperates with the Agency in many areas, mainly safety, security and safeguards. Euratom has extensive experience with safeguards, verification and nuclear research for peaceful uses, and by sharing its know-how with IAEA it contributes to the development of the Agency's methodologies, equipment and facilities (IAEA 2011b; Lundin 2012: 7). For instance, the Agency and Euratom cooperate on inspections and together they have a kind of combined inspection team. This cooperation is of great value as it sets a good example for other states. Through the IAEA the EU is thus able to influence nuclear safety and security in other states and thereby strengthen the international non-proliferation regime – an influence that the EU otherwise would not have. Because the Agency has a worldwide reach, it has a much higher

Table 7.2 EU member states' national and voluntary contribution to the IAEA, 2012

	National contribution to the regular budget (assessed amount) (€)	Voluntary contribution to Technical Cooperation Fund (target share) (€)
Austria	2,301,784	255,440
Belgium	2,908,115	322,727
Bulgaria	87,177	11,526
Cyprus	123,510	13,707
Czech Republic	814,189	104,668
Denmark	1,990,206	220,862
Estonia	89,533	11,837
Finland	1,532,654	170,086
France	16,567,257	1,838,547
Germany	21,692,947	2,407,369
Greece	1,826,392	207,467
Hungary	678,491	87,224
Ireland	1,347,389	149,526
Italy	13,524,406	1,500,867
Latvia	87,177	11,526
Lithuania	148,437	19,625
Luxembourg	244,215	27,102
Malta	38,771	4,984
Netherlands	5,019,016	556,984
Poland	1,880,198	248,587
Portugal	1,349,226	153,264
Romania	402,899	53,269
Slovakia	322,790	42,677
Slovenia	277,897	30,840
Spain	8,595,207	953,851
Sweden	2,880,042	319,612
UK	17,866,922	1,982,777
Total	104,596,847	11,706,951

Source: IAEA 2012b, attachments 1 and 3.

international legitimacy than the EU. Our conversations reveal that the EU has to accept that, although the EU and Euratom are more experienced in safeguards than the IAEA, this does not automatically provide them with the legitimacy to lead the work and to tell other states how things are done. But the EU and Euratom can 'use' to some degree the Agency's legitimacy by working together with the Agency and change practice in other states through this cooperation. The EU thus reforms the Agency's work from the inside, so to speak, by trying to change best practice in small steps. At the same time, by having much higher internal requirements, it can set a good example and be a role model for other states without directly imposing its own standards on these states.

Finally, the EU seeks to strengthen the IAEA and its work more directly through political measures. Two good examples are the safeguards system resolution and the dispute over Iran's nuclear programme. Regarding the former,

Western and many developing states disagree on the Agency's safeguards system and whether it should be strengthened. To verify the correctness and the completeness of states' declarations about their nuclear material and activities, the IAEA inspectors use an extensive set of technical measures called safeguards. Today, the IAEA safeguards nuclear material and activities in more than 140 states (IAEA 2012d). Some states, including the EU member states, want to further strengthen the IAEA's inspection capabilities and have signed the voluntary, so-called Additional Protocol, a legal document which complements the regular safeguards agreements and provides the Agency with additional verification tools to inspect both declared and undeclared activities.

According to EU policy the Additional Protocol should be mandatory for all non-nuclear-weapon states party to the NPT. However, leading Non-Aligned Movement (NAM) and G77 states like Egypt and Brazil, respectively, are opposed to this. They require that the nuclear-weapon states make substantial progress on their nuclear disarmament obligations before they will accept further commitments in non-proliferation beyond NPT. At the General Conference, the EU traditionally sponsors a safeguards resolution, which stresses the importance of the safeguards system and promotes the Additional Protocol. To get the resolution adopted, the EU must compromise with NAM and G77; often the adopted resolution recognizes the Additional Protocol as an important measure but does not endorse it as a verification standard. In 2011, due to disagreements between the Western states and NAM, in particular the Arab states, the General Conference failed to adopt the resolution (Mukhatzhanova 2012). This was a heavy blow to the EU, politically speaking. Although the previously adopted resolutions did not explicitly endorse the Additional Protocol as a new standard, recognition of the Protocol in itself is an important political step towards making it universal. The Union therefore worked very hard at the 2012 General Conference to get the resolution adopted – and succeeded, because of improved tactics and a strong effort by all EU member states. The adopted resolution was seen as a great team effort where 27 member states vigorously lobbied the other states for support. The case thus shows that when acting together the EU does have the ability to affect the IAEA's decision making.

The EU also plays a leading role in the conflict with Iran over its nuclear programme. While the West suspects that Iran is planning to build nuclear weapons, Teheran maintains that its nuclear reactors are for energy and research purposes only. To support the IAEA inspection team in Iran, France, Germany and the UK – the so-called E3 – in 2003 began negotiations with Iran regarding its nuclear programme (these negotiations were conducted outside the IAEA framework but in support of the organization). Later they aligned with the US, Russia and China – the so-called E3+3 (or P5+1, depending on one's view) – with the EU High Representative, Catherine Ashton, as leader of negotiations. Furthermore, the US and the EU have imposed strict sanctions on the Iranian regime to force cooperation, but the conflict remains unresolved. The EU is thus highly involved in the Iran case and, as argued by Van Ham, Iran is a litmus test for the EU and its non-proliferation strategy. It is a very difficult case, which has lasted more than a decade, and the EU risks that its dual-track approach of multilateralism and economic coercion will fail publicly (Van Ham 2011). However, if the EU together with P5+1 succeeds in persuading Iran to sign the Additional Protocol and allow IAEA inspections, it will not only be a victory for the EU but for the IAEA and the non-proliferation regime as well.

Summing up, the EU is a major supporter of the IAEA in terms of financial and technical assistance. It also seeks to strengthen the Agency politically, but as the member states' support to the political reforms showed, this political support to the Agency is limited by the member states' national interests. A grand political reform of the IAEA is thus not sought by the EU. Rather, it seeks to strengthen the Agency from the inside using financial and technical means to change best practice. Furthermore, as shown in the next section, the political outreach and visibility of the Union enabling it to influence the political agenda of the Agency has also been strengthened with the Lisbon Treaty. As a result of the Treaty, the internal effectiveness has increased by streamlining the communication process not only between the EU delegation and the EU member states but also between the EU and third states.

The question remains whether these measures have made the IAEA more effective, and that is very difficult to answer. For example, it is EU policy that more states should sign the Additional Protocol to make the Agency safeguard system more effective. In the period 2004 to 2011, the number of signed additional protocols in force grew from 29 to 108, an impressing increase of 272.41 per cent (Grip 2011b: 4–5). But as noted by Grip, it is difficult – if not impossible – to make a direct causal link between EU policy and the IAEA results. Nevertheless, as Grip concludes it is likely that the increase has been encouraged by EU support and targeted actions, but more research is needed on this subject in order to confirm this conclusion.

Internal reform: making the EU more effective in the IAEA

Following the Lisbon Treaty, the EU delegation in Vienna has played a much more central role in coordinating EU positions in the IAEA. The delegation has one ambassador, Mrs Zanathy, and consists of two sections, the UN section, including the IAEA, and the OSCE section (see Chapter 9 of this volume for an analysis of the EU in the OSCE). Prior to the Lisbon Treaty the EU delegation was merely a Commission delegation; since its task was only to represent the Commission at the IAEA, the size of the delegation was very small. With the Lisbon Treaty the EU delegation has acquired a new task and has thus been reinforced with experienced staff from member states. At the time of writing, eight diplomats work in the UN section, so the size of the team is comparable to the delegation of a large EU country. But compared to the delegations of the US or Russia, it is still relatively small. Also at headquarter level the situation has improved; relevant working groups like CONOP (Working Group of Non-Proliferation) now have permanent chairs provided by the European External Action Service, which improves the work processes between the EU delegation, the Vienna ambassadors and the Brussels working groups like CONOP (Lundin 2012: 4).

The Lisbon Treaty has changed the internal relationship between the EU member states, the presidency and the delegation, giving a much stronger role to the latter – a role that it fulfils. Over the last few years, the delegation has changed from being a rather passive EU actor to chairing the meetings with all the EU member states in Vienna. Earlier the rotating presidency was in charge of chairing meetings and preparing and coordinating all EU statements. Now the team from the EU delegation takes care of all coordination between the EU member states and of drafting EU positions, while the rotating presidency still formally represents the EU in the IAEA's decision-making bodies and reads out the common EU declarations. The Lisbon Treaty seems to have improved the internal relationship between the EU delegation and the member states thereby making the EU more effective.

One clear advantage of the Lisbon Treaty is continuity, both internally and externally. Starting with the former, the treaty has in a few years streamlined the work process, drafting and problem solving by giving the responsibility to the delegation. Previously the ownership of these tasks changed along with the rotating presidency and everything had to be done from scratch every six months. Diplomats in Vienna indicate that this administrative reform does not solve the problem of reaching agreement among strongly divided interests on issues like disarmament or the competence issue (further elaborated below). Reaching an agreement sometimes requires a creative approach, but the EU delegation might be better suited for this than the national delegations, because it can build up a certain routine and experience in handling internal conflicts. At a more practical level, the reform also positively affects the EU's internal 'infrastructure' making communication and coordination much easier: the delegation has a meeting room, contact lists and an internal system to post documents and so on.

External continuity has also improved. Before Lisbon, much depended on the rotating presidency state, and non-EU states had to cooperate with different EU states which had different ways of doing things. Today non-EU states contact the same people at the EU delegation if they have matters to discuss with the EU. As a result, coordination among the EU and other states has become much better. The EU now behaves more as a state (and not a group of states) and the EU delegation increasingly looks and acts like an ordinary national delegation. Importantly, this has not only improved the contact between the EU and third states but has also given the EU a much more competent profile. The informal outreach of the EU has thus improved, and the EU delegation is now better at systematically promoting political dialogue with non-EU states compared to 'the rotating presidency's six-monthly planning perspective' (Lundin 2012: 3–4). However, there are still many states for which the EU is an unknown quantity and the double representation by the EU presidency and the delegation does not make it easier. In fact, third states diplomats tend to see the EU member states as their main contact with the EU. Yet it seems fair to argue that the physical presence of the EU delegation combined with an increased mandate has increased the visibility of the EU.

To reiterate, the EU delegation has over the years taken over more and more responsibility and is in charge of internally coordinating EU policy and informally promoting the EU position at conference meetings in the Agency. However, its role as chair ends here; as the delegation still does not have the formal right to speak on behalf of the EU at conference meetings, this is instead done by the rotating presidency.

Effectiveness: the EU as a key player?

As argued above, the Union's internal administrative effectiveness has increased as a result of the Lisbon Treaty, which has streamlined the coordination process. The question is whether it also improves the Union's effectiveness in the Agency. The size of the EU coalition alone has proven to be rather effective. By having a common position and thus automatically 28 votes in the IAEA in favour of this position, the EU can be a rather decisive factor in the Agency's decision-making bodies. The EU can thus use its size strategically – not only in terms of voting together but also in terms of lobbying together. But *not* having a common position can also be an effective negotiation strategy. For instance, the EU member states avoided defining a common position on a controversial Russian resolution proposal at the 2012 General Conference in the hope that it would be withdrawn. This kind of 'silent diplomacy' can be very effective as well.

Another way to assess the EU's effectiveness is to look at how the EU is perceived by other actors. Do they see the EU as an important player in the IAEA and do they seek the EU's support? First, the relationship between the EU Commission and the IAEA Director General has improved. In 2008 former IAEA Director General, Mohammed El-Baradei, and the current President of the Commission, José Manuel Barroso, made a joint statement which confirmed the importance of working together (IAEA 2008). According to Lundin (2012: 8), the IAEA's lobbying of Commission services has intensified after this statement, especially in the technical field. In January 2013, the statement was followed up by a first ever senior-level meeting to discuss enhanced cooperation between the two organizations. The EU (including Euratom) and the IAEA thus seem to have a rather unique relationship with strong cooperation thereby increasing the interdependency between the two.

Second, non-EU states also seem to increasingly value the EU as an important player and have intensified their lobbying of not only the member states but also the EU delegation. Because the EU increasingly acts in the Agency as a unified group and has shown the ability to deliver results, there has been an increased interest in the EU. Other states are slowly realizing that if they make an agreement with the delegation or the presidency, it is real and all EU member states will actually vote for it. In contrast, if there is no support from the EU, it generally means that the Agency will have difficulty agreeing on a project. Not only are the EU statements in the Agency's political bodies 'looked at carefully', the support of the EU to a given policy is also considered important. Third states diplomats note that the EU would be in an even stronger position if it had a formal seat in the Agency. As it stands today, the EU delegation does not act with the same vigour as the leading countries of the EU.[6]

Although the EU's effectiveness in the Agency has apparently improved, two issues especially threaten it. One is the question about competence, which is an issue in all international organizations where the EU speaks on behalf of its member states (see also Chapters 2 and 9 in this volume). Along with the change of government in the UK in 2010, the question of competence was brought up by the new conservative government. According to the UK, the EU's competence varies depending on the issue and the EU thus does not have the right to speak on behalf of its member states in all issues. In the IAEA, the EU only has full authority on CFSP issues to speak on behalf of the EU on non-proliferation issues, such as Iran and Syria. On safety and security, the competence is mixed, which means that any EU statement is made on behalf of both the EU *and* its member states. Finally, the UK sees budget as an entirely national competence and the EU is thus not allowed to make statements on this. It is important for the UK to keep the different mandates clearly apart. Our conversations in Vienna indicate that the competence issue complicates the internal negotiation process and makes drafting of statements very time consuming, as every single paragraph of the text has to be in accordance with the EU's assigned competence. The outcome is often a compromise; however, at the General Conference in 2011 the EU delegation did not succeed, because the legal services were not prepared, and the EU presidency was therefore not able to deliver a common EU statement at the Conference. Learning from experience, the EU in 2012 delivered an EU statement solely on behalf of the EU and subjects on budget issues and technical cooperation, which are normally included in the statement, were left out.

The other potential threatening issue is disarmament. Establishing a common position on disarmament has often been blocked by either the two nuclear-weapon states in the EU, France and the UK, or pro-disarmament countries like Sweden and Ireland. Despite these internal disagreements, the EU member states have made disarmament a 'non-issue' in order not to bring internal disagreements into the Agency. The argument goes that disarmament is formally not part of the Agency's mandate and hence belongs to Geneva not Vienna. Every year at the General Conference, NAM and G77 states such as Egypt and Brazil insist on making reference to the disarmament in the adopted resolutions, for example in the safeguard resolution. Following these states, whilst the non-proliferation measures have been strengthened over the years, the nuclear disarmament side of the Treaty bargain has yet to be realized. They thus question the argument by the EU and the nuclear-weapon states that disarmament is not a part of the IAEA pointing to the fact that the IAEA statute mentions 'safeguarded worldwide disarmament' as one of its main functions (IAEA Statute, Article 3, par. 7 B.1). Nevertheless, the EU has decided to follow the line of the US and vote against the disarmament language in the resolutions and as a result, the disarmament demands are not included in the adopted resolutions. The EU seems to be highly aware of its own shortcomings and avoids bringing internal disagreements into the Agency which would weaken its position. However, this policy may backfire and in the long run impede the Union's work on non-proliferation and its leading role in the global non-proliferation regime. According to Meier and Quille (2005), 'there is a real danger that the EU will devolve from being a constructive force in the NPT to being simply a microcosm of global divisions on nonproliferation and disarmament between nuclear-weapon states and non-nuclear-weapon states'. Hence, the (non)issue of disarmament may in the long run decrease the legitimacy of the EU and damage its credibility as an international actor.

Reform: better yet?

As shown above, the internal effectiveness of the EU in the IAEA seems in many respects to be quite high; the Lisbon Treaty has improved the internal communication and coordination both between the EU delegation and Brussels and between the delegation and the member states. The result is improved negotiation tactics in the Agency and internal awareness that the EU as a group stands strong and is a key player in the Agency. There are also some indications that the Treaty has increased the visibility and external awareness of the EU in the IAEA Secretariat and in third states resulting in increased lobbying of the EU.

But is it good enough or could the EU do even better? Has the internal reform process based on the Lisbon Treaty succeeded? In relation to the internal administrative practice, there is room for improvement despite the many good results since the Lisbon Treaty. According to Lundin (2012: 13), the EU institutions working with the IAEA are still short on institutional and budgetary resources to deal with the many often technical tasks. Following Lundin (2012: 6):

> EU member states often do not realize that other groups, such as the Group of 77 and the Arab group, are very well organized and that the delegations from countries such as the USA and Russia are staffed at a far higher level than the EU delegation.

This conclusion is in line with the findings by Delaere and van Schaik, who have investigated the EU's effectiveness at the Organisation for the Prohibition of Chemical Weapons (OPCW), where the EU also seems to underestimate how strategically other states negotiate (Delaere and van Schaik 2012).

Furthermore, despite the Lisbon Treaty's many positive effects on the internal effectiveness in the EU, it has not changed the EU's status at the Agency – at least not formally. While the other states have accepted that the EU delegation can speak at informal meetings, only the presidency can speak on behalf of the EU in the political bodies of the Agency. This partial implementation of the Lisbon Treaty seems to reduce the importance of the Union. Because of its huge financial, technical and political assistance to the Agency, the EU should be taken more seriously. One obvious obstacle to a full implementation of the Lisbon Treaty in the Agency is of course the lack of support by other states. While some states, especially G77 states, do not want to give the EU more power, other Western and more EU-friendly states fear similar demands by other regional groups like the Arab League and thus are also very hesitant to give the EU any formal rights. Giving the EU observer status could establish precedence for allowing formal representation of and thereby more power to other regional groups in the IAEA.

Furthermore, also internal hesitation has for a long time seemed to character- ize Brussels' approach to a reform of the EU's status in the IAEA. Given the problems the reform created in New York (for an elaboration of this see Chapter 2) there seemed to be no indication that Brussels would push for a reform at the IAEA as well (Lundin 2012: 5). However, at the time of writing this seems to be changing. The EU Commission adopted in December 2012 an internal commu- nication suggesting to enhance the status of the EU in not only the IAEA but in a number of international organizations (see Introduction). Following this docu- ment, the EU's visibility at the Agency could be improved by either requesting observer status alongside Euratom (following the New York model) or by chang- ing the IAEA–Euratom agreement to include a representation of the EU in the Agency. Indeed, improving the EU's formal status at the IAEA could increase its visibility and status among other states. However, having a formal speaking right does not automatically improve either the Union's or the Agency's effec- tiveness. Hence, effective multilateralism must still be pursued actively follow- ing the already established dual-approach: by directly applying its political strength in the IAEA political bodies to get resolutions adopted and by indirectly changing best practice of IAEA procedures in members of the Agency through financial and technical assistance.

Conclusion

This chapter has investigated whether the EU's external and internal reform measures have made not only the EU but also the IAEA more effective. Because the IAEA's main work concerns 'high politics' issues addressing key aspects such as the sovereignty and security of its members, one would expect it to be a hard case for the EU both internally and externally to put its influence into effect, as great power interests often dominate such issues. Nevertheless, the analysis of the external reform in the Agency shows that, although the EU does not support the political reform of the Agency's decision-making bodies or a reform of the legal mandate of the IAEA Secretary, it does support smaller reform initiatives making the Agency's work on especially non-proliferation, security, safety and safeguards more effective. The strategy of effective multilateralism is thus being pursued using political, financial and technical means. It is difficult to assess the direct impact of these various measures and whether they actually increase the effectiveness of the Agency or the effectiveness of the EU within the Agency. Nevertheless, by supporting the Agency financially and technically in various projects and various ways, the EU reforms the Agency from the inside by changing best practice.

The analysis of the internal reform showed that although the Lisbon Treaty is not yet fully implemented in Vienna, it still has had a huge impact on the work process between not only the EU delegation and the EU member states but also between the EU and third states. While the internal coordination process has been streamlined, the EU has gained more visibility externally; the reform has thus improved how other states perceive the EU and has resulted in intensified lobbying of the Union by both the Agency and third states. Moreover, by its size alone, the EU makes a powerful coalition in the Agency and by using its total sum of delegates wisely it can have eyes and ears everywhere and thus stands a better chance of affecting the end result in the Agency's decision-making bodies. Hence, there is a strong indication that the Lisbon Treaty has increased the EU's effectiveness in the IAEA, but has the improved effectiveness also increased the effectiveness of the Agency? In the sense that it has united the approach of the EU and thus made the Union better equipped to reach its goals, including goals to strengthen the IAEA, the answer is yes. Having made the EU more internally effective, the EU can use this increased internal effectiveness to strengthen the effectiveness of the IAEA either politically in the Agency's political bodies or by more indirectly changing best practice through financial and technical means. However, effective multilateralism is not only a question of heavy financial funding and technical assistance as means to change best practice. The EU must also live up to its political responsibilities and support important political initiatives such as reforms of the IAEA legal mandate, although they are not in accordance with the narrow self-interest of its member states. Likewise, it ought to take seriously the demands for global disarmament by leading NAM and G77 states – if not in Vienna then at least in Geneva. Otherwise it risks damaging its own legitimacy as a role model preaching best practice.

Notes

1 In the following when referring to the EU this includes the 'total' of the EU, i.e. EU member states, the EU delegation and the EU institutional bodies, unless otherwise specified.

2 This chapter builds upon 12 interviews with key diplomats in Vienna; seven of the interviews were conducted with EU representatives (EU Delegation and EU member states; September 2012); five with diplomats from third states (March 2013). Both representatives from nuclear- and non-nuclear-weapon states and nuclear- and non-nuclear-energy states have been interviewed. Due to the rather sensitive subjects the interviews are anonymous. That said, the author would like to thank the interviewed diplomats for taking the time to be interviewed. It is greatly appreciated.

3 Because the EU is not itself a member of IAEA, all financial contributions from the EU institutions to the Agency are categorized as voluntary contributions (Grip 2011b: 3).

4 Contributions to the TCF are part of IAEA budget and the specific contribution from each country is based on the UN's basis of budget allocation. The contributions from the states to the TCF are thus 'mandatory' voluntary payments.

5 Belgium, Germany, Italy, the Netherlands and Spain.

6 The issue of formal status is elaborated below.

References

Council of the European Union (2003) *EU strategy against proliferation of weapons of mass destruction*, (15708/03), 10 December 2003.

Council of the European Union (2013) *Six-monthly progress report on the implementation of the EU strategy against proliferation of weapons of mass destruction*, (2013/C 37/04), 9 February 2013.

Delaere, V. and van Schaik, L.G. (2012) 'EU representation in OPCW after Lisbon, still waiting for Brussels', *Clingendael Paper # 7*, The Hague: Clingendael Institute.

European Council (2003) *A secure Europe in a better world: European Security Strategy*, 12 December 2003.

Findley, T. (2012) *Unleashing the nuclear watchdog: strengthening and reform of the IAEA*, Ontario: The Center for International Governance Innovation.

Grip, L. (2011a) 'Mapping the European Union's institutional actors related to WMD non-proliferation', *EU Non-Proliferation Consortium, Non-Proliferation Papers*, No. 1, May 2011.

Grip, L. (2011b) 'Assessing selected European Union external assistance and cooperation projects on WMD non-proliferation', *EU Non-Proliferation Consortium, Non-Proliferation Papers*, No. 6, December 2011.

IAEA (2008) *Reinforcing cooperation on nuclear energy for peace and development: a joint statement of the International Atomic Energy Agency and the European Commission.* Online. Available www.iaea.org/newscenter/news/pdf/iaea_euratom070508.pdf (accessed 14 May 2013).

IAEA (2011a) *Technical cooperation report for 2010. Report by the Director General. Supplement*, (GC(55)INF/2/Supplement), June 2011.

IAEA (2011b) *Communication dated 16 November 2011 received from the Delegation of the European Union to the international organizations in Vienna on international cooperation by the European Union in support of peaceful uses of nuclear energy*, (INFCIRC/830), 30 November 2011.

IAEA (2012a) *Provisional agenda. Supplementary item for inclusion in the provisional agenda*, (GC(56)/1/Add.2), 27 August 2012.

IAEA (2012b) *Statement of financial contributions to the Agency*, (GC(56)/INF/7), 14 September 2012.

IAEA (2012c) *Committee of the whole. Record of the tenth meeting*, (GC(56)/COM.5/OR.10), 21 September 2012.

IAEA (2012d) *Factsheets and FAQs. IAEA safeguards overview: comprehensive safeguards agreements and additional protocols.* Online. Available www.iaea.org/Publications/Factsheets/English/sg_overview.html (accessed 11 December 2012).

IAEA Statute. *Statute of the IAEA.* Online. Available www.iaea.org/About/statute.html (accessed 14 May 2013).

Lundin, L.-E. (2012) 'The European Union, the IAEA and WMD non-proliferation: unity of approach and continuity of action', *EU Non-Proliferation Consortium, Non-Proliferation Papers*, No. 9, February 2012.

Meier, O. and Quille, G. (2005) 'Testing time for Europe's non-proliferation strategy', *Arms Control Today*, May 2005.

Mukhatzhanova, G. (2012) *Fact Sheet #1. Information relevant to the IAEA General Conference. Topic: IAEA General Conference. Overview and issues for the 2012 meeting*, James Martin Center for Nonproliferation Studies and Vienna Center for Disarmament and Non-proliferation. Online. Available http://cns.miis.edu/stories/pdfs/120911_cns_ iaea_factsheet_overview.pdf (accessed 14 May 2013).

Müller, H. (2010) 'Between power and justice: current problems and perspectives of the NPT regime', *Strategic Analysis*, 34(2): 189–201.

Pomper, M.A. (2012) *Fact Sheet #4. Information relevant to the IAEA General Conference. Topic: IAEA and nuclear safety*, James Martin Center for Nonproliferation Studies and Vienna Center for Disarmament and Non-proliferation. Online. Available http://cns.miis.edu/stories/pdfs/120911_cns_iaea_factsheet_nuclear_safety.pdf (accessed 14 May 2013)

Van Ham, P. (2011) 'The European Union's WMD strategy and the CFSP: a critical analysis', *EU Non-Proliferation Consortium, Non-Proliferation Papers*, No. 2, February 2011.

8 From 'effective' to 'selective multilateralism'

The European Union's relations with NATO

Margriet Drent

Introduction

Even though the European Security Strategy of 2003 (European Council 2003) explicitly referred to the importance of its 'strategic partnership' with the North Atlantic Treaty Organization (NATO), and despite some operational successes, it would be misleading to view EU–NATO relations as a convincing example of 'effective multilateralism'. Whilst important developments, institutionalizations and joint projects were advanced between 1999 and 2004, relations between the two organizations have remained disappointingly stale during the last decade. Even though both organizations launched major reform efforts at their respective Lisbon meetings in 2007 (EU) and 2010 (NATO), the NATO–EU relationship itself has remained rather unaffected by these reform processes. Therefore, this chapter will highlight particularly external change, as it seems that exogenous, systemic developments have had most influence and provided a new context to EU–NATO relations. Indeed, in the context of the framework of this volume, the EU's relations with NATO represent presumably the most limited case of effective cooperation or EU enhancement of its partner. Instead of 'effective multilateralism' we view the EU–NATO relationship at best as a case of 'selective multilateralism'.[1] At worst, the relationship can also be seen as a prolonged case of 'nihilateralism', i.e. complete absence of formal cooperation, with little reform momentum.

It is argued that EU–NATO relations should be understood within the context of the tendency in security and defence governance in Europe to pragmatically work around and outside the official multilateral frameworks. It is not self-evident anymore that policies and operations are initiated and organized within the multinational diplomatic frameworks of the EU and NATO. This also means that scope for fundamental reform is limited; although the 'two Lisbon reforms' of both organizations could have provided an important impetus, they largely failed to have significant impact. This chapter looks in particular at three areas of relevance for the EU–NATO relationship, in which this pragmatic tendency can be observed: (1) crisis management operations, (2) cooperation on capability generation and (3) the proliferation of informal EU–NATO staff relations.[2] When the systemic level of European security governance is increasingly heading towards flexible arrangements, both in time, scope and membership, it will inevitably have its effects on EU–NATO inter-organizational relations. The pragmatic approach to security governance means that duplication, waste of time and money and clinging to political and institutional dogmas risk diminishing the relevance of both organizations. And in terms of understanding 'effective multilateralism', there is a clear need to rethink whether we are still referring to the same 'multilateralism' as when the 2003 European Security Strategy was written.

Setting the scene: phases in EU–NATO relations

Roughly four phases can be distinguished in the EU–NATO relationship since 1993, when the EU aspirations for a security and defence policy were officially voiced in the Maastricht Treaty (Art. J.4 TEU 1993). The first is the phase of *competition*, the second a phase of *formalization*, and the third a phase of *impasse* or *status quo* (Varwick and Koops 2009). The fourth phase is the one which has been emerging in recent years and which can be characterized by a tense '*normalization through informalization*'. Somewhat artificially, since the phases overlap temporally, the first three phases are considered briefly in this section and the second part of the chapter will further elaborate on the fourth phase.

A rivalry between the two organizations has been inherent from the moment it became clear that after the Cold War the European integration project would incorporate a security and defence dimension. The first phase of the EU–NATO relation, the competition phase, is driven by a political and functional rivalry, but can also be understood in terms of processes of identity-differentiation (Drent 2010; Koops 2012: 178). Independent of how the EU–NATO relationship is understood theoretically, the bottom line of this relationship remains one of rivalry and competition. The competition phase actually runs through the EU–NATO relationship until today, thereby rendering competition as a defining feature of the relationship. However, the form and nature of this competitive relationship has changed over the years in which three other phases can be distinguished.

The formalization phase runs from 1999 onwards, as informal contacts between the newly established European Security and Defence Policy (ESDP) and NATO paved the way for a formalized cooperation arrangement between the EU and NATO. An exchange of letters between the NATO Secretary-General and the EU Presidency in January 2001 defined the scope of cooperation and modalities of consultation on security issues between the two organizations. After prolonged negotiations, in which Turkey showed concerns for losing the privileges it had enjoyed through its associated membership of the Western European Union (WEU), a declaration could be concluded at the Copenhagen EU Council summit in December 2002.

The 'EU–NATO Declaration on ESDP' established a 'strategic partnership' between the two institutions (2002). Cooperation further developed by the formalization of an exchange of letters between the Secretary-General of NATO and the High Representative of the Common Foreign and Security Policy, Javier Solana, in March 2003, also known as the Berlin Plus framework agreements (2003). The immediate necessity for this framework for cooperation resulted from the ESDP operation *Concordia* taking over from the existing NATO operation *Amber Fox* in Macedonia. The full negotiated relationship involved not only Berlin Plus, but also provision for scheduled meetings (at least one per presidency) between the EU's Political and Security Committee (PSC) and the NATO North Atlantic Council (NAC) and at lower levels, as well as crisis consultation arrangements. The Berlin Plus arrangements in particular provide for EU access to NATO planning capabilities to contribute to military planning for EU-led operations and the establishment of a list of NATO assets and capabilities that could be made available to the EU for use in EU-led operations. Since *Concordia* in Macedonia, only one ESDP operation made use of the Berlin Plus provisions; this is operation *Althea* in Bosnia and Herzegovina, which started in 2004 and continues, although considerably downsized. Considering the evolved strategic context and the changed security profiles of both the EU and NATO a revised Berlin Plus is long overdue. A renewed 'strategic partnership' between the two organizations is however a political impossibility considering the troublesome relations of Cyprus and Turkey to NATO and the EU respectively, blocking all progress on the issue.

The EU–NATO agreements, including the letter exchange between the Secretary-General and the EU Presidency, laid the groundwork for a formal EU–NATO relationship, but they were also the beginning of the gridlock of a further development of EU–NATO cooperation. This phase can be called the *impasse* phase. As Turkey does not diplomatically recognize the Republic of Cyprus, it does not allow sensitive NATO information to be exchanged with the EU in general or Cyprus in particular at joint EU–NATO meetings. The EU also does not allow engagement in broader discussions with NATO without all of its members present.

The so-called 'participation' problem emerged at an early stage, as Turkey could foresee the EU membership of Cyprus in the near future (Latek 2012). Under the terms of agreements between NATO and the EU for strategic partnership, only EU member states who belong to the Partnership for Peace (PfP) and have a security agreement with NATO can participate. Since Malta's signing of the Partnership for Peace Agreement, Cyprus is the only EU member state that does not qualify, as Turkey blocks its membership to PfP and is therefore excluded from meetings or information exchanges related to EU–NATO strategic cooperation. Ankara has taken a very broad view of what constitutes 'strategic cooperation' thereby narrowing the scope of contact between the two full organizations in any formal setting. According to Turkey, the Berlin Plus agreement also stipulates that Cyprus cannot take part in formal EU–NATO meetings where civilian missions are discussed, even though there were no civilian ESDP missions when Berlin Plus was concluded.

It was however also clear that some EU member states were making use of the Cyprus–Turkey impasse to keep ESDP away from NATO influences. France particularly was instrumental in limiting the agenda of the inter EU–NATO discussions to protect the nascent ESDP. However, by 2007, when president Nicolas Sarkozy came to office, France had already become a member of all of NATO's politico-military bodies, with the exception of the Defense Planning Committee, the Nuclear Planning Group and the Integrated Military Command. In 2009, France also re-entered these NATO bodies (with the exception of the Nuclear Planning Group) and became again a full NATO member, increasing the pressure on Nicosia and Ankara to free the path to a true cooperation between the Union and the Alliance (Irondelle and Mérand 2010). To date, however, this has not happened and the informal 'tip toeing' of staffs around the 'red lines' imposed by the two states is continuing.

External reform: changing contexts

'Effective multilateralism' as understood by the EU is about the centrality of multilateral organizations in pursuing its foreign and security policies. In the context of the Iraq war 'effective multilateralism' was originally formulated as a contrasting principle to the perceived unilateralism and bypassing of multilateral organizations by the Bush government (see Introduction). It had in that sense a strong connotation with 'institutionalized' multilateralism which was created in the twentieth century. At that time, 'formal multilateral organisations took the place of loose, informal agreements' (Bouchard and Peterson 2010: 8).

However, since the aspiration to become a 'stronger actor in the international system' (Kissack 2010: 3) was conveyed through the European Security Strategy of 2003, both the internal and external context of effective multilateralism have changed. Externally, the systemic conditions in which the EU–NATO relationship operates have changed considerably. There is a widely shared consensus that the world is becoming a less cooperative place (Drent and Landman 2012; Layne 2012; Rood and Dinnissen 2013). The character of the international system is moving away from the multilateral arrangements of the past decades towards a system in which non-state actors are emerging and states that have not been equally involved in building the post-Second World War multilateral institutions are on the rise. The question arises as to what extent 'effective multilateralism', central to the 2003 strategy, is still applicable in the new strategic context. For instance, the report of the European Global Strategy project (initiated by the foreign ministers of Italy, Poland, Spain and Sweden) does not mention 'effective multilateralism' and replaced it with the EU's goal 'to effectively manage multipolarity' (EGS 2013: 4).

Part of this changing international system is a tendency in security and defence governance in Europe to pragmatically work around and outside the institutionalized multilateral frameworks, which include the EU itself (Penttilä 2009; Van der Lijn and Teftedarija 2012; Rood and Dinnissen 2013). While UN Security Council legitimacy remains politically desirable and there is still a role for multilateral organizations, it is not self-evident anymore that policies and operations are initiated and organized within the multinational diplomatic frameworks of the

EU and NATO (cf. Slaughter 2004). This development is in line with the tendency to create a range of innovative arrangements, such as coalitions of the willing, 'friends of' groupings and public-private partnerships which characterized global governance in the past decade (Forman and Segaar 2006).

The EU's understanding of multilateralism as an 'institutionalized' multilateralism can now be more aptly described as 'selective' multilateralism. There is cooperation, but it is much more ad hoc on a case by case basis, informally organized and it involves non-state actors as well. A cause and consequence of this trend to select the most suitable forum for achieving results seems to be that EU–NATO relations have been in an impasse since 2004, as described earlier. Other issues are that decision-making within the EU and NATO are politically too cumbersome, too slow and too bureaucratic to enable flexible responses to problems. In other words, effective multilateralism on the issue of security and defence is not working well and has been replaced by a sort of 'selective' multilateralism.

While the context of the changing international system is affecting the *modus operandi* of the EU–NATO relationship, this system level occurrence can also be seen on different levels of this relationship. There are two areas in particular which both function on the actor-level of the two organizations and member (state)s in which this tendency can be observed: first, crisis management operations and, second, cooperation on capability generation. A third EU–NATO inter-organizational phenomenon that is connected to this trend – in the sense that it is an expression of the same pragmatism – is the proliferation of informal EU–NATO staff relations. This is manifesting itself on the level of the individual.

The following paragraphs will explain in more detail how the lever of the two organizations is influenced by external changes by considering recent practices in crisis management operations and capabilities development. Consecutively, the next sections will deal with how the external, systemic changes play out at the level of EU–NATO staff relations. In the context of this volume, these can be considered as 'internal reforms'.

Crisis management operations

Circumventing traditional multilateral organizations in security governance in Europe is particularly visible in the area of the conduct of operations. The coalitions of the willing that intervened in Afghanistan in 2001 is a typical example. At a later stage the ad hoc arrangements were formalized when NATO took command of most of the military operation in Afghanistan and the EU was brought in as well with capacity building and border management missions. In urgent and complex situations, requiring rapid response, the institutional constraints of an international organization are increasingly circumvented, but still international organizations (IOs) are selectively involved for their advantages. The EU and NATO provide international legitimacy, representativeness, continuity, the ability of resource mobilization and assets in personnel and materiel.

Another example is operation *Unified Protector* in Libya in 2011, with NATO providing the 'tools' and *post hoc* legitimacy. It constituted a mission-specific coalition of the willing using NATO assets without overt US leadership. Moreover, it involved non-NATO countries such as Sweden, Jordan, Qatar and the UAE (SIPRI 2012). This model might well be used again in future crisis management operations. In addition, the complexity of responding to crises demands coordination among a whole range of actors, involving states, (specialized) intergovernmental organizations, NGOs and international companies. A pragmatic solution to attempt to coordinate the range of tasks and actors (including non-state actors) involved in counter-piracy operations is the Contact Group on Piracy off the Coast of Somalia (CGPCS) in which EU and NATO are active members and share the lead in the five different working groups: military, shipping, financial, communication and legal aspects (Van Ginkel and Gardner 2012).

Particularly in the area of operational cooperation the limitations of official EU–NATO interaction come to the fore. EU–NATO competition over missions is already built in, in the sense that NATO's non-Article 5 missions overlap to a large extent the EU's Petersberg tasks. The organizations have taken on similar responsibilities. NATO and the EU have conducted or are both conducting operations in Macedonia (*Allied Harmony, Concordia*), Afghanistan (ISAF/NTM-A, EUPOL-A), Kosovo (KFOR, EULEX), Sudan and off the coast of Somalia (*Ocean Shield, Atalanta*).

Capability generation in clusters

Another illustration of the selective use of multilateral security organizations in Europe can be found in the area of capability generation. NATO's 'Smart Defence' and the EU's 'pooling and sharing' initiatives have mainly focused on enablers and training, but developing capacities in multinational context has not been very successful. Cooperation on capability generation is therefore increasingly taking place in small 'clusters' of countries among the member (state)s of the EU and NATO, but outside these multilateral organizations (Valasek 2011). The cluster approach can be defined as the attempt to mitigate the effects of defence budget cuts by working together in some form of formalized setting in a small group of countries on multiple aspects of military capabilities to attain efficiency and advantages of scale. Examples of clusters are the French–British Defence Treaty, the Benelux cooperation, German–Dutch cooperation, the Visegrad 4, the Weimar triangle and the Nordic Defence Cooperation (NORDEFCO).

Although military cooperation in bi- or trinational settings is not a new phenomenon, this method of capability cooperation has been given more priority in recent years. The financial and economic crisis has led to particularly harsh cuts in defence budgets, while at the same time the pressure from the United States to carry more of the defence burden has increased. The European share of defence spending in NATO dropped to 23 per cent of the total and, even worse, that amount is not spent wisely because of duplication and fragmentation (Rasmussen 2012). Moreover, European countries are confronted with the challenge that the American strategic interest is turning away from Europe in the direction of Asia and the Pacific, leaving the EU and the European NATO-countries in the driving seat of security in Europe and its neighbourhood. The urgent necessity to preserve capabilities and to modernize their armed forces in a situation of growing austerity led to increased activity in the area of cluster cooperation.

The pragmatic turn which capability cooperation is taking holds a potential risk of developing capabilities in isolation and thereby not contributing to the collective security and defence needs of the European countries. So far, there is no overall coordination between the clusters taking place. Therefore, clusters might invest in capacities that are already abundantly available to European countries elsewhere. In order to effectively contribute to improving overall capabilities, clusters should particularly address European shortfalls. The EU and NATO are the right organizations to take on this coordinating and monitoring role. On the supply side, the EU is able to counter the fragmentation and inefficiency of the European defence industry by 'promoting a well-functioning defence market, in particular through the effective implementation of the directives on public procurement and on intra-EU transfers' (European Council 2012). The fact that the Common Security and Defence Policy will be discussed at a European Council meeting in December 2013 for the first time since 2005 shows that the EU member states acknowledge the urgency of sustaining serious military capacities in Europe and the complementary role the EU has to play in that goal.

The phenomenon of 'selective' multilateralism affects both the EU and NATO. In the area of security, defence and crisis management, they both struggle to show their relevance, added value and legitimacy to their member (state)s. The question is which organization will be innovative and flexible enough to adjust to this new reality. When European security governance is increasingly heading towards flexible arrangements, both in time, scope and membership, it will also have its effect on the EU–NATO inter-organizational relations. The pragmatic approach to security governance means that the demands for effective EU–NATO cooperation will rise and that this cooperation will be increasingly evaluated by its effectiveness. Duplication, waste of time and money and clinging to political and institutional dogmas will diminish the relevance of both organizations.

EU–NATO relations: asymmetry and rivalry

Asymmetry

A feature which also characterizes EU–NATO relations is their asymmetry in terms of the organizations' differences in size, seniority, constraints, scope and traditions. The EU's Common Security and Defence Policy structures are considerably smaller than the structures that NATO has at its disposal, not only regarding the sheer numbers of staff, but also the degree of specialization. This is visible both at the top and at more technical levels of staff. For instance, the head of the Crisis Management and Planning Department (CMPD), currently Didier Lenoir, has to deal with at least three separate NATO interlocutors at his level. While strategic planning on military and civilian operations and missions and capability planning for CSDP is combined within the CMPD, these tasks are spread among NATO's institutions into various divisions. This generally means that in the area of EU–NATO relations, the EU staff has to cover a broader area of expertise and has less hours available than their NATO-counterpart. The European Defence Agency (EDA) and Allied Command Transformation (ACT) in Norfolk, US, are institutional interlocutors, but their number of personnel is incommensurable, with EDA only employing a total of approximately 100 and the ACT alone totalling 800 personnel. EDA has to divide its attention between the International Staff, the International Military Staff at NATO Headquarters and various NATO agencies. Moreover, the small military planning staff (CMPD and EU Military Staff (EUMS) combined do not even reach 200 personnel) of CSDP is not comparable to the sizeable Headquarter facilities of NATO with around 10,000 staff. In fact, the EU does not have a headquarter facility of its own: it needs to borrow this from willing and able member states or from NATO under the Berlin Plus provisions.

Moreover, the EU only gained a defence dimension in 1999, while NATO as a military organization has been around since 1949. That is five decades of experience and the development of tradition that sets the two organizations apart. Thematically the EU and NATO have a considerable overlap, although the two organizations are very different international organizations. NATO is a collective defence organization with a considerable military infrastructure and a transatlantic membership of which the United States is by far the most influential. Decisions within NATO are made strictly on an intergovernmental basis within the North Atlantic Council, but it is clear that the United States is more equal than others. The EU is an organization with mixed communitarian and intergovernmental decision-making modes whose core business is much more extensive and covers policies in the areas of economics, trade, development, justice, home affairs, social and cultural affairs, and also foreign and security and defence policies. These differences between the scopes of the two organizations define a natural limit to EU–NATO relations.

Political and functional rivalry

The areas of potential duplication and competition between the EU and NATO are also the areas where cooperation and coordination are most essential. The availability of relevant military capabilities, crisis management operations and civil emergency or disaster response are areas in which both organizations have an interest and claim competences. But the same goes for wider strategic issues, such as cyber defence and energy security. Moreover, EU and NATO member (state)s share interests in the Middle-East, North Africa, the Caucasus, the Black Sea area and Central Asia. In fact, the NATO–EU Declaration on ESDP of 2002 aspires to a 'coherent, transparent and mutually reinforcing development of the military capability requirements common to the two organizations'. However, the NATO Response Force and the EU Battlegroups are seeking similar contributions from mostly the same states. This is an area in which the EU and NATO are in dire need of cooperation as military capabilities are scarce and getting scarcer with the deepening of the financial and economic crisis.

Paragraph 25 in the NATO strategic concept of 2010 raised eyebrows among observers: 'form an appropriate but modest civilian crisis management capability...; 2. identify and train civilian specialists from member states, made available for rapid deployment by Allies for selected missions...'. Where the EU was chastised for wanting to duplicate capabilities NATO already has (such as a headquarters facility), the same member states doing the chastising were encouraging NATO to set up civilian capabilities and acquire civilian specialists, an expertise in which the EU is increasingly specializing. However, NATO formulates its comprehensive role in crisis management restrictively and will only take on this role if other actors have not yet arrived, are incapable or if the situation is insecure. With the 'civilian crisis management capability' NATO wanted to improve its planning as operations are increasingly taking place in theatres where also civilian actors are needed or present. The EU might even make use of this civilianized planning capacity, as planning is one of NATO's strengths. Also, NATO experienced in Afghanistan that it is in need of a civilian-to-civilian interface to be able to operate with and alongside civilian organizations. NATO plans to increase this capacity significantly and has already put it into practice in the operation over Libya. In operational terms, CSDP might benefit from this development in NATO, as the asymmetry of an EU civil-military approach to crisis management versus NATO's military one can be better accommodated by NATO in future operations when these ambitions are implemented. A prerequisite is that the Civilian Planning and Conduct Capability of the EEAS and NATO's civil crisis management capability remain in close contact.

Since the adoption of NATO's new Strategic Concept at the Lisbon Summit in November 2010, which identifies the need for the Alliance to address emerging threats, several new areas of cooperation with the EU are under consideration. This concerns in particular energy security issues and cyber defence. These issues lie predominantly in the realm of the Commission (although cyber security is since 2012 also part of EDA's work programme) and informal staff level consultations are taking place. Piracy is also an issue that is discussed at staff level, as well as the rise of China and India.

Particularly in the area of operational cooperation the limitations of EU–NATO cooperation come to the fore. EU–NATO competition over missions is already built in, in the sense that NATO's non-Article 5 missions overlap to a large extent the EU's Petersberg tasks. The organizations have taken on similar responsibilities in the field, such as in operations and missions in Afghanistan, Kosovo, Sudan and off the coast of Somalia. The impossibility of reaching generic security agreements between EU and NATO, because of the non-recognition of Cyprus by Turkey and Cyprus not being a Partnership for Peace member, is potentially harmful for the safety of personnel from both organizations (but particularly from the EU) on the ground. A few minor incidents have been reported where, despite the lack of a security agreement, NATO forces have worked outside these official frameworks and used common sense to save lives. However, this is a most unsatisfying situation and it seems that it has only been on account of extremely lucky circumstances that no fatal incidents have occurred so far.

Unofficial meetings have taken place on a regular basis in crisis areas where both organizations are encountering each other in the field. One example is Afghanistan, where the NATO Senior Civilian Representative regularly meets with the EU Special Representative, and also in Sudan, where staff-level contacts have been productive. In October 2009, the presidency of the EU took the initiative to brief the NAC informally on operation *Atalanta* (General Secretariat of the Council 2009). It is damaging to the causes of both organizations that EU-personnel in Afghanistan are limited in their operations because NATO is prioritizing staff from NGOs and other IGOs instead of their EU-colleagues when there is a seat left in a transport helicopter.

Internal reform: EU–NATO institutions going informal

Particularly the inability, and unwillingness, of key actors within both organizations to address the shortcomings of the EU–NATO Berlin Plus arrangements – and thereby reform the relationship overall – continues to render formal EU–NATO relations highly inefficient. It is therefore also not the formal reforms of the Lisbon Treaty that are a central consideration of this volume that play the largest role in this relationship. When reviewing influence of formal EU changes it is rather the 2004 EU membership of Cyprus that influenced EU and NATO inter-organizational practices. Indeed, it needs to be kept in mind that in the context of this volume, the EU–NATO relationship presents an odd *sui generis* case of the EU's role *within* international organizations. Unlike the EU's relations with the United Nations or OSCE, the EU is structurally and politically prevented from 'speaking with one voice' *within* NATO as various nation-states seek to avoid the formation of an 'EU caucus' within NATO. EU member states sometimes act in official NATO organs with EU-interests in mind, but rarely as a bloc (Graeger and Haugevik 2011: 749), despite the obligation in the Lisbon Treaty that member states 'shall coordinate their action in international organisations.... They shall uphold the Union's positions in such forums' (TEU Art. 34, 2009; see also Chapter 2 of this volume). There is no permanent EU representation in NATO at the political level, nor is there one of NATO within the EU. The creation of an EU caucus in NATO is resisted by non-EU NATO-members, particularly the United States and Turkey, and there is no pre-negotiated, common EU-position within NATO. The concerted action that is displayed by EU member states in the United Nations in recent years has not been possible in NATO (Gowan and Brantner 2008). Yet, as we argue below, despite these challenges and stalemate at the formal level, more effective coordination and cooperation opportunities still emerge at the informal level of the relationship.

Although internally, the entering into effect of the Lisbon Treaty had institutionally a profound effect on the representation of the EU and its member states to international organizations, the influence of the Lisbon Treaty on EU–NATO relations is less extensive. If anything, the EU's internal reforms have rendered the EU slightly less effective vis-à-vis NATO. After the Lisbon Treaty, a number of minor changes have had their effect on EU–NATO relations. While the crisis management structures of CSDP have been integrated into the European External Action Service (EEAS), decision-making remains intergovernmental. The Political and Security Committee (PSC) is now officially chaired by the High Representative (HR) Catherine Ashton. However, the HR has many responsibilities, among which are setting up and heading the EEAS, chairing the Foreign Affairs Council, taking her role as vice-president of the Commission and heading EDA. In practice, she is leaving the permanent chair of the PSC to an EEAS official, currently the Belgian diplomat Walter Stevens. Stevens previously headed the CMPD and, while consistency and continuity is safeguarded by a fixed chair, the political influence which the chairmanship of an ambassador of the presidency enjoyed has diminished. Also, Ashton has skipped informal ministers of defence meetings and EDA-meetings (although she was always present at the EDA Steering Board meetings). In fact, while NATO's Secretary-General Rasmussen was present at an informal EU defence ministers meeting in February 2010, Ashton was elsewhere, leaving Rasmussen to monopolize the discussion (Howorth 2011). Another example of how the institutional reform has caused a backlash is that of the briefings taking place under the Berlin Plus Agreement of non-EU NATO members. They were briefed four times a year by the presidency troika of the EU. This ended after the Lisbon Treaty entered into force and no other formal structures have replaced these briefings (Graeger and Haugevik 2011: 750), although there are formats such as the 'PSC+7 or 9',[3] where non-EU NATO allies (sometimes including candidate countries) are informally briefed.

Internal reforms have therefore had little effect on EU–NATO relations. The EU–NATO relationship also knows an intra-organizational form of 'selective multilateralism', which in the context of EU–NATO relations is the tendency by EU and NATO staffs to avoid non-productive formal formats and to meet off the record. This practice has markedly increased since Cyprus joined the EU in 2004.

From the perspective of the EU, there are basically two varieties of institutional actors who have formal relations with NATO. First, there is a number of EU institutions, among which are the High Representative, the Political and Security Committee (PSC) and the EU Military Committee. NATO's counterparts for these institutions are the Secretary-General, the North Atlantic Council (NAC) and NATO's Military Committee. These are all institutions that function at the political or intergovernmental level. Second, there is the international staff level. Since the EU gained a European Security and Defence Policy, the natural functional interlocutor to NATO has been the CSDP (as it is now known), its institutions and their staff, also including the EU Military Staff (EUMS), the European Defence Agency (EDA) and even, although to a lesser extent, the

Civilian Planning and Conduct Capability (CPCC). However, increasingly, the European Commission has also become an interlocutor of NATO. Both of these categories have developed their own 'informal' way of doing business; a practice that is underresearched but of vital importance for understanding the EU and NATO's relationship.

The growing scope of informal relations is also discernible with the meetings between the PSC-ambassadors of the EU and the NAC-ambassadors of NATO. Since 2004, representatives of the Commission have been participating at these joint PSC–NAC meetings. They have, however, diminished in frequency, with eight joint meetings on average per year in the period 2001–4 and not even four per year on average in the period 2005–8 (Yost 2007: 92). Judging by the official websites of NATO and EU the joint meetings between the PSC–NAC have almost ceased to exist as a practice: there was only one PSC–NAC meeting per year in 2009, 2010 and 2011. Informal meetings, such as the PSC+7 or PSC+9 formats, have stepped into the place of the ritualistic, insubstantive PSC–NAC format. Also, two lots of ambassadors often gather informally over lunches or dinners to discuss subjects barred from their formal agenda.

In September 2005, EU and NATO foreign ministers held their first informal dinner, and since then these so-called 'Transatlantic dinners' have taken place twice a year. They often coincide with the General Assembly meeting in New York in the autumn period. These events are not strictly EU–NATO meetings, despite the attendance of top-level representatives from both institutions. The NATO Secretary-General (SG), the High Representative and (pre-Lisbon) the Commissioner for External Relations are also present. These meetings have no agenda and there is no press conference or a public statement afterwards. The same Transatlantic formula has been applied to meetings involving NATO and EU ambassadors, also including the NATO SG, the HR and the Commissioner of External Relations (again, pre-Lisbon). These sessions on ambassadorial level were devoted to a single topic, such as Darfur and Kosovo. The High Representative is invited to NAC meetings in foreign ministers format and the GAERC (in foreign ministers' format), and the post-Lisbon Foreign Affairs Council meetings are attended by the NATO Secretary-General.

Informal, bilateral meetings between Secretary-General Anders Fogh Rasmussen and High Representative Catherine Ashton take place on an irregular basis. Rasmussen does not get much room for manoeuvre in setting the agenda for these meetings as the NAC wants to be involved in determining the topics they are going to discuss. This hampers the desired leeway to discuss EU–NATO matters of common interest off the record. There is also a tendency to meet with only a few officials present. This might be an effort to regain some space, but it also has consequences for the feedback from these meetings into their organizations.

On the staff-to-staff level, contacts on capabilities are particularly intense and exemplary of the development of these informal contacts. The EU–NATO Capability Group is a formal body for coordination on capability development. It met for the first time in May 2003 and has since then convened regularly (approximately every four-six weeks), alternating between the Council building and NATO headquarters in Brussels. The only EU or NATO member (state) that is not able to be present at these meetings is Cyprus. Turkey managed to negotiate the membership condition of the Group to include a Partnership for Peace membership, a status Cyprus does not have. Therefore, there is no Cypriot representative sitting at the table. The EU is further represented by the Planning and Policy Unit of EDA, the Crisis Management Planning Department and the Commission. NATO is represented by the Defence Policy and Planning Division (also the coordination), the International Military Staff, the Defence Investment Division and defence counsellors and advisers from the missions and capitals (Sturm 2010). Although Cyprus is not officially sitting at the table of the EU–NATO Capability Group, it was agreed by both staffs that, in advance of an official Capability Group meeting, Cyprus is informally briefed on the substance of the meeting by the other EU member states. Also, beyond the Capability Group there are numerous contacts at staff level. The official EDA website distinguishes between its contributions to the formal and informal level. On the informal side, 'EDA has a wide network of staff-to-staff contacts with NATO counter-parts in Allied Command Transformation, NATO Headquarters and NATO Agencies' (EDA 2013).

The track record of the EU–NATO Capability Group has been poor. The objective to 'deconflict' the EU's European Capability Action Plan (ECAP 2001) and NATO's Prague Capabilities Commitment (2002) did not succeed well and overlaps were occurring regularly, despite some informal staff attempts at coordination. The formation of NATO–EU subgroups of technical experts who could actually coordinate on, or propose joint solutions to, specific capabilities development tasks was blocked (Michel 2007). However, with the financial crisis and the ensuing budget austerity in defence, the EU and NATO seized the opportunity to launch new initiatives on defence capability cooperation among their member (state)s. When the EU informal ministerial in Ghent launched the 'Ghent Initiative', the NATO Secretary-General followed with a similar initiative called 'Smart Defence'. These two initiatives seem to be synchronized much better with the help of staff-to-staff relations with complementary projects on the provisional lists on European capability cooperation (Zandee 2011).

Despite the taboo on producing documents in an informal setting, joint papers were written and presented on Counter-Improvised Explosive Devices, Medical Support, and chemical, biological, radiological and nuclear (CBRN) weapons. This is regarded as a widening of the margins of what has been possible so far under the watchful eyes of Cyprus and Turkey.

Informality: the dominant *modus operandi* between EU and NATO

EU–NATO relations can be characterized by a proliferation of informal staff-to-staff relations at many levels and on all kinds of subjects, particularly since 2004. These informal relations do require a particular sensitivity of all involved not to cross the so-called 'red lines' which Cyprus and Turkey have imposed on formal EU–NATO contacts, but on the informal ones as well. These red lines vary from a ban on official flags on tables when staffs meet informally to the ban on the exchange of official documents or the writing of reports on the basis of joint informal meetings. As long as these staff-to-staff relations remain under the radar of public acknowledgment, do not reach the media or official declarations, informal contacts seem to be working relatively well. A complication is that the position of the 'red line' can be different from theme to theme and from period to period. This requires complex diplomatic manoeuvring from staffs, which is mostly cumbersome and time-consuming. Although a growing normalization of informal practices of cooperation between staffs is occurring, this is not to say that it is an optimal situation. There is a clear pattern that whenever the Cyprus–Turkey blockade is subjected to official diplomatic efforts to find a solution, the leeway for informal contacts shrinks considerably. In short, cooperation is possible, as long as it remains invisible to the wider world.

As was attempted by his predecessor secretary-generals George Robertson and Jaap de Hoop Scheffer (De Hoop Scheffer 2007), a renewed diplomatic initiative was launched by the fresh Secretary-General Anders Fogh Rasmussen in 2010 (Ames 2010). He tried to officially find a solution to the deadlock between the Turkish refusal to accept Cypriot participation in anything that has to do with NATO and the Cypriot and Greek ban on rapprochement of the Turks to the EU and CSDP. In exchange for accepting Cyprus as eligible for a NATO security clearance, making it possible for official EU–NATO meetings to take place, Turkey could be granted a security agreement with EDA and an enhanced involvement in CSDP-meetings. However, the Turks did not accept any deal in which the Cypriots were involved, since this country *de jure* does not exist for them. This episode led to a hardened position of Turkey on the draft Strategic Concept, particularly on the phrasing of NATO's relationship to the EU. Neither the provisions on missile defence, nor the relationship of NATO to Russia were causing most difficulties in concluding the Strategic Concept of 2010: in fact, the articles on the European Union were the last ones to be finalized. Rasmussen had clearly crossed a red line and has not attempted to launch new official initiatives to solve the problem since (Szymanski and Terlikowski 2010).

In an off-the-record comment, which was subsequently leaked through Wikileaks, David Leakey, at the time the Director-General of the EUMS, was pessimistic on the prospects for improved NATO–EU relations. He mentioned the detrimental effect on the staff-to-staff contacts when senior EU and NATO officials try to cast light on positive examples of existing areas of informal cooperation. Highlighting these informal relations gave the opportunity to Greece and Turkey for 'political grandstanding'. 'Both Greece and Turkey are growing increasingly combative on NATO–EU cooperation', he complained, 'and try to impede NATO–EU cooperation' (Wikileaks 2009). His comment testifies to the tendency that although informal contacts are functioning well, they have to function in a covert way, because visibility is crossing the diplomatic boundaries set by the Cypriot and Turkish camps.

It is widely reported that EU–NATO staff-to-staff relations have in recent years become more relaxed; there are less reservations and a diminished mistrust between personnel. As it is impossible to launch visible projects, cooperation necessarily remains within practical areas. This clearly has its limitations: EU and NATO cooperation remains underdeveloped on strategic issues as there is no dialogue about shared strategic interests, such as strategies vis-à-vis the Middle East, the Caucasus, the Gulf or North Africa. However, successes of the staff-to-staff method can be reported. The Ghent Initiative on pooling and sharing of military capabilities and the follow-on initiative by Rasmussen called 'Smart Defence' were potentially duplicating initiatives. However, due to the informal consultation mechanisms in the forefront of the official EU–NATO Capability Group, two complementary lists of projects have been produced. Also, the division of labour in Kosovo with EULEX taking the lead on the wider diplomatic effort of political transformation and NATO taking care of security is working out quite well and are named as successes of the informalization of EU–NATO contacts (Cadier 2011).

Conclusion

Ten years after the European Security Strategy featured 'effective multilateralism' as a key method and aspiration to how and to what end the European Union wants to assert itself as an external actor, there is a need to revisit it. In the case of the relationship of the EU with NATO, this chapter had little to say about internal reforms in the last ten years. The Treaty of Lisbon did not significantly alter those parts of the EU that deal with NATO. It certainly did not decisively improve EU–NATO relations as it left the underlying functional and political rivalry of the two organizations intact. Instead, this chapter focused more on the external *changes* (rather than reform) that now provide a new context to the EU–NATO relationship. In fact, these external changes have had their influence on the practice of how the EU and NATO work together on different levels. This was identified as taking place at the system level, which provides the external context in which the two organizations function. The influence of the changing context on operations and missions and capability development takes place at the level of the member (state)s. The *modus operandi* of informal staff-to-staff relations is a notable feature which not only defines the shape of EU–NATO relations, but at the same time sets its limits. This informal practice can be positioned at the individual level.

The type of multilateralism to which the EU has adhered in the past years can be called 'institutional' multilateralism. The EU wanted to strengthen and work through a well-functioning system of formal international organizations. However, particularly in security governance, multilateralism in formal organizations has weakened and a shift to informal forms of multilateralism is discernible. There still is cooperation, but this cooperation is much more in informal, ad hoc settings and on a case-by-case basis. Also, non-state actors are increasingly involved in this type of multilateralism as well. 'Selective multilateralism', so it is argued, is more and more replacing the former 'institutional' multilateralism as propagated by the EU. NATO and the EU are both affected by this changing context and are also coming under pressure from this tendency because it is they, as formal institutions, that are increasingly sidelined.

It should be a warning call to the EU and NATO that they are regarded as not being flexible, capable and fast enough to function as a first-instance crisis management organization, as the cases of Afghanistan, Libya and Mali have shown. They are selectively used as a legitimizer of an operation and take on roles as facilitators, toolboxes and *fora* through which longer-term development and stabilization can be organized.

Also in the crucial area of cooperation on military capabilities the roles of the EU and NATO have lost ground to small groupings or 'clusters' of countries. Instead of going through the cumbersome multinational decision-making structures, like-minded countries are initiating defence cooperation projects which have not been possible in the 20+ member (state) setting of the EU and NATO. Relatively good results are achieved in safeguarding and generating new capabilities in this cluster setting, but eventually EU and NATO must show that they are capable of channeling these initiatives to the benefit of European security in general.

This, however, requires cooperation between the EU and NATO. Although, particularly on cooperation and coordination in the area of capability development, progress has been made, this has been to a large extent due to the ability of informal 'under the radar' staff-to-staff relations. In operations where both the EU and NATO are present, such as off the coast of Somalia (*Atalanta* and *Ocean Shield*), Afghanistan (EUPOL and NTM-A/ISAF) and Kosovo (EULEX and KFOR), the informalization of EU–NATO relations has also managed to at least allow some kind of working relationship on the ground. Hence the term 'normalization through informalization'. However, the situation is suboptimal and not sustainable in the long term.

In sum, 'effective multilateralism' barely applies to the EU–NATO case, neither in terms of the EU having any formal representation in NATO nor in the sense that their relationship has been much conducive to provide multilateral solutions to international security issues. Their relationship remains problematic and is marked by political and functional rivalry. What is more, under changing conditions of multilateralism becoming more 'selective' they have to be able to prove their added value and are therefore dependent on each other's ability to start working together effectively. Putting a stop to duplication, waste of time and money and to holding on to political and institutional dogmas is imperative; the alternative is a diminished relevance of both organizations. Staffs of both organizations have already shown their flexibility in this regard, now it is time for a grand bargain on EU–NATO cooperation at the political level.

Notes

1 I owe thanks to Joachim Koops for suggesting this term.
2 The author conducted a range of interviews with EU and NATO officials in the period from November 2011 to February 2012 in Brussels.
3 PSC+7 is a briefing of non-EU NATO members; PSC+9 format is a briefing of non-EU NATO members and candidate countries.

References

Ames, P. (2010) 'Rasmussen seeks to break deadlock', *Europolitics*, 26 February.

Assem, A. van den, and Drent, M. (forthcoming) 'The institutionalization of the European security field: securitization and Bourdieu's practice theory', *European Security*.

Berlin Plus Agreement (provided by Mr. Tim Waugh, NATO) Online. Available www.europarl.europa.eu/meetdocs/2004_2009/documents/dv/berlinplus_/berlinplus_en.pdf (accessed 5 February 2012).

Bouchard, C. and Peterson, J. (2010) 'Conceptualising multilateralism: can we all just get along?', *MERCURY E-Paper*, No. 1, February.

Cadier, D. (2011) 'EU mission in Kosovo (EULEX): constructing ambiguity or constructive disunity?', *Transatlantic Security Paper*, 3: 5.

De Hoop Scheffer, J. (2007) 'NATO and the EU: time for a new chapter', speech at Berlin, 29 January.

Drent, M. (2010) 'A Europeanisation of security: the security identities of the United Kingdom and Germany', unpublished dissertation, University of Groningen.

Drent, M. and Landman, L. (2012) 'Why Europe needs a new European Security Strategy', *Clingendael Policy Brief*, No. 9, July 2012.

EDA (European Defence Agency) (2013), *EDA Annual Report 2012*, Brussels.

EGS (2013) *Towards a European global strategy: securing European influence in a changing world*. Online. Available www.euglobalstrategy.eu (accessed 29 May 2013).

EU–NATO Declaration on ESDP (2002) 16 December 2002. Online. Available www.nato.int/docu/pr/2002/p02–142e.htm (accessed 5 February 2012).

European Council (2003) *A secure Europe in a better world: European Security Strategy*.

European Council (2012) *Conclusions*, Brussels, 13–14 December, EUCO 205/12.

Forman, S. and Segaar, D. (2006) 'New coalitions for global governance: the changing dynamics of multilateralism', *Global Governance*, 12: 205–25.

General Secretariat of the Council (2009) 'PMG recommendations on concrete measures improving EU–NATO relations', 8 December, 17344/09.

Ginkel, B. van and Gardner, M. (2012) 'Foreword. Testing the waters: assessing international responses to Somali piracy', *Journal of International Criminal Justice*, 10(4): 723–5.

Gowan, R. and Brantner, F. (2008) *A global force for human rights? An audit of European power at the UN*, London: European Council on Foreign Relations.

Graeger, N. and Haugevik, K.M. (2011) 'The EU's performance with and within NATO: assessing objectives, outcomes and organisational practices', *Journal of European Integration*, 33(6): 743–57.

Howorth, J. (2011) 'The "new faces" of Lisbon: assessing the performance of Catherine Ashton and Herman Van Rompuy on the global stage', *European Foreign Affairs Review*, 16: 303–23.

Irondelle, B. and Mérand, F. (2010) 'France's return to NATO: the death knell for CSDP?', *European Security*, 19(1): 29–43.

Kissack, R. (2010) *Pursuing effective multilateralism: the European Union, international organisations and the politics of decision making*, London: Palgrave Macmillan.

Koops, J. (2012) 'NATO's influence on the evolution of the European Union as a security actor', in O. Costa and K.E. Jørgensen (eds) *The influence of international institutions on the European Union: when multilateralism hits Brussels*, New York: Palgrave Macmillan, pp. 155–85.

Latek, M. (2012) 'EU-NATO partnership in stagnation', *Library Briefing*, Library of the European Parliament, 4 September.

Layne, C. (2012) 'This time it's real: the end of unipolarity and the Pax Americana', *International Studies Quarterly*, 56(1): 203–13.

Lijn, J. van der, and Teftedarija, A. (2012) *Continuïteit en onzekerheid in een veranderende wereld. Clingendael Strategische Monitor 2012*, The Hague: Clingendael.

Michel, L. (2007) *NATO-EU Cooperation in Operations*, NATO Defense College, Research Paper No. 31, February.

Penttilä, R. (2009) *Multilateralism light: the rise of informal international governance*, London: Centre for European Reform.

Rasmussen, A.F. (2012) Keynote speech at NATO Parliamentary Assembly, Prague, 12 November.

Rood, J. and Dinnissen, R. (2013) *Een wereld in onzekerheid. Clingendael Strategische Monitor 2013*, The Hague: Clingendael.

SIPRI (2012) 'Chapter four: Europe', *The Military Balance*, 112(1): 71–182.

Slaughter, A.-M. (2004) *A new world order*, Princeton: Princeton University Press.

Sturm, P. (2010) 'NATO and the EU: cooperation?', *European Security Review*, 48, ISIS Europe, February.

Szymanski, A. and Terlikowski, M. (2010) 'The policy of Turkey towards EU–NATO cooperation', *Bulletin*, No. 122, November, Warsaw: PISM.

Valasek, T. (2011) *Surviving austerity: the case for a new approach to EU military collaboration*, London: Centre for European Reform.

Varwick, J. and Koops, J. (2009) 'The European Union and NATO: shrewd interorganizationalism in the making?', in K.E. Jørgensen (ed.) *The European Union and international organizations*, Milton Park: Routledge, pp. 101–30.

Wikileaks (2009) *EU military staff head on opportunities for US–EU relations, 20 May*. Online. Available http://wikileaks.org/cable/2009/05/09USEUBRUSSELS716.html (accessed 22 December 2011).

Yost, D.S. (2007) *NATO and international organizations*, Rome: NATO Defence College.

Zandee, D. (2011) 'EU–NAVO: minder politiek, meer pragmatisme', *Internationale Spectator*, 65(12): 637–41.

9 Effective multilateralism between unequal partners
The EU in the OSCE

Niels van Willigen

Introduction

The European Security Strategy of 2003 mentions the Organization for Security and Cooperation in Europe (OSCE) alongside the Council of Europe (CoE) as one of the organizations whose strengthening benefits the EU (European Council 2003).[1] In 2002, the High Representative for the Common Foreign and Security Policy of the European Union, Javier Solana, had referred already to the OSCE and the EU as 'natural born partners' (Solana 2002). This qualification was echoed in publications on the relationship between the EU and the OSCE (Doyle 2002; Wohlfeld and Pietrusiewicz 2006: 186; Van Ham 2009: 131). In terms of membership, objectives, activities and tasks there is indeed much overlap between the two organizations. Nonetheless, effective cooperation between the two organizations is not obvious and the value of the EU–OSCE relationship needs constant reaffirmation. This is mainly because it is a relationship between unequal partners; the EU has a much stronger political, legal and economic position compared to the OSCE. Moreover, with 28 member states the EU is the dominating bloc within the OSCE. Its dominant position is attractive in terms of effective multilateralism, because it offers the EU the opportunity to influence the OSCE's agenda and thus strengthen the organization if it desires to do so. Effective multilateralism with respect to the OSCE is therefore contingent upon the extent to which the EU is able to use its position within the OSCE.

Focusing on the question of reform, the purpose of this chapter is to analyse the EU's functioning within the OSCE from 2003 to 2013. The relationship between the two organizations has been described and analysed before, but most of these publications either were written before the implementation of the Lisbon Treaty or do not analyse the EU–OSCE relationship from the perspective of effective multilateralism (Wohlfeld and Pietrusiewicz 2006; De Graaf and Verstichel 2008; Van Ham 2009; Galbreath and Brosig 2013). This chapter analyses the external and internal effectiveness of the EU within the OSCE before and after the Lisbon Treaty.[2]

The chapter starts with an overview of the most important issues the organization has been dealing with in the last ten years. Second, I delve into the issue of external reform. External reform is defined as the contribution of the EU to the strengthening of the OSCE. In other words: in what way(s) did the EU contribute to the OSCE's effectiveness as a multilateral organization? Third, the relationship between the EU and the OSCE is described. The fourth part of the chapter elaborates on internal reform and addresses the question to what extent the Lisbon Treaty has been implemented and to what extent this has affected internal EU-coordination and effectiveness. The analysis is wrapped up in the conclusion by elaborating on the impact of the Lisbon Treaty on the internal and external effectiveness of the EU in the OSCE.

Institutional crisis and reform attempts

When the drafters of the European Security Strategy coined effective multilateralism in 2003 it came at a good moment for the OSCE. The organization was heading towards an institutional crisis and could use some help from the EU. The OSCE increasingly suffered from the (relative) success of the EU and the North Atlantic Treaty Organization (NATO). Reflecting on his six-year term as Secretary-General of the OSCE, Marc Perrin de Brichambaut referred to the OSCE as the 'Cinderella of European security organizations' (Brichambaut 2012: 34). De Brichambaut did not explicitly mention the two evil stepsisters, but because of overlapping membership and competencies these would logically be the EU and NATO. Even if one does not agree with the analogy, it is widely recognized that the EU and NATO are partly responsible for the institutional crisis the OSCE has been in since the start of the twenty-first century. The membership and mandates of the three organizations increasingly overlap. Both the EU and NATO have expanded and now include many countries that were formerly part of the Eastern Bloc. In many ways the EU and NATO have more to offer to these countries than the OSCE. In spite of the economic and financial crisis, the EU is still a powerful economic actor with an expanding foreign policy profile. NATO is still the most effective military alliance in the world and can give credible and hard security guarantees to its members.

The added value of the OSCE in European security is often summarized by referring to its inclusiveness and its comprehensive concept of security. Indeed, the OSCE's predecessor, the Conference on Security and Cooperation in Europe (CSCE), was innovative in the sense that it adopted a comprehensive approach to security in the Helsinki Final Document (1975). The CSCE balanced political-military affairs (the first dimension), economic and environmental affairs (the second dimension), and humanitarian affairs (the third dimension). However, after the Cold War NATO and the EU transformed into international organizations dealing with similar comprehensive security issues. Both the EU and NATO adopted multifaceted and multidimensional conceptions of security. Therefore, when it comes to the question how the EU, NATO and the OSCE came to define European security after the Cold War, there is much overlap in their basic security assessments. The added value of the OSCE's inclusiveness was further undermined by the enlargement of NATO and the EU, as well as competition of the CoE.

The OSCE's emphasis on the human dimension in the 1990s created significant overlap with the CoE. While giving due attention to human rights the CSCE emphasized managing geopolitical conflict between East and West. The CSCE facilitated *Détente* and contributed to the end of the Cold War (Leatherman 2003). When the CSCE transformed into the OSCE in the 1990s, more emphasis was put on the human dimension (Galbreath 2009). This is illustrated by the establishment of three autonomous institutions dealing with humanitarian issues: the High Commissioner on National Minorities (HCNM), the Office for Democratic Institutions and Human Rights (ODIHR), and the Representative on the Freedom of the Media (RFOM). Further, field operations were established in Eastern Europe, South-Eastern Europe, South Caucasus and Central Asia, with the purpose to promote conflict resolution, democratization and respect for human rights. In spite of the OSCE's human rights profile, in some ways the EU seems to prefer cooperation with the CoE over the OSCE. While both were mentioned in the same sentence in the European Security Strategy, and although the CoE is not mentioned in the Report on the Implementation of the European Security Strategy, the EU signed a memorandum of understanding with the CoE in which common interests were identified (Council of Europe 2007). Tellingly, in spite of several attempts, there is no comparable arrangement between the EU and the OSCE.

At the initiative of the EU the Platform for Cooperative Security was adopted during the Istanbul Summit in 1999 with the aim to form the basis of cooperation between the OSCE and other international organizations, including the EU (Lundin 2012). More specifically, in 2003 the EU attempted to strengthen the cooperation with the OSCE on a structural basis and this led to the 'European Council Draft Conclusion on EU–OSCE Co-operation in Conflict Prevention, Crisis Management and Post-conflict Rehabilitation' (Council of the European Union 2003). It was followed by the 'Draft Assessment Report on the EU's Role vis-à-vis the OSCE' in 2004 with the aim to 'strengthen the relationship between the EU and the OSCE' and to 're-enforce the performance of the EU in the OSCE' (Council of the European Union 2004). When having the rotating presidency in 2006, Austria proposed to draft an EU–OSCE declaration 'to reaffirm the complementary way the two groupings work together' (Lööf 2006: 15). It was meant to be a document that would give guidance to practical cooperation, but also provide a 'step towards a real strategic partnership between both organizations' (Van Ham 2009: 145). However, none of the drafts mentioned above was followed up and significant progress in structural cooperation between the EU and the OSCE remained absent (Stewart 2008: 280). Policy officials indicated that there were internal divisions within the EU. Upgrading the status of the EU within the OSCE could lead to demands for access from other international organizations or non-governmental organizations which not all EU member states looked forward to.

While not denying the role of NATO, the EU and the CoE in the OSCE's crisis, it seems to be the case that the major problem is the OSCE itself. The core of the institutional crisis revolves around the OSCE's identity. On the international political strategic level, the success of the CSCE during the Cold War could not be replicated by the OSCE in the 1990s and beyond. The last significant political-military arrangements were made during the Istanbul summit in November 1999 when the Charter for European Security and the Adapted Conventional Armed Forces Europe Treaty (Adapted CFE-Treaty) were adopted. The summit took place against the background of the war in Chechnya, NATO's military intervention in Kosovo (spring 1999) and failed efforts by Russia to prevent and later condemn that intervention (Van Santen 2000: 8; Ghebali 2005: 378). Russia had pushed for a larger role of the OSCE in European security, including a significant role in Kosovo. The Charter for European Security was meant to strengthen the OSCE as a security actor, but did not live up to Moscow's ambitions (Lynch 1999: 62–3; Ghebali 2005: 378).

The 1999 summit can therefore be seen as the inception of the OSCE's institutional crisis. More specifically, Russian grievances about the direction which the OSCE headed into during the late 1990s and early twenty-first century became 'the crux of the OSCE crisis' (Ghebali 2005: 12). The grievances focused on what Russia (often supported by countries in the former Soviet Union) sees as the adoption of double standards, the overdevelopment of the human dimension, the political self-marginalization of the OSCE and the lack of organizational oversight by the participating states. The double standards refer to the accusation that the human dimension exclusively focuses on countries in the former Soviet Union and the Balkans. For instance, Moscow accused the ODIHR of applying double standards in its election monitoring. Related to the double standards is the accusation that the human dimension expanded at the expense of the political-military and economic-environmental dimension. That led to the claim that the OSCE lost focus on what Moscow sees as the really important security issues, which it left to the EU and NATO. According to Russia, the result was the OSCE's political self-marginalization. Finally, Russia argues that the weak institutional structure of the OSCE allowed the West to make the OSCE agenda a reflection of its foreign policy priorities. In particular, the autonomous institutions are given too much leeway as far as Russia is concerned (Ghebali 2005: 14).

The Russian grievances led to an institutional crisis and forced a search for a new role of the OSCE in European security. In 2004 the majority of member states of the Commonwealth of Independent States (CIS) issued the Moscow Declaration and the Astana Appeal in which they urged the need for reform. Responding to the pressure, the OSCE's ministerial council in 2004 established a Panel of Eminent Persons with the mandate to reflect on how the effectiveness of the OSCE could be strengthened. Their report 'Common Purpose: towards a more effective OSCE' addressed the grievances to some extent and made concrete recommendations for reform (OSCE 2005). However, due to a lack of consensus only a few and mostly marginal reforms have been implemented. Large reforms supported by Russia, such as giving legal personality to the organization, did not take place.

The crisis lingered on, as evidenced by Russia's president Vladimir Putin's reference to the OSCE as 'a vulgar instrument' of a group of (Western) countries during the 2007 Security Conference in Munich (De Graaf and Verstichel 2008: 270). During the parliamentary elections in 2007 and the presidential elections in 2008, Russia imposed such stringent conditions on election monitoring that the OSCE decided not to send election observers at all. Moreover, the 2008 war between Russia and Georgia, and the Western support for Kosovo's unilateral declaration of independence, seriously hampered relations between the Western participating states and Russia. The so-called Corfu process, launched in June 2009 by the Greek Chairman in office of the OSCE, was meant to renew dialogue on European security writ large (Kropatcheva 2012: 378). In their declaration the OSCE ministers of foreign affairs pledged to: 'Reconfirm our acquis, Review the state of play of European Security and Renovate our mechanisms to deal with traditional and new challenges' (OSCE 2009). The Corfu process was also meant to channel the Russian proposal for a new European security treaty which had been communicated by Russia's President Dmitri Medvedev in October 2008 (Kropatcheva 2012: 378). This treaty would restructure the entire European security architecture and not only affect the OSCE, but also NATO, the EU, the CIS and the Collective Security Treaty Organization (CSTO) (Zagorski 2010: 43). While the proposal did not get support in the West, the Corfu process facilitated a dialogue on key security concerns which were also part of Medvedev's proposal.

The Corfu process was followed by the Astana Declaration in 2010. For the first time since 1999 a summit of OSCE heads of state or government convened in order to discuss the future of the organization. The Astana Summit issued the 'Astana Commemorative Declaration Towards a Security Community', which aims at continuing the security dialogue, which was reinvigorated in Corfu, with the purpose of working towards a security community based on the confirmation of existing commitments across the three dimensions (OSCE 2010).

The Astana Summit failed to adopt a concrete action plan, mainly because of lack of consensus about the unresolved conflicts in Georgia and Nagorno Karabakh (Kemp 2010: 261; Kropatcheva 2012: 379). At the 2012 ministerial council meeting in Dublin the Astana Declaration was complemented by a strategic roadmap; the Helsinki+40 Process. It is a multi-annual roadmap towards the establishment of the security community as defined in the Astana Declaration. By 2015, when the 40th anniversary of the Helsinki Final Act is celebrated, the process should have resulted in 'visible progress, an updated agenda and a realistic workplan' (OSCE 2012c). The Helsinki+40 initiative can be seen as the latest initiative to resolve the crisis within the OSCE and to 'reinforce and revitalize the organization' (OSCE 2012e). However, the Dublin ministerial council meeting failed to adopt clear priorities. Policy officials indicate that the resulting problem is that Helsinki+40 is process rather than issue orientated. This seems to be born out of necessity, because while all participating states can agree on the necessity of talking about reforms, they disagree when it comes to concrete proposals.

As a result, Helsinki+40 means different things for different participating states. On the one hand, the Russians see the initiative as 'a window of opportunity to strengthen the role, reputation and relevance of the OSCE'. This would include giving the OSCE legal personality by way of a founding charter (OSCE 2013d). The United States of America (US) on the other hand rejects such a charter as well as major reforms (OSCE 2012f). The EU did not explicitly take a position on legal reform during the ministerial council meeting in December. In general, the EU is in favour of legal reform (De Graaf and Verstichel 2008: 273). However, views on what kind of legal reform and whether the OSCE should get a charter differ. That could be the reason that the EU simply stated that Helsinki+40 should result in a stronger OSCE without further qualifications (OSCE 2012g).

It would be too easy to conclude from the EU position that it could play a mediating role between the US and Russia. That might be the case with respect to the legal status (because it adopts a nuanced position falling between the American and Russian position), but with respect to the human dimension the EU is very close to the American position and far removed from Moscow's views. Moreover, the EU is hardly trusted as an impartial mediator. The EU has its own reform priorities and the question is to what extent these priorities match the reform needs of the OSCE. That being said, to what extent did the EU contribute to the effectiveness of the OSCE?

External reform: making the OSCE more effective?

As pointed out above, the EU regards the OSCE as an important organization to reach its foreign policy aims. In the 'Report on the Implementation of the European Security Strategy' the European Council emphasized that 'It is important that countries abide by the fundamental principles of the UN Charter and OSCE principles and commitments' (European Council 2008: 2). The same report recognized that 'Lasting stability in our neighbourhood will require continued effort by the EU, together with UN, OSCE, the US and Russia' (European Council 2008: 10). More recently in her statement during the ministerial council meeting in Dublin, High Representative of the Union for Foreign Affairs and Security Policy (High Representative) Catherine Ashton stressed the importance of the OSCE remaining 'a robust pillar in Europe's security architecture' and promised: 'you can count on the European Union to play its part' (OSCE 2012b: 3). To what extent has the EU lived up to its promises and contributed to the effectiveness of the OSCE since 2003?

According to the Report on the Implementation of the European Security Strategy, the relationship with the OSCE has been deepened since 2003, 'especially in Georgia and Kosovo' (European Council 2008: 11). To a large extent this is true. There is extensive cooperation between the EU and the OSCE in the field. In Kosovo, for example, the EU and the OSCE deployed large field missions and cooperation between them is characterized by 'a division of labour which allows organizations to occupy the same policy area and maintain institutional autonomy' (Galbreath and Brosig 2013: 279).

In relative terms the EU is a large financial supporter of the OSCE. About 65 per cent of the unified budget is paid for by EU member states. Moreover, the

European Commission is a relatively large contributor to the extra-budgetary funds of the OSCE. That being said, the EU member states have cut back their contributions to the OSCE in the last few years. This fits the overall decrease of financial contributions by the participating states. If financial commitments are an indicator for the level of importance which states attribute to an international organization then the OSCE is in trouble. The unified budget of the OSCE decreased from €182.2 million in 2002 to €149.3 million in 2011. The same trend can be recognized with the extra-budgetary contributions, which decreased from €43 million in 2002 to €17 million in 2011 (OSCE 2003, 2012h). EU countries are also increasingly less willing to allocate staff for OSCE related work. Policy officials indicate that in the capitals only few work on the OSCE and the field missions are increasingly difficult to fill with competent staff members.

In spite of a decreasing financial commitment, the EU's share in funding is still large and that, together with the 28 seats in the decision-making institutions, makes the EU an influential actor. Even more so, because often (potential) candidate states also align themselves with EU statements. In the last ten years the EU has used its influence mainly by focusing on implementing the existing commitments of the OSCE participating states. In terms of making the OSCE more effective there is no grand strategy. Instead, the EU prefers focusing pragmatically on concrete issues that need to be addressed by the OSCE.

This pragmatic approach sometimes raises concerns that the EU uses the OSCE primarily instrumentally for its own foreign policy purposes. A concrete example is the way the EU uses the OSCE to get information about a (potential) candidate country for its progress reports. The field missions of the OSCE in (potential) candidate countries are well informed and can help the EU in assessing the progress of the country concerned (De Graaf and Verstichel 2008: 266; Galbreath and Brosig 2013: 274). Another example is that the OSCE is considered to be very useful for shaping European policy towards the Eastern neighbourhood. For example, policy officials often emphasize that communication between the OSCE and the Central Asian states is facilitated by the fact that they as participating states regard the OSCE as their organization, whereas the EU is an external third party. At the same time, it should be realized that the OSCE's involvement in Central Asia has its limits too. The Central Asian governments generally have 'strong reservations about the OSCE's involvement within their borders, particularly when it comes to reinforcing democracy, human rights or the role of civil society' (De Graaf and Verstichel 2008: 267–8).

The EU's instrumental use of the OSCE regularly receives criticism. Some policy officials indicated that they would prefer to see the OSCE treated more as a partner and not just as an implementing agency. At the same time it should be recognized that the OSCE uses the EU in a similar way. Especially EU-candidate countries are sensitive to pressure from Brussels. When the OSCE deals with an issue in a candidate country it often involves the EU to apply pressure. It seems therefore that the EU–OSCE relationship is characterized by strategic calculation from both sides (Galbreath and Brosig 2013: 276). The overlapping policy priorities (i.e. human rights, democratization) of both organizations facilitate this instrumental cooperation.

The EU has an official agenda, which focuses on four particular policy priorities (OSCE 2010):

1   Improving capabilities for preventing, managing and resolving conflicts, and making progress on resolving the protracted conflicts;
2   Strengthening conventional arms control including security- and confidence-building measures;
3   Strengthening implementation of norms, principles and commitments, in particular in the human dimension, including full support for the work of the relevant OSCE institutions;
4   Tackling transnational and emerging threats and challenges.

While in statements the EU pays due attention to all four priorities, in practice the EU emphasizes the implementation of OSCE commitments in the human dimension. According to policy officials that explains why the EU strongly supports the work of ODIHR, HCNM and RFOM, and why it emphasizes the value of the field missions. Through the extra-budgetary funds, the EU and individual EU member states implement projects aimed at promoting human rights and democracy. These funds do not need approval by the Permanent Council, which enables the EU to avoid resistance from, for example, the CIS.

Some, particularly Russia, regard the EU's approach to comprehensive security as being unbalanced. This is not just a hollow accusation. In fact, the EU admits it too. This is nicely reflected in an EU statement from January 2013: 'Security cannot be achieved without respect for human rights and fundamental freedoms. The EU cannot accept a weakening of existing commitments and their implementation' (OSCE 2013e). In other words, while the EU considers the first and the second dimension as being part of the OSCE's comprehensive security concept, the human dimension clearly comes first.

The paradox of the EU's emphasis on the human dimension is that it made the OSCE both more and less effective, depending on the answer to the question: effective for whom? For the EU the OSCE has become more effective, because the strengthened human dimension led to many concrete projects funded through the extra-budgetary funds and to the establishment of the autonomous institutions and field operations. The institutions and missions have much leeway in carrying out their mandates and are therefore not hampered by the stalemates in the decision making bodies in Vienna. Their ability to operate independently 'in some of the most sensitive areas of the OSCE's remit' made De Brichambaut (2012: 38) call the autonomous institutions 'one of the greatest assets' of the organization. However, the autonomy of the institutions and the field missions is part of the reform discussion. Russia would like to see a stricter control over the institutions and missions; something which is successfully resisted by the United States and the EU. On the one hand, these differences of opinion fuel the institutional crisis and make the OSCE less effective as a forum for consultation between the countries 'East and West of Vienna'. On the other hand, the EU's striving for effective multilateralism is meant to strengthen international organizations in such a way that they provide global governance in line with European norms, values and interests. An OSCE which weakens the human dimension is therefore not 'effective' from the perspective of the EU; on the contrary. That implies that at least in the context of the OSCE 'effective multilateralism' cannot be seen as a politically neutral concept. Instead, it is strongly linked with EU foreign policy priorities.

The EU in the OSCE

The EU–OSCE relationship is an old one. All EU member states are participating states in the OSCE and the EU's predecessor, the European Community (EC), was involved in the CSCE from the beginning. Respectively, the European Commission and the rotating presidency were involved as negotiator and signatory of the Helsinki Final Act in 1975. Since then the EC/EU has been recognized as a political actor within the CSCE/OSCE. Until the Lisbon Treaty, the EC/EU was represented by the rotating presidency and by the delegation of the European Commission. Alongside the rotating presidency the European Commission was a signatory of the Charter of Paris for a New Europe in 1990 and the Charter for European Security in 1999. Nonetheless, it is important to stress that the European Commission had no autonomous position within the CSCE/OSCE; it was always forced to team up with the rotating presidency. The European Commission's dependence on the rotating presidency was reaffirmed in the 2006 Rules of Procedure of the OSCE: 'At the meetings of the decision-making bodies, the European Commission shall have one seat next to the participating State holding the EU Presidency' (OSCE 2006a: 8). As a participating state, the Council Presidency is entitled to speak first and the European Commission 'may take the floor immediately after the participating State holding the EU Presidency' (OSCE 2006a: 10).

EU representation changed because of the Lisbon Treaty. The delegation of the European Commission was replaced with the mission of the European External Action Service (EEAS). The Vienna delegation of the EEAS covers both the OSCE and the International Atomic Energy Agency (IAEA) – the latter is discussed by Glavind in Chapter 7. Excluding the head of delegation, the OSCE-section consists of about eight staff members at the time of writing. This is just a small increase compared to the European Commission delegation, which consisted of about four members (excluding the head of delegation). As I explain below, the role of the rotating presidency has not changed in spite of the fact that its role in foreign policy has diminished considerably since the Lisbon Treaty.

Next to the representation through the rotating presidency and the EEAS, the current relationship between the two organizations is based on several other frameworks for cooperation. Following the Lisbon Treaty, these frameworks have changed somewhat. First, there are regular contacts between officials on the highest levels of both organizations. There is for example an annual

EU–OSCE meeting, in which the OSCE troika (the former, current and next chairman in office) and the EU's High Representative or the rotating presidency participate (OSCE 2011, 2012a: 115; Cyprus Presidency 2012). The High Representative also speaks at the ministerial council meeting of the OSCE. Before the Lisbon Treaty, the EU addresses were made by the rotating presidency and the European Commissioner for External Relations and European Neighbourhood Policy (OSCE 2006b, 2006c, 2007a, 2007b, 2008). Meetings also take place between the OSCE Secretary-General and the European Commissioner for Enlargement and European Neighbourhood Policy. On 10 April 2013, for example, European Commissioner Stefan Füle and OSCE Secretary-General Lamberto Zannier discussed 'possibilities to further enhance cooperation between the two organizations, as well as recent developments in areas of mutual interest' (European Commission 2013). Second, on the working level, there is an annual meeting of officials from the OSCE secretariat and their counterparts in Brussels. The meetings rotate between Vienna and Brussels. Policy officials indicated that before the Lisbon Treaty, these meetings were twice a year (following the schedule of the rotating presidency). Further, officials from the OSCE secretariat are in touch with colleagues from the EU on a daily basis. OSCE representatives are regularly invited to participate in formal and informal meetings with relevant EU committees and working groups. Given the overlap in activities of both organizations, this occurs quite often.

The overview above shows that there are plenty of institutionalized contacts between the OSCE and the EU. From the OSCE side a lot of this work is coordinated by the OSCE's Secretariat's Section for External Co-operation. In Brussels, the Council's Working Party on the OSCE and the CoE (COSCE) (established in 2004) has a coordinating function. Its main purpose is to negotiate a common EU position within the OSCE and the CoE. However, the COSCE only meets once a month while the EU delegation coordinates positions on a weekly basis. According to policy officials, the coordinating role of the COSCE is therefore small compared to the coordinating role of the delegation in Vienna (see below).

Internal reform: making the EU more effective within the OSCE

With the 'big bang' of EU enlargement in 2004 there were concerns among the other participating states that an enlarged EU would dominate the agenda of the OSCE (Wohlfeld 2003: 52). To a certain extent this has become true. If the EU has a coordinated position it unites a group of 28 participating states out of 57. Moreover, the EU is often successful in gaining support from several non-EU countries too. However, size is only one factor in determining whether the EU is an effective actor in the OSCE. The other factor is the ability to agree on a common position. This section looks into that particular question and addresses how the Lisbon Treaty has affected internal EU-coordination and effectiveness.

To start with, assessments of EU internal effectiveness before the Lisbon Treaty are often quite negative. The literature mentions rivalry between the different EU institutions as well as lack of unity and coherence when it comes to external representation towards the OSCE (Van Ham 2009: 144). In that sense the Lisbon Treaty was expected to make a positive change (Stewart 2008: 275). At the same time, an effectively coordinated position does not automatically mean a strong position. Two problems can be identified with EU coordination. First, negotiations between 28 member states often lead to the lowest common denominator, or general and cautious positions. Second, it leads to inflexibility. Positions cannot be easily abandoned, because that would require a reopening of negotiations (De Graaf and Verstichel 2008: 275). The changes in the Lisbon treaty did not help to solve these two problems. Many policy officials recognized the fact that an EU position is still always some sort of compromise and that renegotiating an EU position is not always easy. However, some of them stressed that the problem of inflexibility should not be overstated.

The Lisbon Treaty has not been fully implemented with respect to the external representation in the OSCE. In formal meetings the EU is still officially represented by the rotating presidency rather than by the EEAS. Policy officials indicated three reasons for this. First, the EEAS lacks capacity. The transformation of the Commission-delegation to the EEAS delegation led to a small strengthening in numbers only and it is too small to cover all meetings and responsibilities. This led to a pragmatic approach, which leaves ample room for deciding who represents the EU on what occasion. Second, EU member states are simply used to the rotating presidency. The country holding the rotating presidency still feels responsible for EU foreign policy and acts accordingly. And third, the status of the EU as an actor within the OSCE is contested. As pointed out above the EU does not have any formal status within the OSCE as a result of which non-EU participating states – Russia in particular – prefer representation by the rotating presidency rather than the EEAS. Policy officials indicated there was an attempt to adapt the 2006 Rules of Procedure in such a way that the Lisbon Treaty could be fully implemented. The OSCE secretariat explored some options to this end, but lack of political consensus among the participating states prevented its adoption. As a result, the rotating presidency maintained its formal function. It seems that an enhanced status of the EU could possibly gain support from Russia, but only under certain conditions. During the Dublin ministerial council meeting Russia declared that it would be willing to consider changing the rules of procedure in such a way that the EU can be formally represented by the EEAS, but only if the changes would also grant access to other international organizations such as the Collective Security Treaty Organization and the Eurasian Economic Commission (OSCE 2012d).

The continued function of the rotating presidency has not led to serious coordination problems with the EEAS. In practice the role of the rotating presidency has diminished extensively. Before the Lisbon Treaty it took the floor and fully represented the EC/EU. The delegation from the European Commission, sitting next to the rotating presidency, almost never spoke. Since the Lisbon Treaty the rotating presidency still takes the floor, but immediately transfers its role to the EEAS representative. Therefore in official meetings the rotating presidency functions as facilitator rather than as the substantial EU representative. In informal meetings, the rotating presidency also still has a function. EU-coordination meetings take place three times a week; the permanent representatives meet on Monday afternoons and Thursday mornings and the deputy permanent representatives on Wednesday afternoons. Policy officials indicate that the EU coordination meetings are presided over by the EEAS, unless a lack of capacity forces the EEAS to hand that task over to the rotating presidency. The meetings of the deputies, however, are still presided over by the rotating presidency. The purpose of these meetings is to prepare a common EU-statement for the weekly Permanent Council meeting on Thursday afternoons. Thus, EU coordination mainly takes place in Vienna rather than in Brussels. According to policy officials, the recommendations which the EEAS receives from Brussels are taken as a starting point for discussion, but the outcome is often different as a result of the negotiations between the European country delegations in Vienna. This differs from the situation before the Lisbon Treaty. The delegation of the European Commission had a coordinating function, but coordination was mainly done by the rotating presidency. In that sense, the diminished role for the rotating presidency is good news for internal coordination. Before the Lisbon Treaty the EU's commitment towards the OSCE heavily depended on the commitment of the EU-member holding the rotating presidency and some of them gave more attention to the OSCE than others (Van Ham 2009: 136). With the EEAS in place, the problem of the lack of commitment of some rotating presidents has for a large part been solved.

While the continued role of the rotating presidency has not led to major issues, there has been a problem regarding the competencies of the EU and therefore the competence of the EEAS to act as EU representative. The Lisbon Treaty identifies three different EU competencies: exclusive, shared and supportive. In the fall of 2011 the UK voiced that it wanted more clarity with respect to the EU-competencies in EU-statements (see also Chapter 2). In response to that the EU's COREPER hammered out the 'practical arrangements'. These arrangements were concluded in October 2011 and are meant to assist the EU countries in answering the question which competence is involved in relation to the specific topic being discussed.

The arrangements offer three different formulations. First, when an issue concerns the exclusive competencies of the EU the statement will start with: 'The EU'. An example is the 'EU statement on the Human Rights situation in Azerbaijan' (OSCE 2013a). Second, in the case of shared and supportive competencies, the first few sentences of the statement will read: 'The EU and its member states'. This phrase was, for example, used in the 'EU statement in response to the reports by the Chairpersons of the three Committees' (OSCE 2013b). Finally, when the issue deals with the exclusive competencies of the member states the EU statement will start with: 'The European Union member states'. This was for example the case with the 'Interpretative Statement ... regarding the adoption of the Unified Budget for 2013' (OSCE 2013c).

According to policy officials, the majority of EU-statement concerns the exclusive competency of the EU and the vast majority of statements are made as EU with no difficulties. This is mainly because most issues concern the human dimension which, according to the practical arrangements, falls under the exclusive competency of the EU. The statements concerning shared competencies are often related to the political–military dimension. The number of statements in this category comes second after statements dealing with the exclusive competency of the EU. The number of statements which fall under the exclusive competency of the member states is quite small. This is mainly the case with the approval of the unified budget, which consists of contributions from the individual participating states. The EU as a legal entity only contributes to extra-budgetary expenses of the OSCE. Policy officials explain that that is the reason why the UK not only insists that the statement should be made on behalf of the member states, but also that the coordinating presidency rather than the EEAS communicates the statement.

Although according to some policy officials there was an initial backlash, according to others the competencies issue did not seriously hamper the EU's internal effectiveness. A *modus operandi* was found and most EU member states came to accept the UK position regarding the exclusive competency of the member states on the budget issue quite soon. The ability to achieve consensus in spite of the practical arrangements was facilitated by deciding to first discuss the subject matter and only afterwards the competency issue. The fact that most differences of opinion within the EU-group concern procedural issues rather than substance helps in enhancing internal effectiveness. It seems that there are no significant structural differences between the UK position and the other EU member states when it comes to substance. Some officials indicated that the competencies issue had a negative effect on the image of the EU as a coherent and effective actor within the OSCE. According to others, the outside actors do not really care and consider this an internal EU-issue without significant affect on its external representation. All EU statements are titled as 'EU statements', which suggests more unity than one would expect from the discussion above. Some policy officials argued that non-EU states use the coherence issue strategically and only pretend to be confused about who is representing the EU when it suits them to be confused.

Concluding, the Lisbon Treaty enhanced the role of the delegation in Vienna, which was taken over from the European Commission by the EEAS. The role of the rotating presidency changed from being the main representative of the EU to being merely a facilitator. The issue about the competencies was resolved and did not seriously harm internal effectiveness. It seems that not much has changed in terms of the intensity of internal coordination, which according to policy officials was pretty intensive before Lisbon and continued to be intensive afterwards. Although a few officials claimed that coordination became more difficult, it is not clear that this is because of the Lisbon Treaty. It might have more to do with substance. Issues which are difficult to reach consensus on within the EU-group often predate the Lisbon Treaty. The issue of Kosovo is a case in point.

While Kosovo's independence is recognized by the majority of EU member states, five EU member states refuse to do so. Policy officials explained that this often leads to statements based on the lowest common denominator and impedes the EU in being a decisive actor on this topic. In general, however there is a clear common denominator in the EU-group with a strong emphasis on the human dimension. If there are differences of opinion, it seems that these are mainly about details reflecting particular national priorities on human rights issues.

Conclusion

This chapter addressed the question to what extent the EU has internally and externally been effective as an actor within the OSCE. More specifically, I analysed the impact of the Lisbon Treaty on the internal and external effectiveness of the EU. So far, the Lisbon Treaty only had a limited effect. The EU delegation in Vienna got a larger role in coordinating EU policy, but at the same time the rotating presidency remained and executes functions which the Lisbon Treaty formally attributes to the EEAS. The role of the EEAS will probably expand in the future, but that would also require an increase in staff members of the delegation. As I pointed out above, one of the reasons for the rotating presidency continuing is lack of capacity of the EEAS.

It would be an improvement in terms of external representation if the OSCE's rules of procedure were adapted and allowed the EU to represent itself as an international organization. However, an upgraded status would probably result in increased visibility, but it would not necessarily lead to increased internal or external effectiveness. First, in spite of some recent problems concerning the UK position on competencies, internal effectiveness seems to be quite high. A common position is the rule, and lack of consensus or dissenting positions are the exception. This is mainly explained by the fact that the majority of issues concern the human dimension, in which the EU member states pursue a common agenda. That being said, the statements are of a very general nature and often reflect the lowest common denominator. Second, external effectiveness would be served better by increased EU commitment rather than an upgraded formal status. The analysis of external reform showed that with decreasing financial commitments and a focus on the human dimension, the EU is one of the actors fuelling the institutional crisis.

To conclude, for the EU, effective multilateralism within the context of the OSCE primarily means using the organization instrumentally for its own foreign policy purposes. These purposes for a large part clash with the participating states 'East of Vienna', which leads to political deadlocks. Future research should investigate more deeply into the question of what effective multilateralism means for whom. For example, reforming the OSCE in the direction of Russian priorities would not be effective from the EU's point of view. In terms of future policy venues, the EU could make a few steps forward by using the OSCE more genuinely as a platform for cooperation and dialogue between East and West. That would not imply that the EU departs from its foreign policy priorities, but it would imply the development of a strategic vision of what kind of an organization the OSCE should be. Such a vision is currently lacking, and therefore the EU's use of the OSCE as a multilateral platform is not as effective as it could be.

Notes

1 I thank Nora Dörrenbächer and Annika Eberstein for their valuable research assistance, as well as the officials from the OSCE, the EU and national delegations who were so kind to grant me interviews.
2 The data collection consists of primary documents and interviews with officials from the OSCE, the EU and national delegations to the OSCE. The interviews took place in The Hague, Brussels and Vienna, in the winter and early spring of 2013.

References

Brichambaut, M.P. de (2012) 'The OSCE in perspective, six years of service, six questions and a few answers', *Security and Human Rights*, 23(1): 31–44.

Council of Europe (2007) *Memorandum of understanding between the Council of Europe and the European Union*, 11 May 2007.

Council of the European Union (2003) *Draft conclusions on EU-OSCE co-operation in conflict prevention, crisis management and post-conflict rehabilitation*, 10 November 2003.

Council of the European Union (2004) *Draft assessment report on the EU's role* vis-à-vis *the OSCE*, 10 December 2004.

Cyprus Presidency of the Council of the European Union (2012) *Press release: Cyprus' Foreign Affairs Minister chairs meeting with OSCE*, 16 October 2012.

De Graaf, V. and Verstichel, A. (2008) 'OSCE crisis management and OSCE–EU relations', in S. Blockmans (ed.) *The European Union and crisis management*, The Hague: T.M.C. Asser Press, pp. 255–76.

Doyle, D. (2002) 'EU and OSCE: natural born partners?', *European Security Review*, (September 2002), 14: 6–8.

European Commission (2013) *Statement by Commissioner Stefan Füle following his meeting with OSCE Secretary General Lamberto Zannier*, 10 April 2013.

European Council (2003) *A secure Europe in a better world*, 12 December 2013.

European Council (2008) *Report on the implementation of the European Security Strategy: providing security in a changing world*, 11 December 2008.

Galbreath, D.J. (2009) 'Putting the colour into revolutions? The OSCE and civil society in the post-Soviet region', *Journal of Communist Studies and Transition Politics*, 25(2–3): 161–80.

Galbreath, D.J. and Brosig, M. (2013) 'OSCE', in K.E. Jørgensen and K.V. Laatikainen (eds) *Routledge Handbook on the European Union and international institutions: performance, policy, power*, London and New York: Routledge, pp. 271–81.

Ghebali, V.-Y. (2005) 'Growing pains at the OSCE: the rise and fall of Russia's pan-European expectations', *Cambridge Review of International Affairs*, 18(3): 375–88.

Kemp, W. (2010) 'The Astana Summit: a triumph of common sense', *Security and Human Rights*, 21(4): 259–64.

Kropatcheva, E. (2012) 'Russia and the role of the OSCE in European security: a "forum" for dialog or a "battlefield" of interests?', *European Security*, 21(3): 370–94.

Leatherman, J. (2003) *From Cold War to democratic peace*, Syracuse: Syracuse University Press.

Lööf, S. (2006) 'The OSCE and the EU: complementing each other's strengths', *OSCE Magazine*, July 2006.

Lundin, L.-E. (2012) *'Working together: the OSCE's relationship with other relevant international organizations'. Nine steps to effective OSCE engagement*, Food-for-thought paper commissioned by the CiO, 9 July 2012.

Lynch, D. (1999). 'Walking the tightrope: the Kosovo conflict and Russia in European security, 1998 – August 1999', *European Security*, 8(4): 57–83.

OSCE (2003) *Financial report and financial statements for the year ended 31 December 2002*, 26 September 2003.

OSCE (2005) *Common Purpose: towards a more effective OSCE. Final report and recommendation of the panel of eminent persons on strengthening the effectiveness of the OSCE*, 27 June 2005.

OSCE (2006a) *Rules of procedure of the Organization for Security and Co-operation in Europe*, 1 November 2006.

OSCE (2006b) *Finnish presidency of the Council of the European Union. Statement by Erkki Tuomioja, minister for foreign affairs on behalf of the European Union*, 4 December 2006.

OSCE (2006c) *European Commission. Benita Ferrero-Waldner. 14th OSCE Ministerial Council Meeting*, 5 December 2006.

OSCE (2007a) *Speech by Benita Ferrero-Waldner, European Commissioner for External Relations and European Neighbourhood Policy* (OSCE Ministerial Council Madrid), 29 November 2007.

OSCE (2007b) *Closing statement of the Portuguese Presidency of the Council of the European Union* (OSCE Ministerial Council Madrid), 30 November 2007.

OSCE (2008) *Statement by the European Union at the opening session of the sixteenth meeting of the OSCE Ministerial Council. Minister of Foreign and European Affairs H.E. Bernard Kouchner* (OSCE Ministerial Council Helsinki), 4 December 2008.

OSCE (2009) *Corfu informal meeting of OSCE foreign ministers on the future of European security. Chair's concluding statement to the Press*, 28 June 2009.

OSCE (2010) *Astana Declaration by the Chairperson-in-Office*, 30 June 2010.

OSCE (2011) *OSCE Troika, EU High Representative Ashton discuss co-operation*, 18 July 2011.

OSCE (2012a) *OSCE annual report 2011*, 30 March 2012.

OSCE (2012b) *Statement by the Head of the EU Delegation, High Representative of the Union for Foreign Affairs and Security Policy Catherine Ashton to the OSCE Ministerial Council*, 6 December 2012.

OSCE (2012c) *Opening remarks by Secretary General Lamberto Zannier to the OSCE Ministerial Council* (OSCE Ministerial Council Dublin), 6 December 2012.

OSCE (2012d) *Statement by Mr Sergey Lavrov, Minister for Foreign Affairs of the Russian Federation, at the Nineteenth Meeting of the OSCE Ministerial Council*, 6 December 2012.

OSCE (2012e) *Press release: OSCE Chairperson, at Dublin Ministerial Council, announces agreement on future road map for OSCE*, 6 December 2012.

OSCE (2012f) *United States mission to the OSCE. Closing statement for the OSCE Ministerial Council in Dublin*, 7 December 2012.

OSCE (2012g) *19th Meeting of the OSCE Ministerial Council. EU closing statement*, 7 December 2012.

OSCE (2012h) *Financial report and financial statements for the year ended 31 December 2011 and the opinion of the external auditor*, 19 July 2012.

OSCE (2013a) *EU statement on the human rights situation in Azerbaijan*, 14 February.

OSCE (2013b) *EU statement in response to the reports by the Chairpersons of the three Committees*, 31 January 2013.

OSCE (2013c) *Statement by the European Union at the 940th meeting of the OSCE Permanent Council. Interpretative statement under paragraph IV.I(A)6 of the rules of procedure of the Organization for Security and Co-operation in Europe regarding the adoption of the united budget for 2013*, 7 February 2013.

OSCE (2013d) *Press release. Russian Deputy Foreign Minister in his address to OSCE outlines Russia's priorities*, 14 March 2013.

OSCE (2013e) *EU statement in response to the Minister of Foreign Affairs of Ukraine, H.E. Leonid Kozhara*, 17 January 2013.

Solana, J. (2002) *Address to the Permanent Council of the Organization for Security and Cooperation in Europe* (OSCE), 25 September 2002.

Stewart, E.J. (2008) 'Restoring EU–OSCE cooperation for pan-European conflict prevention', *Contemporary Security Policy*, 29(2): 266–84.

Van Ham, P. (2009) 'EU–OSCE relations', in K.E. Jørgensen (ed.) *The European Union and international organizations*, London and New York: Routledge, pp. 131–48.

Van Santen, H. (2000) 'The Istanbul Summit: a moderate success', *Helsinki Monitor*, 11(1): 8–10.

Wohlfeld, M. (2003) 'EU enlargement and the future of the OSCE: the role of field missions', *Helsinki Monitor*, 14(1): 52–65.

Wohlfeld, M. and Pietrusiewicz, J. (2006) 'EU–OSCE cooperation', in A. Ricci and E. Kytömaa (eds) *Faster and more united? The debate about Europe's crisis response capacity*, Brussels: European Commission, pp. 186–90.

Zagorski, A. (2010) 'The Russian proposal for a Treaty on European Security: from the Medvedev initiative to the Corfu process', in Institute for Peace and Security Policy at the University of Hamburg/IFSF (ed.) *OSCE Yearbook 2009*, Baden-Baden: Nomos Verlagsgesellschaft, pp. 43–59.

10 Between effective multilateralism and multilateralism light

The EU in the G8

Judith Huigens and Arne Niemann

Introduction

For nearly 40 years, a group of arguably the world's most powerful state leaders has come together in an informal setting to discuss a multitude of international issues. Born out of frustration with the inefficiency and slow decision-making of existing international institutions such as the International Monetary Fund and the World Bank, the summits were intended to bring together a small party of powerful state leaders for a 'direct, unscripted, unbureaucratic exchange between a few heads of government' (Bayne 1995). Apart from these heads of state/government, the summit has also seen the permanent representation of the European Union, since as early as 1977.

Without a secretariat, a formal founding treaty, or a permanent body of representation, the G8 summit has always remained an ad hoc conference, which is hosted by a different state each year. The G8 has therefore been described as a case of informal global governance, which was to create an intimate and small setting for those of the highest authority to exchange views, hereby reducing the transactions costs in international relations in general. This 'multilateralism light', as Penttilä (2009) calls it, is best suited for coordinating policies, tackling acute crises and launching new initiatives.

These characteristics place summitry, and the G8 specifically, into a special category of multilateralism, of which the relationship with *effective* multilateralism as envisaged by the EU is not evident. In fact, 'multilateralism light' and effective multilateralism are only two interpretations of a variety of multilateralisms that exists out there in the international domain. One of the first questions that needs to be addressed here, is whether these two interpretations of multilateralism are conflicting or compatible, because the answer to this question provides us with indicators of an EU acting in pursuit of effective multilateralism.

The definition of effective multilateralism as used in this volume indicates that informal governance at most indirectly contributes to effective multilateralism, since it lacks any kind of enforcing rules or charters (see Introduction). However, the G8 does have the ability to stimulate and facilitate other forms of international cooperation, by endorsing principles, stimulating activities, showing leadership and promoting reform (Putnam and Bayne 1987: 158;

Penttilä 2005: 85; Gstöhl 2007: 3). For this reason, Dobson (2007: xvii) refers to the G8 as 'plate spinner'. The overarching role of the G8 enables it to put into motion other tools of global governance, thus 'spin the plates'. This suggests a possible division of labour between formal and informal global governance (Penttilä 2009: 2).

On a more critical note, informal governance can also have harmful effects on more institutionalized arrangements. For example, the exclusive membership of the 'Gs' and the lack of enforceability of the agreements can possibly undo trust that has previously been created by more formalized tools of multilateralism (Penttilä 2005: 84; Jokela 2011: 59). However, the most fundamental critique on summitry is that it constitutes a form of multilateralism that is based upon interests as opposed to norms, thus incorporating the 'old vices' of realist power politics (Tedesco and Youngs 2009; Jokela 2011: 51). Still, the G8, more than other summits such as the G20 or the G77, is a summit of like-minded Western states, which makes it more suitable than other Gs to act as a form of norm-based multilateralism.

As a result, in this case two scenarios of EU operationalization of effective multilateralism within the G8 can be distinguished. The first scenario is that the EU tries to make the G8 a more effective 'plate spinner', and thus able to contribute to effective and efficient performance of other, more formalized forms of global governance. The second scenario is of a more radical nature and constitutes an EU that aims to enlarge and formalize the G8, as well as make it more focused on norms as opposed to interests. We will observe the extent to which the EU tries to operationalize effective multilateralism by looking at its contribution to recent reforms of the G8, and the EU's position at the G8. Two simultaneous reforms have taken place in 2009–10. The first reform was the establishment of the G20 in 2009 (see Chapter 11 of this volume), and the consequences of this development for the future of the G8. The second reform constituted the implementation of the Treaty of Lisbon, which resulted in the replacement of the rotating presidency by the permanent president of the European Council.

We now continue this chapter with a look at the effects of internal and external reform respectively on the ability of the EU to realize effective multilateralism, the main conclusion being that throughout these two reforms, the relation between these two forms of multilateralism remains awkward, with the EU generally lacking the formal tools to pursue the radical scenario and producing moderate results at the 'plate spinner' scenario.[1]

External reform: the future of the G8 in a G20-world

The EU has been presented with an interesting opportunity to operationalize its notion of effective multilateralism due to increasing criticism of the G8, and pressures to reform. The G8 has, for example, been condemned for its lack of representativeness, for not being sufficiently democratic and for its inability to deal with urgent global (especially financial) issues (cf. Cooper 2007: 4; Hajnal and Panova 2012). Most reform proposals have focused on questions of 'out-reach' (the extension of participation or membership), whereas the dimensions of 'in-reach' (institutionalization of the summit system) and 'down-reach' (involvement and participation of civil society) have received considerably less attention (Kirton 2008: 1). In this chapter we will take up the 'out-reach' dimension since it constitutes the most important aspect of the G8 reform debate. In this section, we set out to show that the reform discussion has ultimately been settled in favour of a division of labour between the G20 and the G8, with the EU playing a substantial role in both forums.

The discussion in the context of G8 reform has been marked by a multitude of proposals, ranging from expanding or reducing the G8's membership, supplementing it with additional bodies, or abolishing the G8 altogether. Two issues have been taken up repeatedly: the legitimacy and the effectiveness of the G8. Most positions have, broadly speaking, followed at least in part one of the following two lines of argumentation. On the one hand, a small number of participants would lead to more cohesion, homogeneity concerning values, flexibility and thus more effectiveness. On the other hand, a more inclusive membership would lead to more representativeness, legitimacy and also effectiveness, in the sense that all key actors are included (cf. Kirton 2008: 3; similarly Gnath 2010: 5f.).

One can broadly distinguish between the following approaches to G8 reform (cf. Hajnal and Panova 2012: 65ff.): (1) expansion of the G8 with the goal of including especially the emerging powers as full members of the G8 (e.g. Sachs 1998); (2) G8+G5: these approaches stress an institutionalized dialogue between the G8 countries and the emerging powers (G5), rather than pressing towards a full membership of the G5; (3) G20 as substitute for the G8, the so-called L20 initiative; (4) replacement of the G8 by some other grouping with a different membership composition (e.g. Kenen *et al.* 2004; Roach 2004); (5) coexistence of the G8 and G20 (e.g. Dobson 2001; Brown and Berlusconi 2009); (6) coexistence of the G8 and a new group (e.g. Bergsten 2004; Haynal 2005); (7) variable geometry: this approach has the G8 at the core of discussions while leaving appropriate room for wider participation, involving various combinations, depending on the agenda (Hajnal and Panova 2012: 77).

Subsequently, we examine the positions and roles played by the EU, its member states as well as other G8 countries and the BRICs in the (external) reform debate, before analysing the extent to which the EU has furthered the notion of effective multilateralism in the external reform debate.

The role of the EU and its member states in the G8 reform debate

For many years *Germany*'s position concerning G8 reform has been ambiguous. While part of the Red-Green coalition, Finance Minister Steinbrück argued that the G8 would become superfluous in the medium term, would need to be replaced by a more representative body and advocated for an expansion of the G8 (Fues 2007: 11). Subsequently, Chancellor Merkel showed her reluctance concerning 'forward-looking positions on the reform of the global-governance architecture'. She clearly rejected formal membership of the 'Outreach 5' in the G8 (Fues 2007: 19). At the G8 summit in Heiligendamm (2007), Germany proposed a new model for the outreach process (G8+5) by introducing the 'Heiligendamm Process'. This process went beyond previous ad hoc invitations as it foresaw an institutionalization, without implying full membership within the summit structure (Fues 2007: 19). This change of attitude towards the G8 reform has been interpreted as a compromise within the Christian Democrat/Social Democrat coalition in order to reconcile the positions of Steinbrück and the Chancellor (Cooper 2007). After the Heiligendamm Process and with the emergence of the financial crisis Merkel became a clear advocate of broadening the G20 to the leaders' level (Seith 2009). Merkel still appreciates the G8 as a forum for opinion building among leaders on global issues and thus favours a coexistence of both groupings. However, she regards the G20 as the more salient forum (Dullien and Herr 2010: 28), and prefers a greater degree of institutionalization of the G20.

The *United Kingdom* has played an integral part in the debate concerning G8 reform especially from 2005 onwards (G8 Research Group 2005: 41). Prime Minister Blair advocated turning the G8 into a G13, building on the 'G8+G5' formula that was tested at the G8 Gleneagles summit in 2005. Blair thus sought to make China, India, Brazil, South Africa and Mexico full members of the G8 (Hajnal and Panova 2012: 71). Gordon Brown followed a similar policy, but went a step further: even after the success of the Heiligendamm Process he called for a deeper involvement of the 'Outreach 5' states in the central proceedings of the G8 (Gnath 2010: 8). But in contrast to French president Sarkozy, he opposed a formal inclusion of those countries as full G8 members. He argued that the informal outreach process was sufficient to make the G8 more representative and that his experience in the EU-27 proved that effective decision-making is difficult in larger groups (Pilling 2008). Brown has been a 'leading advocate of the G20 format' and argued 'that the old G8 club of rich, industrial countries was no longer acceptable for directing world affairs' (Parker 2009, cited in Hajnal and Panova 2012: 71). He proved his commitment to the G20 by hosting the second G20 summit in April 2009 in London (Pettifor 2010: 39). Current Prime Minister Cameron has shown similar commitment to the G20 as a complementary part within the international global governance architecture. He advocated strengthening the role of the G20, however, without substantially formalizing it for example by establishing a permanent secretariat (Cameron 2011).

France has been a strong advocate of G8 reform over the past decade. Former President Chirac repeatedly highlighted the 'importance of adapting the G8 to global evolutions in the power-base if the institution is to remain successful as a coordinating body'. He pointed to the lack of legitimacy of the G8 and stressed that it is 'necessary to hear from those that represent a growing proportion of international economic activity or population' (cf. G8 Research Group 2005: 13). However, the French government seems to have been reluctant to clearly state its position on the formal expansion of the G8 (G8 Research Group 2005: 42).

Under President Sarkozy this changed decisively. Even after the success of the Heiligendamm Process, Sarkozy clearly demanded the permanent extension of the G8 to a G14 – including China, India, Brazil, South Africa, Mexico and Egypt (Gnath 2010: 8) – and played an important role in the establishment of the G20. He also showed strong support for the G20 by advocating, together with Chancellor Merkel, the institutionalization and valorization of the G20 within the global governance system.

Italy was one of the first countries calling for G8 reform. Since the Genoa summit of 2001, Italy has been committed to expand the dialogue with emerging and developing countries. Since 2004 Italy seems to advocate the expansion of the G8 and to include China and India as full members. Berlusconi underlined at the Sea Island Summit of 2004 that 'it doesn't make much sense for us to talk about the economy of the future without two countries that are protagonists on the world stage' (cited according to G8 Research Group 2005: 23). For the period since the financial crisis there is evidence for two types of preferred reform scenarios. On the one hand, Italy seems to foster a strategy of 'variable geometry', where the G8 remains at the core while leaving room for various other participants and/or forums, depending on the issue at stake (Hajnal and Panova 2012: 77). On the other hand, Italy seems to support the coexistence of the G8 and the G20 (Brown and Berlusconi 2009). Italy clearly refuses the replacement of the G8 by the G20 but rather stresses their complementarity. Italy's attitude makes sense considering its strategic interests: its place as a member of the G8 gives it a disproportionately large amount of political power relative to its economic size (G8 Research Group 2005: 24; Stella 2010: 49). Italy accepts an important role of the G20 during the international financial crisis, but it does not support an extension of its mandate to other areas, such as climate change, international security and development, since those issues can be discussed effectively in other formats such as the (expanded) G8 (Stella 2010: 50).

The *European Union* has for most part taken a low profile role in the G8 reform debate. However, it seems that Commission President Barroso has played a key role in the establishment of the G20 at leader's level in 2008 (European Commission 2010; Larionova and Renard 2012). Two weeks after Lehman Brothers announced its bankruptcy, Barroso and Sarkozy went to Camp David and are said to have convinced US President Bush (hardly a multilateralist) to support the broadening of the G20 to leaders' level. At the same time, Barroso is said to have secured EU membership in that new forum (Griesse 2010: 31). Interestingly, in contrast to France and Britain, the EU does not seem to support the idea of (greater) institutionalization of the G20. Although there are no official public statements to this effect, internally Barroso and Van Rompuy seem to hold the view that the G20 should remain an informal leaders-driven process that should focus on content and not on structures. Moreover, informal solutions are thought to suit the EU better than formal ones, because in informal settings there is no need for the EU to define itself, while this is more difficult in more formal ones, such as in the United Nations.

The other G8 countries and the BRICS in the G8 reform debate

How are the positions of the EU and its (G8) member states to be situated within the broader range of positions? Among the other G8 countries, *Canada* has by far been the staunchest supporter of broadening the G20 to the leaders' level since the late 1990s. Although Canada strongly advocated the L20 initiative, it never regarded it as a substitute for the G8 (G8 Research Group 2005: 7). *The United States*, by contrast, regarded the creation of a Leader's G20 for a long time with caution. The same applies to initiatives to expand and reform the G8. This reluctance can be explained through the predominant US perception that such reform of the international summit architecture would likely go hand in hand with a diminished US influence (cf. G8 Research Group 2005: 47; Cooper 2007: 19). This view gradually changed over the years and from around 2009 onwards the US seems to have become one of the stronger supporters of the Leader's G20 (Anderson 2010: 74). *Japan* has been highly ambivalent on G8 reform as well as on the creation of the L20. On the one hand, Japan considers itself as a 'bridge between the predominant European or North Atlantic nations of the G7/G8, and the emerging powers, particularly within the Asian region'. On the other hand, Japan also tries to preserve its unique position as the only non-Western country in the G8 (G8 Research Group 2005: 28). Towards the end of last decade, Japan became more supportive of the L20 initiative (cf. Kirton 2012: 8). Similar to the US, *Russia* has been skeptical about the extension of the G8. It has been suggested that Russia 'would not want to demote itself to a club where it is equal to financially delicate emerging economic middle powers like Indonesia or Argentina' (G8 Research Group 2005: 37). Russia's position in the reform of the international summit architecture is to some extent special: on the one hand, it is a full member of the G8. On the other hand, Russia is also a member of the BRICs forum. Due to an often complicated relationship with the Western G8 states, Russia tends to put more emphasis on bilateral relations, and also focuses common interests within the BRICs grouping (Hajnal and Panova 2012: 72).

The *BRICs* countries faced a certain dilemma in the debate on the reform of the international summit architecture. On the one hand they would benefit from close engagement with the G8 or even a full membership, especially in terms of trade and foreign investment, but on the other hand they would lose their credibility and legitimacy to be the leaders of the global South once they joined the exclusive 'club of the rich' (e.g. Chin 2008: 84). In contrast to the G8, the G20 is a forum that better allows them to cope with this dilemma (e.g. Hurrell 2010).

The outcome of the debate

It seems that the issue has, at least temporarily, been settled in favour of coexistence between the G8 and the G20, with some elements of variable geometry (at least on the fringes). The G20 seems to have solved the issues of legitimacy and representation that haunted the G8. Also, the installment of the G20 has enabled the G8 to return to its original small-scale informal attire. The relocation of the 2012 summit from Chicago to the much more secluded location of Camp David serves as an example of this trend. In line with the Italian position, a division of labour seems to have developed between the two forums, with the G20 as the financial and economic forum, and the G8 focusing more on political issues. In terms of effectiveness the renewed informality of the summit seems to have made the G8 more humble in its intentions. The G8 once again serves as a catalyst for ideas, leaving more ambitious decision making up to other institutions, among which the G20.

What was the effect of this external reform to the position of the EU at the summit? A hypothetical question of relevance in this regard, is what would have happened to EU representation within the G8, if the Group had indeed been enlarged? It is not unlikely that a restructuring of the G8 would have called into question the legitimacy of the EU's double representation. If the G8 had been enlarged, the goal of small-scale intimacy may have justified a debate on the appropriateness of having as many as six European representatives. The financial crisis, however, changed the direction of the transformation completely, and resulted in co-existence. In this situation, both the EU institutions and the individual member states are able to play a role in both institutions. The EU even managed to become a fully-fledged member of the G20 from the start (as opposed to the rather vague status of participant at the G8 summit), an indicator of its position within the G8. Thus the external reform ensured a large role of the European members both in the G8 and in the G20. More specifically, the reinforcement of the original informal setting of the G8 summit continues to serve the interests of the EU. In addition, through its early presence within the G20, the EU has secured (continued) participation at the top tables of global governance (cf. Jokela 2011: 66).

It (thus) seems that the EU has furthered the notion of effective multilateralism only moderately in the external reform debate. Overall it seems that in terms of the two scenarios that we elaborated in the introduction, the EU has rather worked towards more effective plate-spinning in the G8 and G20, as well as towards potentially more effective cooperation between the EU, the G8 and the G20. Interestingly, the EU has done so (at least indirectly) by strengthening the informality of both the G8 and the G20. What the EU seems *not* to have done, is use this opportunity to transform the G8 and the G20 into more formalized and/ or norm-based institutions, contrary to the wishes of some of its individual member states. Despite the EU's preference for effective multilateralism, formalizing the Gs seems not to be in the EU's interest, whose (undefined) position seems to be tied to the informal nature of the summits. The next section assesses whether internal reform has been more successful in the pursuit of either scenario.

Internal reform: the EU in the G8 before and after the Treaty of Lisbon

This second section looks at the changes to the EU's representation in the G8 following the implementation of the Lisbon Treaty and what this entailed for the EU's ability to pursue its ambitions within the G8. The prime focus is the extent to which the EU representation is able to operationalize effective multilateralism in the G8, and hence has been able to influence the G8. Given the fact that the G8 is an informal group within which no formal decision making takes place, our interpretation of influence, or effectiveness, focuses on the ability to take part in the social processes of the summit. We start with a general overview on the EU's specific status within the G8 and how this is related to its (in)ability to pursue effective multilateralism in this forum. Second, we turn to the changes that were implemented under the Treaty of Lisbon. We finish this section by addressing the question of whether the EU manages to either act as an effective 'plate spinner' or to expand and formalize the G8 now the Lisbon Treaty has altered the form of its participation within the G8.

The EU's specific status and position in the G8

While the G8 remains primarily a gathering of heads of state, since 1977, only two years after the first summit in Rambouillet, the EU/EC has been officially represented at every summit. Originally an economic forum, and with efficiency and authority as the main goals of the summit, the need for EU involvement was recognized right from the start. After some internal disagreements on the nature of the representation, the member states compromised on a parallel approach that allowed for the EU to be represented at the summit by the president of the European Commission, as well as the rotating president of the EU Council (alongside the individual EU member states). However, no formal mandate was instated and close oversight mechanisms were installed.

Despite (or perhaps even because of) this precarious starting position, the European Commission was able to establish itself as a nearly fully-fledged participant at the summit table. Although initially restricted to participation in discussions on trade, the Commission was already involved in every aspect of the summit by 1981 (Niemann and Huigens 2011: 426). Also, the various oversight mechanisms fell into disuse (cf. Putnam and Bayne 1987: 153).

While not a sovereign state like the other G8 members, the European Commission is now generally treated like one at the summit. Other G8 members encourage the EU's involvement because of what it can contribute. The Commission delegation participates independently in all components that make up the summit structure, including the on-site and independent ministerial forums and meetings that have grown to be a part of the G8 infrastructure. The EU's performance and compliance, as measured by the G8 Research Group, has been on par with that of other G8 members, suggesting that it has been successful as an autonomous delegate (Huigens and Niemann 2011: 647). The position of the

Council Presidency, on the other hand, has been marginal. With a different EU member state joining the summit each year, the Council Presidency tended to join ranks with the Commission, but remained largely excluded from the preparatory process. Also, when represented by a G8 EU member, the position of Council Presidency became a neglected one.

Formally, only two aspects distinguish the EU from other G8 members, namely the exclusion from the name 'G8' and the fact that the EU cannot host a summit. This last aspect is of more value than one may suspect, since the summit hosts play an important part in defining the atmosphere and agenda of the summits. Especially in a setting as informal as the G8, every summit host has the liberty to organize a summit on the terms it prefers. This inability of the EU to organize the summit leaves it devoid of a significant tool to shape the summit in terms of inclusiveness and formalization. On the other hand, individual EU member states have been known to organize more inclusive and outreach-oriented summits, while the Atlantic states tend to focus more on informality and exclusiveness. Thus one may conclude that the radical scenario of effective multilateralism is pursued only in indirect terms.

Proactive EU involvement differs per issue area. This variation is explained by diverging levels of competence as well as by other factors, such as experience, national interests or international context. As a result the EU is a more effective plate spinner for some issues than for others, despite the fact that the informal nature of the summit makes the issue of whether or not the EU has the competence to speak less stringent. Such issues include climate change and development aid, for which the EU has often attempted to use the G8 summit as a forum not only to foster understanding and promises, but also to enforce more formalized international agreements. For example, the EU delegation has repeatedly identified the commitment to emission cuts of 50 per cent by 2050 as a summit objective (see, for example, Kwok *et al.* 2008: 129). Similarly, on the issue of development aid, the EU has consistently advocated a fixed share of GDP reserved for Official Development Assistance (ODA) (see, for example, Kwok *et al.* 2008: 131–2). In these attempts to formalize and institutionalize international agreements, which have repeatedly appeared on the EU's list of summit priorities, the goal of effective multilateralism can be identified. However, while a certain extent of plate spinning occurs thanks to these efforts, and other more formal initiatives are endorsed and explored, the EU has mostly failed in formalizing agreements at the G8 level. In most cases, the wording of the G8 communiqués is such that extensive liberty is granted to each member state on whether and how to execute the agreements that were made at the summit, which does not align with the aim of effective multilateralism.

In addition, the EU delegation is not completely independent, despite its distinctive infrastructure. This to some extent limits the EU's ability to operationalize effective multilateralism in the G8. The European Commission, unlike individual EU G8 members, must always take into account the positions of the other EU G8 participants, and is therefore less likely to be pressing for the more radical approaches (Putnam and Bayne 1987). Division among the ranks of the

EU members is possible, and the Commission does choose sides, but only after at least one other EU member has expressed support for that side. In contrast, individual member states do not hesitate to act independently. Relating back to the question of effective multilateralism, this makes the EU more of a general *norms chaser* than most other G8 members, who are more focused on the pursuit of interests. The EU is there to offer a broader, more general perspective.

There is neither a coordinated EU position within the G8, nor a formal policy among European delegations on how to deal with diverging goals in the summit. Nevertheless, behind the scenes, coordination does take place occasionally, usually by the Commission, and only when it suits the member states. Still, in terms of output, the four member states and the EU are quite cohesive, since there are few international issues on which the EU states have not already established a common position. However, most G8 members agree that too much EU unity could lead to the polarization within the G8 – the Europeans *versus* the rest – which would be counterproductive. This results in a balancing act between not coming across as divided, while not appearing a unified bloc either.

An interesting relationship thus exists between these two forms of multilateralism, with the informality of the G8 *enabling* the formalized necessity of EU presence. On the one hand, the transfer of competences from individual member states to the EU level deemed EU participation on some issues not only logical, but even legally necessary. On the other hand, this necessity was facilitated by the informality of the summit, which enabled the EU to participate alongside some but not all individual EU member states. But this same formalized necessity, or the EU agreements that deem EU participation legally mandatory, also made the parallel arrangement inevitable. At the same time, the informal nature of the summit did not only enable the parallel structure, but also encapsulated it through a logic of path dependency and power politics, in the sense that it is unlikely that the four largest EU member states will give up their G8 seat.

Referring back to the question of how 'effective' the EU is as a participant at the summit, we conclude that the EU is almost a fully-fledged participant at the summit, with its main challenges stemming from its lack of true independence. This limited independence makes it difficult for the EU to pursue the more radical scenario of formalizing the G8. Evidence does exist, however, of the EU endorsing the principle of the G8 as a plate spinner, albeit only in certain topic areas. The structure of EU representation has made EU participation somewhat more delicate than that of regular G8 members. At the same time, however, the informality of the summit counterbalances these delicacies. Thus, it seems not so much the setting of 'multilateralism light' that challenges the EU's ability to pursue effective multilateralism, but rather the internal EU arrangements. This begs the question whether recent internal reforms, namely the Treaty of Lisbon, have solved this issue.

The influence of the Lisbon Treaty

Up until 2009, the European Union was represented by the European Commission and the rotating president of the European Council. Under these circumstances only the Commission managed to approximate the status of regular G8 members. The single most important reason for this fact was consistency. In a personalized intimate forum such as the G8, social relations need time to develop. Under such circumstances, the changing face of the Council Presidency was a distinct disadvantage. By the time the Treaty of Lisbon was to be implemented, it was obvious that the representation of the Council would need a different attire.

The Lisbon Treaty solved this issue by instating a permanent President of the European Council. One of the main goals of the Treaty was to make the Common Foreign and Security Policy a more integral part of the EU and to enhance coherence in EU external action generally (Bache *et al.* 2011: 213; Gebhard 2011: 121). The position of the permanent president of the Council was therefore designed to do just that: manage *coherence*, in terms of organizational unity, and *consistency*, or organizational continuity, by for the first time representing the Council as a self-contained institutional actor (European Union 2008: Article 13.1). Thus, as of 2010, the EU is represented at the summit by both the Commission president and the permanent president of the European Council. The question that is discussed in this final section is how EU representation at the summit changed and the effect of these changes on the aforementioned goals of the Lisbon Treaty.

The practical implication of this change was that a new division of labour developed between the Commission and the Council. The two institutions were to be more tightly connected and form one single EU delegation, with in effect 'two heads'. Since each summit participant is entitled to one sherpa and three sous-sherpas, these positions are crossways divided for both the G20 and the G8. Hence the Commission provides the G20 sherpa and the Council the G8 sherpa, while in return both sherpas act as sous-sherpa in the other forum. Both summit teams are supported by a small Commission-team, which connects the summit input and output to the daily affairs of the Commission DG's. Apart from the expertise input by the Commission, the G8 representation of the Council is first and foremost directed by Van Rompuy's cabinet, and not by specific input from the European Council or its individual members.

This infrastructure is complemented by an informal division of tasks between Van Rompuy and Barroso. In typical G8 fashion, the division of labour is not exactly according to legal competences, but the result of a practical exchange of subjects that are considered relevant that particular year by one or the other. Competences play a part here, but only indirectly, as the Council President has been more involved in foreign policy issues, such as Syria or Afghanistan, while the Commission focuses on certain other topics that are either an exclusive competence, such as trade, or a so-called 'pet' issue, such as climate change. On some issues both presidents speak, for example because they speak from different angles. Development aid budgets can, for instance, be a topic on which the representative of the individual EU member states represents a different perspective than that of the Commission, which has its own aid budget.

What these changes most significantly improved was the *consistency* of the EU Council delegation, an important determinant for effective participation within the informal setting of the summit.[2] Previous studies have found that leaders with more summit experience tend to perform better, both in terms of interaction and in effectiveness (Kokotsis 2002). Initial disadvantages – that the Council delegation may have had in this respect – were quickly neutralized, due to the fact that the Council team was manned by highly experienced diplomats, who were able to integrate into the G8 network smoothly. Also, through its close cooperation with the Commission, the Council was able to benefit from its lead and experience as well. In relation to its ability to pursue effective multilateralism, this increased continuity enabled the Council to become a more credible and proactive advocate of certain objectives (as opposed to varying, member state specific objectives), testifying to an increased ability to pursue the scenario of plate spinning.

The second goal of the Treaty constituted *cohesion*. Since the Lisbon Treaty added new (and more) actors to represent the EU internationally, increased cohesion was not evident. This was also the case for the G8, in which one reasonably effective EU representative, the Commission, was replaced by two separate EU institutions. Initially, this put fellow G8 members off, who were expecting to encounter a more united EU and instead had to deal with another EU representative. Although this development would thus seem detrimental for cohesion, in practice this does not seem to be the case. Cooperation between the Council and the Commission seems to have run smoothly so far, as their interests seem not only to align, but to be similar, as both bodies represent the EU interest. Additionally, the Commission deems cooperation and coordination with the permanent Council president significantly easier than with a different rotating president each year. Officials from non-EU G8 members have confirmed the image of one EU actor. Some of them were not even aware that both institutions were part of the G8, since they only dealt with one (as double representation only takes place at the very highest level).

What has not increased since the Lisbon Treaty is the internal coordination between member states and the EU delegation, both G8 member states and non-G8 member states. Even though Van Rompuy represents the European Council, his position is only indirectly the result of Council deliberations. Thus the position of the EU delegation(s) remains as restricted by certain internal conditions, such as competences and double representation, as it ever was.

Probably the most significant change was an aspect not explicitly envisaged by the Lisbon Treaty: the fact that the EU is now always represented by two people (see also Chapter 11). But it is not merely the strength of numbers, but also that the Council and the Commission bring different angles, which usually complement each other. Such different perspectives bring different arguments to the table, amplifying the chances of convincing other G8 members.

Consequences for the EU's efforts to pursue effective multilateralism

The above elaboration on the implementation of the Lisbon Treaty begs the question whether increased consistency and, to a lesser extent, increased cohesion, has boosted the EU's effectiveness in the G8. In fact, the two elements, consistency and cohesion, seem to almost work against each other in this context, by adding a consistent new EU representative to the original set-up. The ability of the Council to take full part in the summit processes has increased considerably. But at the same time, the Commission now has to share its position as prime EU representative, in effect adding an extra head to the beast. In this light, the EU seems to have done rather well, in its smooth cooperation between the Commission and the Council. Also, in terms of performance as well as compliance, no significant effect of the changes can be detected.

The special position of the European Union as a participant, but not quite an official member, has not altered since the Lisbon reforms and thus not solved the EU's main predicament to the pursuit of effective multilateralism. Two important challenges remain, namely the inability to host a summit, and the parallel structure of having both the EU and four individual member states present. These challenges continue to make it difficult for the EU to pursue effective multilateralism in an informal forum such as the G8. A consistent addition in numbers has probably added to the EU's ability to make the G8 a plate spinner. However, the structure of the representation, with two EU representatives as well as four member states, remains such that more institutionalization is probably not in favour of the EU. Therefore, the conclusion seems to be that in terms of effectiveness, things do not seem to have regressed, but have not significantly improved either.

Conclusion

This chapter has introduced a fascinating relationship between different interpretations of multilateralism, namely 'multilateralism light' and 'effective multilateralism'. The question explored was if and how the EU balances these multilateralisms through membership in the G8. We have focused our analysis on the EU's positioning in the debate on G8 reform and on the conditions related to its own specific status within the G8 as well as the reforms in that regard implemented after the entry into force of the Lisbon Treaty.

First, we looked at the external reform dimension. Of the two scenarios introduced at the beginning of this chapter, the EU seems to have eschewed transforming the G8 (and the G20) into a more inclusive, formalized or norm-based institution, despite its preference for effective multilateralism. Instead, it has rather worked towards more effective plate-spinning as well as towards potentially more effective cooperation between itself and the G8. The most obvious explanation for this behaviour seems to be that the more radical scenario might possibly have constituted a threat to the EU's own position at the summit.

Next, we illustrated that the EU's position in the G8 summit, as a representative that acts in parallel with four individual member states, approximates that of the real G8 members, with two important exceptions. The EU is unable to host a summit, and its position is slightly more formal and less independent than that of other summit members, due to its not being a state. This position prevents the EU from shaping the contours of the summit and thus pursue the more radical scenario of institutionalizing and legitimizing the summit. This restricts the EU to the pursuit of the first scenario, of making the G8 more of a plate spinner. The EU attempts to do this by using the summit as a pusher for its norms-based agenda in certain issue areas, but has only been moderately successful.

Finally, we concluded that the Treaty of Lisbon mainly elevated the position of the European Council, giving it a much more consistent position at the summit. But despite promises made to non-EU summit members, the EU position has not become more unified than it was before. If anything, the group gained a participant. In terms of effectiveness, the main gain for the EU delegation was another integrated member to plead the European case, or effective multilateralism. The somewhat delicate position of the EU, however, was not altered through the Lisbon Treaty, thus maintaining the delicate balance between effective multilateralism and multilateralism light for now.

Notes

1 Our analysis has drawn on interviews with various officials from the EU G8 delegations, as well as the individual G8 member delegations, which were conducted between 2008 and 2013.
2 These results must be considered preliminary, since the new representation structure has only been in place for three consecutive summits. Future research should reveal whether or not the trends that we detect here have persisted.

References

Anderson, S. (2010) 'Länder-Fact-Sheet – USA', in C. Pohlmann, S. Reichert and H.R. Schillinger (eds) *Die G-20: Auf dem Weg zu einer 'Weltwirtschaftsregierung'?*, Berlin/Bonn: Friedrich Ebert Stiftung, pp. 73–5.

Bache, I., George, S. and Bulmer, S. (2011) *Politics in the European Union*, Oxford: Oxford University Press.

Bayne, N. (1995) 'The G7 summit and the reform of global institutions', *Government and Opposition*, 30(4): 492–509.

Bergsten, C.F. (2004) 'The euro and the dollar: toward a "Finance G-2"?', paper prepared for the conference on 'The Euro at Five: Ready for a Global Role', 26 February. Online. Available www.iie.com/publications/papers/bergsten0204.pdf (accessed 2 June 2013).

Brown, G. and Berlusconi, S. (2009) Joint article by President of the Council Berlusconi and British Prime Minister Brown, taken from the Prime Minister's Office website. Online. Available www.g8italia2009.it/G8/Home/News/G8-G8_Layout_locale-119988 2116809_InterventoBerlusconi.html (accessed 2 June 2013).

Cameron, D. (2011) *Governance for growth: building consensus for the future*, Prime Minister's Office, London. Online. Available www.google.de/url?sa=t&rct=j&q=&esrc =s&source=web&cd=1&cad=rja&ved=0CCoQFjAA&url=http%3A%2F%2Fwww. number10.gov.uk%2Fwp-content%2Fuploads%2F2011%2F11%2FGovernance-for-growth.pdf&ei=i5hQUPWqI8bXtAa4l4CQDg&usg=AFQjCNHcESX4yHRagFzbYf-pFdzUl_BlcA&sig2=bMVqF2EIDEH6HQeKTcnuJw (accessed 2 June 2013).

Chin, G. (2008) 'China's evolving G8 engagement: complex interests and multiple identity in global governance reform', in A.F. Cooper and A. Antkiewicz (eds) *Emerging powers in global governance: lessons from the Heiligendamm process*, Waterloo: Wilfrid Laurier University Press, pp. 83–113.

Cooper, A. (2007) *The logic of the B(R)ICSAM. Model for G8 reform*, The Centre for International Governance Innovation, Policy Brief, No. 1. Online. Available http://dspace.cigilibrary.org/jspui/bitstream/123456789/10127/1/The%20Logic%20of%20the%20BRICSAM%20Model%20for%20G8%20Reform.pdf?1 (accessed 2 June 2013).

Dobson, H. (2007) *The Group of 7/8*, Abingdon: Routledge.

Dobson, W. (2001) *Broadening participation in G7 summits*, Letter of transmittal to the leaders of the G-8 member countries, Turin, 21–22 January. Online. Available www.iie.com/publications/papers/g8–2001.pdf (accessed 2 June 2013).

Dullien, S. and Herr, H. (2010) 'Länder-Fact Sheet – Deutschland', in C. Pohlmann, S. Reichert and H.R. Schillinger (eds) *Die G-20: Auf dem Weg zu einer 'Weltwirtschaftsregierung'?*, Berlin/Bonn: Friedrich Ebert Stiftung, pp. 27–9.

European Commission (2010) *Conseil Européen – Bruxelles 16 septembre 2010. Conclusions de la présidence*, Brussels. Online. Available www.google.de/url?sa=t&rct=j&q=&esrc=s&source=web&cd=2&cad=rja&ved=0CC0QFjAB&url=http%3A%2F%2Feuropa.eu%2Frapid%2FpressReleasesAction.do%3Freference%3DDOC%2F10%2F3%26format%3DPDF%26aged%3D1%26language%3DFR%26guiLanguage%3Den&ei=dIRRUOHWIuen4gTExYGgDg&usg=AFQjCNEQEZIbrdzTJsjlUaMhIAcXK6gkiA&sig2=qSblu2-xXR28zt3mMwsO2g (accessed 2 June 2013).

European Union (2008) 'The treaty on the functioning of the European Union', *Official Journal of the European Communities*, C 115/47, 5 September.

Fues, T. (2007) 'Global governance beyond the G8: reform prospects for the summit achitecture', *Internationale Politik und Gesellschaft*, 2: 11–24.

G8 Research Group (2005) *G8 Reform: expanding the dialogue. An overview of the G8's ongoing relationship with the emerging economic countries and prospects for G8 reform*, Toronto: G8 Research Group. Online. Available www.google.de/url?sa=t&rct=j&q=&esrc=s&source=web&cd=2&cad=rja&ved=0CDYQFjAB&url=http%3A%2F%2Fwww.g8.utoronto.ca%2Fevaluations%2Fcsed%2Fed_050707.pdf&ei=_2FPUPjWFMKF4gTHzoHADw&usg=AFQjCNEh0mLyiBsANsloY_RqQcW_sd-C0Q&sig2=pWPCp9ozfKZSzNxhheEqoA (accessed 2 June 2013).

Gebhard, C. (2011) 'Coherence', in C. Hill and M. Smith (eds) *International relations and the European Union*, Oxford: Oxford University Press, pp. 101–27.

Gnath, K. (2010) *A group's architecture in flux: the G8 and the Heiligendamm Process*. Robert Schuman Centre for Advanced Studies, EUI Working Papers, 2010/06. Online. Available http://cadmus.eui.eu/bitstream/handle/1814/13097/RSCAS_2010_06.pdf?sequence=1 (accessed 2 June 2013).

Griesse, J. (2010) 'Fact sheet – Europäische Union', in C. Pohlmann, S. Reichert and H.R. Schillinger (eds) *Die G-20: Auf dem Weg zu einer 'Weltwirtschaftsregierung'?*, Berlin/Bonn: Friedrich Ebert Stiftung, pp. 30–4.

Gstöhl, S. (2007) 'Governance through government networks: the G8 and international organizations', *Review of International Organizations*, 2(1): 1–37.

Hajnal, P. and Panova, V. (2012) 'Future role and reform of the G8', in M. Larionova (ed.) *The EU in the G8: promoting consensus and concerted actions for global public goods*, Farnham: Ashgate, pp. 65–81.

Haynal, G. (2005) 'Summitry and governance: the case for a G-XX', in D. Carment, F.O. Hampson and N. Hillmer (eds) *Canada among nations: setting priorities straight*, Montreal, Kingston: McGill-Queens University Press, pp. 261–74.

Huigens, J.C. and Niemann, A. (2011) 'The G8 1/2: the EU's contested and ambiguous actorness in the G8', *Cambridge Review of International Affairs*, 24(4): 629–57.

Hurrell, A. (2010) 'Brazil and the new global order', *Current History*, 109: 60–6.

Jokela, J. (2011) *The G20: a pathway to effective multilateralism*, Chaillot Paper No. 125, Paris: Institute for Security Studies.

Kenen, P., Shafer J., Wicks N. and Wyplosz, C. (2004) *International economic and financial cooperation: new issues, new actors, new responses*, London: Centre for Economic Policy Research.

Kirton, J. (2008) 'The case for G8 reform', lecture delivered at Chuo University, Tokyo, Japan, 26 June. Online. Available www.google.de/url?sa=t&rct=j&q=&esrc=s&source =web&cd=2&cad=rja&ved=0CDYQFjAB&url=http%3A%2F%2Fwww.g8.utoronto. ca%2Fscholar%2Fkirton_reform_080629.pdf&ei=_J9NUPHgGpPU4QTDkICIDw&us g=AFQjCNHwgsDEhs0qnB7Ky6iBwLmgJkijtg&sig2=nu5zaltgCUbAd6SSuA6Mkg (accessed 2 June 2013).

Kirton, J. (2012) 'Japan's contribution to G8, G20 and global governance'. Online. Available www.google.de/url?sa=t&rct=j&q=&esrc=s&source=web&cd=1&cad=rja&ved= 0CCgQFjAA&url=http%3A%2F%2Fwww.g8.utoronto.ca%2Fscholar%2Fkirton-jfi-120321.pdf&ei=ulJQUJLEN8rb4QSUsIDACw&usg=AFQjCNHqQ_pYQgL7gYh QQpDDLh74EJ4gvQ&sig2=3_Y3Kq-B35uEljHb5GnHtg (accessed 2 June 2013).

Kokotsis, E. (2002) 'Compliance and the G7/G8 summits', lecture prepared for G8. Online. Available www.g8.utoronto.ca/g8online/2002/english/2002/06.html (accessed 27 October 2012).

Kwok, A., Seleanu, D., Vanderlinden, C. and Guebert, J. (2008) *2008 Hokkaido Toyako G8 summit country assessment report*, Toronto: University of Toronto G8 Research Group.

Larionova, M. and Renard, T. (2012) 'The European Union in the G20', in M. Larionova (ed.) *The EU in the G8: promoting consensus and concerted actions for global public goods*, Farnham: Ashgate, pp. 151–72.

Niemann, A. and Huigens, J.C. (2011) 'The European Union's role in the G8: a principal-agent perspective', *Journal of European Public Policy*, 18(3): 420–42.

Penttilä, R. (2005) 'Advancing American security interests through the G8', in M. Fratianni, J.J. Kirton, A.M. Rugman and P. Savona (eds) *New perspectives on global governance: why America needs the G8*, Aldershot: Ashgate, pp. 83–104.

Penttilä, R. (2009) *Multilateralism light: the rise of informal international governance*, London: Centre for European Reform.

Pettifor, A. (2010) 'Länder-fact sheet – Grossbritannien', in C. Pohlmann, S. Reichert and H.R. Schillinger (eds) *Die G-20: Auf dem Weg zu einer 'Weltwirtschaftsregierung'?*, Berlin/Bonn: Friedrich Ebert Stiftung, pp. 38–40.

Pilling, D. (2008) 'G8 club under pressure to expand', *Financial Times*, 9 July. Online. Available www.ft.com/intl/cms/s/0/c7454f2a-4dde-11dd-820e-000077b07658.html# axzz25gIiluVd (accessed 2 June 2013).

Putnam, R. and Bayne, N. (1987) *Hanging together: cooperation and conflict in the seven-power summits*, London: Sage.

Roach, S. (2004) 'How to fix the world', *Global Economic Forum*, December. Online. Available www.morganstanley.com/GEFdata/digests/20041217-fri.html#anchor0 (accessed 2 June 2013).

Sachs, J. (1998) 'Global capitalism: making it work', *The Economist*, 348(8085): 23–5.

Seith, A. (2009) 'Gipfel in L'Aquila: G-8-Größen rüsten sich zum Trümmertreff', *Der Spiegel Online*, 7 July. Online. Available www.spiegel.de/wirtschaft/gipfel-in-l-aquila-g-8-groessen-ruesten-sich-zum-truemmertreff-a-634529.html (accessed 2 June 2013).

Stella, F. (2010) 'Länder-fact sheet – Italien', in C. Pohlmann, S. Reichert and H.R. Schillinger (eds) *Die G-20: Auf dem Weg zu einer 'Weltwirtschaftsregierung'?*, Berlin/Bonn: Friedrich Ebert Stiftung, pp. 48–50.

Tedesco, L. and Youngs, R. (2009) *The G20: a dangerous 'multilateralism'*, FRIDE Policy Brief No. 18. Online. Available www.fride.org (accessed 22 December 2012).

11 Effective minilateralism

The EU's pragmatic embracement of the G20

Peter Debaere, Dries Lesage and Jan Orbie

The G20 as a form of 'effective minilateralism'

When launching the objective of 'effective multilateralism' in the 2003 European Security Strategy, the EU clearly did not have a forum such as the G20 in mind. In the 2003 document, no references were made to informal groupings such as the G7, G8 or G20. Only in the 2008 implementation report, was the G8 mentioned once by stating that '[t]he G8 should be transformed', without further specifying what a transformed G8 should look like. This chapter zooms in on the G20 and assesses the challenges and opportunities posed for the EU's principle of 'effective multilateralism' as a result of the G20's exclusive membership and informal nature. These include the risk of the G20 undermining other international institutions and relying on soft law and informal agreements. On the other hand, the G20 has the potential to break the stalemate in several global negotiations such as in trade and climate, thereby making multilateralism more effective.

First, the G20 can be seen as undermining the official multilateral institutions that were established in the wake of the Second World War, such as the United Nations (UN) and the International Monetary Fund (Kirton 2010). Indeed, the relationship between the G20 and multilateral institutions has been contentious from the very beginning of G20 summitry in the fall of 2008. In 2009, then president of the United Nations General Assembly (UNGA), Miguel d'Escoto Brockmann of Nicaragua, explicitly pitted the 'G192' against the G20 as the only legitimate group to bring about the necessary global economic and financial reforms (TWN 2009). He organized a UN counter-summit on the global financial crisis in June 2009 in New York. Input to that meeting was provided by a commission led by the renowned economist Joseph Stiglitz. Its report presented an analysis of the crisis quite different from the Western governments' and the IMF's. Moreover, the 'Stiglitz Commission' advocated the creation of a Global Economic Coordination Council within the framework of the UN as an alternative to the G20 (General Assembly 2009). In 2009 Singapore set up the Global Governance Group (3G) to gather the critics of the G20 (Chowdhury 2010). In this context, the 2010–11 president of the UNGA, Joseph Deiss of Switzerland, launched an intergovernmental initiative on strengthening the role of the UN in global economic governance. It resulted in discussions, papers from members, reports and UNGA resolutions.

Nevertheless, by including the emerging economies, the G20 has also been seen as a more inclusive, and thus more legitimate, forum compared to other forums that have been established since the 1970s, such as the G7 and the G8 (Goodliffe and Sberro 2012). By including countries such as Mexico, Turkey, Saudi Arabia, Argentina and Indonesia it is also more inclusive than the BRICs forum. In addition, agreements reached at the level of the G20 could be seen as a stepping stone towards multilateralism. In this scenario the G20 would be building the consensus for agreements at the multilateral level. This can be witnessed in the case of the governance reform of the IMF which was prepared in the G20 context (see third section below).

Second, the G20 relies on soft law and informal agreements that are reached within a club-like atmosphere, in sharp contrast to highly institutionalized international organizations that produce hard law and binding agreements. Therefore the G20 has, just like the G7 and the G8, sometimes been dubbed as a 'talking shop' that produces no tangible results (e.g. The Economist 2009). However, the nature of the G20 may well make it possible to function as a 'steering committee' of global governance that is more effective than the official multilateral institutions. It is no coincidence that the G20 was upgraded in the context of the financial crisis of 2008, when the subprime mortgage crisis and the Lehman bankruptcy in the US threatened to destabilize the entire world economy. Effective and rapid international action may be achieved more easily through flexible forums such as the G20, which may provide the necessary political impetus for appropriate measures by national governments and international institutions.

Following similar considerations about the 'input' and 'output' legitimacy of the G20, Naím argues that the G20 can be seen as a form of 'effective minilateralism', meaning 'the smallest possible number of countries needed to have the largest possible impact on solving a particular problem'. Whereas 'large-scale multilateral negotiations … stopped yielding results almost two decades ago', agreements reached by a small number of countries could make it possible to 'break the world's untenable gridlock' (Naím 2009). In international relations scholarship the term was first launched by Kratochwil (1993: 468) referring to 'the creation of core groups and the multilateralisation of their agreements'. Thus, both Naím and Kratochwil explicitly state that minilateral groupings aim to reinforce multilateral institutions, even if they recognize the potential tension between the two forms of international governance.

However, the legitimacy of the G20, both in terms of inclusiveness and effectiveness, has not (yet) been firmly established and remains a question for debate. What makes it even more difficult to assess the track record of the G20 is that we are dealing with a moving target: in its early existence the G20 seems to be moving from a 'crisis committee' to a 'steering committee', but it is still uncertain how it will evolve (Cooper 2010). The inclusion of issues such as development cooperation and food security may strengthen the global agenda setting power of the G20 but it is yet to been seen whether this can be achieved.

Within this context, the question arises how the EU has positioned itself towards the G20. Traditionally, the EU is known as a firm supporter of a global order based on rules (Keukeleire and MacNaughton 2008). As a major economic power, the EU has wholeheartedly committed itself to the principle of 'effective multilateralism'. However, since the G20 relies on soft law and possibly under-mines formal multilateral institutions, its effectiveness and contribution to multi-lateralism can be questioned. Hence, to what extent does the EU support the G20 as a legitimate forum for global governance, and has it attempted to build bridges between the G20 and the official part of global multilateralism such as the IMF? And (how) has the EU adapted its internal decision-making system to the emer-gence of the G20 as an informal and barely institutionalized forum of global governance? These are questions this chapter aims to address by focusing on the G20's upgrade to leaders level and the ensuing internal EU reform.

The existing literature only provides tentative answers to this question. Jør-gensen argues that the EU policy-makers have 'mixed views about the merits of minilateralism' even if this would enhance effectiveness, pointing to reasons of legitimacy (Jørgensen 2006). Others have shown that the EU has already embraced minilateralism in the field of security (Attina 2008). However, apart from the work of Jukela (2011), the question has not been systematically ana-lysed, nor has it been applied to the EU's involvement with the G20.

In addressing these questions, the chapter is built up as follows.[1] The next section will examine the EU's role in the creation and evolution of the G20 since 2008 ('external reform'). Subsequently, we shed light on how the rise of the G20 has influenced the position of the IMF and how the EU approaches the G20–IMF relationship. Next, we will analyse how the EU's decision-making procedures have been coping with the G20 ('internal reform'), with particular attention to the involvement of those EU member states that are not members of the G20. The chapter will show that the EU's internal reform processes have largely con-sisted of ad hoc and flexible responses to the new external situation and that the EU, including the small member states, have gradually come to accept the G20 as an effective forum for global governance. In this way, the EU seems to emphasize 'effective' over 'multilateralism'.

External reform: the EU and the creation of the G20

This section focuses on the EU's approach vis-à-vis two aspects of G20-level reform, namely the G20's upgrade to the level of heads of state and government in 2008 and the enlargement of its agenda. It is illustrated that the EU generally supported the upgrade of the G20, notwithstanding the initial critical attitude of some smaller EU member states who saw their national interests endangered. But soon, they advocated for G20 agenda expansion in the benefit of their own foreign policy priorities.

The European Commission and some EU member states played a pivotal role in the establishment of the G20 at leaders' level in 2008. However, there was also some controversy within the EU, with some smaller member states fearing that the G20 would undermine the multilateral institutions and that they would be excluded from key decision-making processes. As such, this resistance may not be surprising given earlier precedents. The creation of the G8[2] in 1975 also provoked criticism from excluded EU countries that feared being considered second-class member states. They therefore insisted that the European Community[3] should be represented at the G8, and later the G7 meeting of finance ministers (see Chapter 10). Only after an intensive struggle with France, the non-G8 member states managed to secure the participation of the European Community in the G8. However, when the G20 was established in 1999 as a club of finance ministers and central bank governors, in the context of the Asian crisis, there was less contestation within the EU. This could partly be explained by the fact that the EU acquired official membership status right from the start. The EU's involvement in the G20 was allegedly motivated by the wish of the non-EU members of the G7 to avoid the direct participation of smaller EU member states in the new forum (Hodson 2011). The EU was represented through the rotating Council presidency and the president of the European Central Bank. However, the EU could not hold the presidency or host a G20 summit, and the Commission was only involved at a technical level. The limited contestation against the pre-2008 G20 can also be explained by its low political salience. It brought together the finance ministers and central bank governors of the member countries, not the heads of state and government, and when the sense of urgency around the Asian crisis faded away it came to be seen more and more as a consultative and consensus-building group (Bini Smaghi 2006).

The G20 as we currently know it constitutes an upgrade of this forum to the level of heads of state and government, in reaction to the outbreak of the global financial crisis in 2008. The decision to convene an international summit at leaders' level in November 2008 was taken at a meeting of the French President Sarkozy, holding the Council presidency, and the European Commission President Barroso with US President Bush at Camp David (Runningen and Viscusi 2008). Sarkozy and Barroso envisaged an enlarged G8 summit but a few days after this meeting, the US announced that it would invite the G20 leaders to the crisis meeting (Alexandroff and Kirton 2010). The upgrade of the G20 also entailed a promotion of the European Commission's status in the G20 from the technical level to the highest political level with the European Commission president representing the EU next to the president of the European Council. The sudden entrance of the Commission at the G20 is probably due to the Commission's involvement in the decision for an international crisis summit and to the Commission's expertise and competences in the area of financial market regulation.

Despite the immediate and upgraded role of the EU in the G20, some EU member states contested the establishment of the new forum. Some critical reactions came from countries that traditionally support multilateralism, namely Sweden, Belgium, Finland, Poland, Luxembourg and Portugal (Nagpal 2009). They condemned the G20's arbitrary membership, its self-proclaimed leadership and its non-transparent decision-making process. Apart from principled considerations, they also quickly realized that the impact of G20 measures would go beyond the G20 membership and could adversely affect their interests. At least in some dossiers this fear proved to be correct. Illustrative are the new bank capital requirements under Basel III, the list of tax havens on which three non-G20 EU member states appeared and the 2010 IMF quota and governance reform. All these reforms have been negotiated in the G20 context, while hitting many non-G20 countries, including smaller EU states.

Other EU member states resorted less to normative arguments, but took a more pragmatic stance in arguing that they also deserved a seat at the table of the G20 because of their economic importance and their financial interconnectedness. More specifically, the government of Poland, Spain and the Netherlands attempted to secure membership of the new forum. After long discussions with the US, France met the Spanish and Dutch concerns. France could offer one of its seats to the leaders of Spain and the Netherlands, because at the end of 2008 it was represented in the G20 both as the EU Council Presidency and in national capacity. The Netherlands managed to secure an invitation for the subsequent three summits, while Spain has acquired the status of permanent guest. Poland remained excluded from the G20 forum, but has not yet put aside its hope to join the club (WBJ 2010; Isler 2012). In a similar vein, the Belgian minister of finance unsuccessfully launched the idea of a joint Belgian–Dutch seat (Visser 2010).

The addition of two more EU member states to the G20 table raised the annoyance of a number of Asian G20 countries about the European overrepresentation (Price 2009). Nevertheless, the G20 puts an end to the numerical dominance of EU member states in the G7 and G8. Moreover, since the Treaty of Lisbon, the European Council or rotating Council presidency and the European Commission form a single EU delegation in the G8 and G20 (see above). This EU delegation replaces the two separate delegations for the European Council and the European Commission as was the case pre-Lisbon. But still, the EU is widely considered as overrepresented in the G20 (Ickes 2010; Fidler 2009), although the discussion on its overrepresentation now seems to be closed.

Rather quickly, critical EU voices against the G20 disappeared. To the extent that there was some resistance against the G20 in 2008–9, the EU member states seem to have gradually accepted the existence of the G20 since 2010 onwards. Even though legitimacy will always remain an issue for the member states, they recognize the G20 as the premier forum for international economic cooperation. Three explanations for this acceptance can be given. First, there is a recognition among the EU member states, including the smaller ones, that the G20 has effectively delivered in the context of the crisis. The G20 is considered to be a new reality that cannot be ignored. For example, in a preparatory note for a meeting between the former Belgian and Spanish prime ministers Van Rompuy and Zapatero, the G20 is described as a 'political reality which must be taken into account'. In the 2011 global governance debate at the UN, the EU made it clear that '[t]he G20 has provided important elements of a global crisis response'. The G20 has 'deliver[ed] through exchange of information, peer pressure and coordination' (European Union 2011). In other words, effectiveness took priority over multilateralism. Importantly, there is also a recognition that, in line with the above-mentioned definition of minilateralism, measures by the G20 have effectively facilitated multilateral policies, including the new Basel regulations, a strengthening of the Financial Stability Board and regional development banks, as well as a reform of the IMF's quota and governance.

The EU emphasizes that its support for the G20 hinges on its ability to support reforms at the multilateral level and to include non-G20 members in the process. The EU praises the G20's efforts on outreach to non-members and UN institutions. However, to 'continue to increase its effectiveness', it encourages the G20 to enhance engagement with non-members, in particular in the context of G20 agenda widening, including development policy. With regard to the relation between the UN, the Bretton Woods institutions, and other international and regional bodies, the EU makes a case for an 'efficient division of labour, coordination and complementary'. Finally, the EU supports 'enhanced cooperation between the United Nations and the G20'. In that framework, it sees a 'catalytic and/or supportive role' for the G20 'in specific areas, such as economic policy, development, financial sector reform, trade, energy safety and security, environment, including climate change, and health'. This way, the EU also iterated its preference for agenda broadening at the G20. For the EU 'the G20 can also provide the political momentum in areas where the UN may find it more difficult to galvanize action. Conversely, the UN's operational agencies provide a critical mechanism for implementation of internationally shared priorities' (European Union 2011).[4]

In addition, the EU soon advocated for an enlargement of the G20 agenda beyond economic and financial issues, to include also issues such as development and climate change.[5] While development has been successfully adopted as a core G20 area, climate change remains largely excluded from the G20 agenda. Several G20 countries including the BRICs do not share the EU's view that the G20 should deal with climate change and prefer the UNFCCC as the main forum for negotiating climate change (Carin *et al.* 2010). Remarkably, precisely those EU countries that were critical at the time of the creation of the G20 have now come to see the G20 as an opportunity to pursue their foreign policy priorities. For example, during its EU Council Presidency in 2009, Sweden pushed hard for the G20 to engage in strong language on climate change. In the area of employment, the Belgian EU Council Presidency organized an International Forum on Decent Work which concluded that employment should be an integral part of the G20 agenda (Eutrio.be 2010). Therefore, under the Belgian leadership, the Forum called for a systematic organization of a meeting of the ministers for employment of the G20 and the G8 prior to each G20 and G8 Summit. Again, pragmatic considerations in terms of effectiveness seem to have guided the EU position, more than an attachment to the principle of multilateralism.

Finally, EU member states that are not members of the G20 shifted focus to the internal EU decision-making process in order to get their voice heard. By being involved in the formation of the EU position, they could at least indirectly be involved in the G20 process. For example with regard to development coop-eration, interviews reveal that many member states do not question the G20's relevance and added value, but now emphasize the transparency of the EU's representation in the G20. Member states want to be informed on what the European Commission is going to say at G20 meetings and whether it represents the interests of all EU member states rather than only the interests of the Commission or the large EU member states. Before proceeding with a discussion of the development of ad hoc and flexible intra-EU coordination mechanisms in the context of the G20, we will first take a closer look at the EU's stance in the G20's relationship with the IMF. The pragmatic attitude of the EU with regard to the notion of effective multilateralism also appears from its position in the G20-IMF relationship and the IMF reform debates.

External reform: the EU between the IMF and the G20

The emergence of the G20 at leaders' level has also repercussions for other international institutions in the global economic governance architecture, in particular for the IMF. With its nearly universal membership, the IMF is traditionally considered as the multilateral organization for global macro-economic and monetary cooperation. When the G20 proclaimed itself as the 'premier forum for international economic cooperation', it is no surprise that analysts and policy-makers believed that the G20 was to become a rival of the Fund. However, over the recent years the IMF and G20 have developed a relationship that is rather mutually reinforcing than competitive. On the one hand, the G20 relies on the IMF as one of its main instruments, next to the Financial Stability Board, to implement and monitor G20 decisions and recommendations. In addition, the IMF provides substantive support by putting its expertise at disposal of the G20. The staff of the IMF, for example, feeds every G20 meeting of finance ministers and central bank governors with a summary of global economic prospects, the so-called 'G20 Surveillance Notes'.[6] On the other hand, the IMF has also benefited from the rise of the G20. By tripling the Fund's lending capacity in spring 2009, the G20 has reaffirmed the central role of the IMF in the international financial system after a decade of waning IMF relevance.

Yet, the relationship between the G20 and the IMF challenges the EU's concept of effective multilateralism. In general, the IMF represents the rule-based, inclusive multilateralism defended by the EU. The constituency system ensures that nearly every country in the world has, at least formally, a voice in the Fund's decision making. The G20, in contrast, is a select informal club and focuses on providing effective solutions to global problems rather than offering a universal platform for dialogue. Nevertheless, the IMF membership risks being confronted with pre-cooked G20 decisions regarding the Fund's governance, resources or policies as a result of the G20's political authority and influence. Given the EU's long-standing support for rule-based multilateralism, one would expect that the EU might prefer to strengthen the IMF instead of the informal and exclusive G20. Officially, the EU indeed calls for a central role of the IMF in global macro-economic coordination (European Council 2009). However, the EU's position in recent IMF reform debates illustrates its reluctance to reinforce the IMF.

First, the EU did not advocate a more prominent role for the International Monetary and Financial Committee (IMFC) to tackle the global financial crisis. This contrasts starkly with the active role of the European Council presidency and the European Commission in the decision to hold a G-summit. As the IMF's political advisory group at minister's level, the IMFC could constitute an alternative to the G20. As a small grouping, with the presence of the world's major economies, it has the potential to provide political steering, while it is still embedded in a universal, treaty-based framework (susceptible to reform). Given their limited role within the IMF structure, working through the G20 enhances the role of the EU institutions in global economic governance. As far as the EU member states are concerned, several of them recognize the need for an upgrade of ministerial involvement in the Fund, but they disagree on whether this should be done by improving the current IMFC procedures or by activating a Ministerial Council with decision-making powers, as foreseen in the IMF's statutes.

Second, the EU member states showed great reluctance and reactive behaviour in the process to agree on a broad reform package of the IMF's quota and governance. Nonetheless, the EU acknowledged the need to adapt the IMF to the new economic realities. In the 2008 implementation report of the European Security Strategy – as well as in many other documents – the EU explicitly states that it is necessary to 'mould the IMF and other financial institutions to reflect modern realities'. Ahead of the first G20 summit in November 2008, France even launched a quite ambitious IMF reform proposal, which eventually did not win the support of the other EU member states (Council of the European Union 2008). But in the ensuing negotiations at IMF and G20 level, the EU member states were visibly dragging their feet. This is not entirely incomprehensible as the EU was put in the defensive due to its perceived overrepresentation in terms of chairs in the Executive Board (EB) and shares of voting power. Possibly, a proactive role for the EU was also hindered by the criticism of some non-G20 EU member states, who are relatively strongly represented in the Fund, about the G20 claiming the political lead in IMF reform.

Only after the Obama administration threatened that the absence of a solution would prompt the US to veto the renewal of the anomalous number of 24 chairs in the EB, the EU agreed to a final deal at the G20 finance ministerial meeting in Gyeongju, Korea in October 2010. A US veto would have reduced the EB to the default number of 20 members and put enormous pressure on the European (over)representation within the EB. Besides a substantial decrease in voting power for most EU member states, the reform package includes a reduction of two advanced European seats in the EB in favour of emerging markets and developing countries. This concession by the EU could give the impression that the EU was in the end sincerely willing to strengthen the voice of the emerging markets and developing countries. However, the reshuffle of the EB seems to benefit in the first place (candidate) EU member states that are classified as emerging markets, which is obviously not in the spirit of the 2010 agreement (Lesage *et al.* 2013).

In the margin of the reform negotiations, the idea of a single EU or euro seat has been discussed within the Eurogroup (Dutch Ministry of Finance 2009). A single euro chair is also regularly proposed by the European Commission (Strupczewsky 2009; European Commission 2012). Even though the 2010 reform round was an ideal opportunity to make a significant progress towards a single seat, the time was far from ripe. In the meantime, the decision by Belgium and the Netherlands to merge their constituencies is meant to be a first embryonic step in this direction, although only seven of the 15 constituency members belong to the EU and four are part of the euro area. In this context, it is also worth noting that the Lisbon Treaty has no direct implications for the EU's representation in the IMF. The European Council President and the High Representative are not involved in the IMF since the Fund does not gather the heads of state and government, nor the ministers of foreign affairs. The rotating Council presidency still delivers a statement at the IMFC meetings on behalf of the EU. Therefore, a single EU/euro chair would certainly address one of Lisbon's core aims, namely to enhance the coherence and continuity of the EU's external representation. The Lisbon Treaty did not alter the internal EU structures and procedures to deal with the IMF either. This is because the EU member states discuss IMF matters in the Economic and Financial Committee and its subcommittee on IMF related issues, SCIMF. Both have a fixed chair without any linkages with the rotating presidency. Hence, apart from the reform of individual EU member states' representation, no internal reform took place in the EU in 2008–12 with regard to the IMF. This contrasts starkly to the EU's intensive internal reform efforts for the G20 in the same period, as will be illustrated in the next section.

To summarize, the EU and in particular the European Commission and the large EU member states seem to prioritize the G20 over the IMF when it comes to political steering. While the EU declares that the IMF should play a central role in the global financial architecture, it fails to strengthen the IMF's institutional structures in a credible way so that it can assume that central role. This contrasts starkly with the active role of the EU in the decision to hold a G-summit and a strong European presence in the subsequent summits.

Internal reform: adapting EU coordination to the G20

This section discusses how the EU has adapted itself internally to the upgrade and expansion of the G20 by developing flexible and ad hoc coordination structures. Here, coordination refers to deliberation and consultation among all EU member states before and/or after G20 meetings, rather than coordination of the positions of the EU participants at G20 level. Intra-EU coordination may take different forms and purposes ranging from information-sharing over avoiding policy divergences to negotiating a common EU position. It is shown that this way of internal reform is a reaction to the external reform of the G20. The upgrade of the G20 evoked protest by non-G20 EU member states making a reform and strengthening of the EU's internal preparatory process for the G20 crucial to accommodate their concerns.

Antecedents of EU coordination for G20-like forums are limited, even though the EU has extensive experience in preparing and coordinating for international summits or processes such as the conferences on Financing for Development in Monterrey 2002 and Doha 2008 or international climate change negotiations. During the early years of the G8, a meeting of the European Council was held shortly before the G8 summit in order to coordinate a common position on key agenda items of the summit (Putnam and Bayne 1987). However, this habit was not maintained since the summits became less result-oriented, according to Putnam and Bayne. Since then, and up till the Treaty of Lisbon, the EU's participation in the G8 was prepared by the office of the European Commission president. Non-G8 EU member states were involved through informative briefings in COREPER by the EU's G8 sherpa (Nasra *et al.* 2009). As for G7 meetings, they were occasionally prepared by the Eurogroup Working Group and informally discussed at ECOFIN Council meetings.

In contrast to the limited coordination efforts for the G8 and G7, no significant attempts were made by the EU to coordinate for the pre-2008 G20 process. The online archives of the Council do not provide any indications that the EU's participation in the G20 finance ministers and central bank governors meeting would have been a subject of discussion within the EU before 2008. Only since the G20's upgrade the non-G20 EU member states have become – to a certain extent – involved in the preparation of the EU's participation in the G20. Under the French rotating Council Presidency, President Sarkozy put the G20 on the EU agenda and organized an informal European Council meeting one week ahead of the G20 Washington summit of 15 November 2008. Now the G20 continues to appear on the agenda of every European Council meeting that precedes a G20 summit.

However, EU coordination for the G20 at European Council level appeared to be insufficient to accommodate the concerns of the non-G20 EU member states. Their demand for involvement became even more pressing given a number of incidents in which they were confronted with a G20 decision with major impact on their interests. For example, at the 2009 London summit, Luxembourg, Belgium and Austria were listed by the G20 as tax havens, despite an internal agreement at the preceding European Council meeting that no EU member states would appear on such a list. Another example is the involvement of the G20 in the IMF quota and governance reform. It was very likely that a G20 decision in this dossier would affect the position of the Netherlands, Sweden and Belgium in the Fund. Hence, an internal document shows that these countries considered a common EU position helpful for the large EU member states to take their interests into account in G20 discussions on this matter.

Two other developments at the end of 2009 spurred the development of an informal EU coordination mechanism for the G20. First, the Copenhagen climate change conference in December opened the eyes of the EU as it was side-lined by the US and emerging powers in the final negotiations on a global climate accord (see Chapter 5). As a follow-up at the informal European Council meeting of 11 February 2010, the 27 heads of state and government decided to improve the European preparation for G20 meetings to strengthen the role of the EU in the G20 (Van Haver 2010).

Second, the Lisbon Treaty, which entered into force after the third G20 leaders' summit, did not provide additional coordination mechanisms either, despite its aim to enhance the EU's performance in external relations. Therefore, the EU had to develop informal practices to prepare for the G20. With regard to the EU's representation in the G20, the impact of the Lisbon Treaty is more substantial as it created a single EU delegation in the G8 and G20. To organize their representation, European Council President Van Rompuy and European Commission President Barroso agreed on a rough division of labour. The former is responsible for the G8 and focuses on political and security issues, while the latter concentrates on economic and financial matters and is in charge of the G20. However, more concretely, they decide on a case-by-case basis who will take the floor (Pop 2010). The External Action Service, another major innovation of the Lisbon Treaty, does not play any role of significance vis-à-vis the G20 since the foreign affairs ministers are not involved in the G20 process.[7]

Setting up a coordination mechanism for the G20 did not prove to be self-evident. Not only were the European G20 countries wary of being left insufficient room for manoeuvre, the informal and confidential nature of the G20 also had a negative impact on EU coordination. For example, in order to prevent distribution of G20 documents outside the sherpa network, documents are sometimes digitally secured or published by posting a copy to a noticeboard. For this reason, the Commission is also reluctant to share G20 documents because it claims that this information belongs to the G20 Presidency. However, within the EU, the Economic and Financial Committee (EFC) was able to address the concerns of some G20 members about possible leaks outside the G20 network. The EFC has a comparable secretive nature and is strictly shielded from the outside world or even other EU bodies and member states' ministries (Grosche and Puetter 2008). Therefore, the EFC was able to guarantee the confidential treatment of internal G20 documents, as some G20 members demand, which allowed for the relatively quick establishment of a coordination mechanism for economic and financial affairs on the G20 agenda, the so-called finance track.

For the G20 finance track, common EU positions are coordinated in the *ECOFIN-filière* with the EFC and its sub-committees preparing the G20 deputy finance minister meetings. Based on background papers drafted by the Commission in liaison with the rotating Council presidency, the EFC negotiates a document of usually about 10 to 15 pages outlining the priorities of the EU as a whole and its member states. Subsequently, these terms of references are forwarded to the ECOFIN Council, which approves them as the non-binding EU position for the G20 finance ministers meetings. This procedure is run for every G20 meeting and automatically invites all the non-G20 EU member states to give input (Debaere and Orbie 2013).

Next to financial and economic matters, the G20 also deals with non-financial issues such as development, agriculture or employment. These issues fall under the responsibility of the sherpas, the personal representatives of the heads of state and government who prepare the G20 leaders' summits. In the area of employment and agriculture, the sherpas tasked the G20 ministers of labour and agriculture to prepare the G20 summits in their respective policy domains. This institutional and substantive expansion of the G20 has led the EU to reconsider its coordination mechanism that was initially led by the *ECOFIN-filière*.

The sherpa meetings are prepared by the Commission that draws up the EU's position primarily relying on existing EU positions. While the non-G20 EU member states are not involved in the preparation of the sherpa meetings, they have the opportunity to provide input for some individual policy areas. In the responsible Council committees[8] all member states formulate texts outlining the non-binding EU position for the respective ministerial meetings, based on a draft by the Commission and the Council presidency. This document is called 'Guidelines for EU participation', in contrast to the 'Terms of reference' for the finance track. Compared to the Terms of Reference, the Guidelines contain only five pages and are less detailed. An anomaly in this process is development. While the G20 work on development is already quite substantial, the involvement of the member states is limited to information-sharing by the European Commission to the 27 development attachés. With regard to development, there is no intention to involve the non-G20 EU member states in the formulation of the EU's position in the G20.

The coordination mechanisms outlined above represent the internal reform undertaken by the EU in reaction to the upgrade of the G20 and the expansion of its agenda. In developing this coordination process, the EU had to adapt to the nature, structure and functioning of the G20. For example, energy-related issues such as fossil fuel subsidies, clean energy and energy efficiency are prepared in the *ECOFIN-filière* by finance experts since energy is situated in the G20 finance track and not in the sherpa track. If energy fell under the sherpas' responsibility, it is likely that EU coordination would be organized in an EU Council committee specializing in energy matters.

As a consequence of the reactive character of this internal EU coordination process, the level of involvement by non-G20 EU member states varies significantly. For finance matters, all EU member states negotiate a detailed, but non-binding EU position, while for employment or agriculture a broad EU message is formulated. For development and general sherpa meetings on the other hand, non-G20 EU countries' involvement is limited to informative briefings. The variety of coordination practices and the involvement of several directorate-generals of the Commission and numerous Council bodies have increased the need for supervision of the EU's preparation for the G20. The Secretariat-General of the European Commission fulfils this role and oversees this process. It acts as a hub through which the separate issues are funnelled and it prepares the position of the EU sherpa in the G20.

Conclusion

This chapter has illustrated that the advent of the G20 at leaders' level was relatively well received by the EU, not least because of its catalysing role in making the upgrade possible. Only a handful of EU member states voiced serious concerns about the G20's legitimacy, especially those countries that are affected by G20 decisions. However, they soon accepted the G20 as a political reality and even tried to instrumentalize the G20 for their own foreign policy priorities in other domains. Since around 2010, they have focused their attention on the quality of EU representation in the G20. Nevertheless, significant differences in opinion on the G20 remain between the ministries within each EU member state. Furthermore, it has been argued that the reform of the external context, i.e. the upgrade of the G20 to the level of heads of state and government in 2008 and the expansion of its agenda, has forced the EU to reform its internal processes to prepare for the G20. In turn, this internal reform contributes to the inclusiveness of the G20 and thus enhances the G20's legitimacy.

Internal reform as a result of the Treaty of Lisbon is only found in the EU's representation in the G20. In contrast, as far as the EU's internal coordination process is concerned, its impact has been limited. First, the Treaty only entered into force after the third G20 summit when informal EU coordination practices were already being developed. Second, the Lisbon Treaty did not provide any new rules to prepare for international conferences. Internal EU coordination was mainly driven by a considerable demand for involvement by non-G20 EU countries who saw their interests endangered by G20 decisions. Besides, it was also a consequence of the broader international context and more precisely the EU's bad experience at the Copenhagen UN climate change summit. Nevertheless, on some issues, EU coordination still hardly takes place, with development as the main example. Further research is needed to explain the differences of non-G20 EU member state involvement across the various policy domains.

To conclude, being an exclusive and informal body, the G20's relationship with the EU gives a revealing image of how the EU implements the idea of effective multilateralism. In its discourse, the EU remains a supporter of effective multilateralism by being concerned about the risks the G20 poses to official multilateralism. It engages in the quest for a harmonious relationship between the informal group of major powers and the universal membership of the UN, in a way that both reinforce each other. However in reality, the EU also acknowledges and appreciates the emphasis on effectiveness in the G20, considering the G20 as a stepping stone to multilateralism. The case of the IMF reform nicely illustrates this point, since the EU went along with the G20's leadership role in this debate. In fact, the EU does not really foster a strengthening of the G20 with a view of supporting the complete UN system including the IMF. Moreover, a reinforcement of the G20 might come at the expense of the UN, which would contradict the EU's core objective in the European Security Strategy of strengthening the UN. Neither can an opening be found in the EU's discourse to the idea of a G20-like 'Council' embedded in the UN system, for example as a part of the IMF. Instead the EU acted in a pragmatic rather than visionary way by reluctantly agreeing to the final IMF reform package. And as the EU's stance in G20 reform and internal reform for the G20 has shown, the EU's pragmatic embracement of the G20 reveals its support for 'effective mini-lateralism' rather than effective multilateralism.

Notes

1 This chapter draws on six interviews with officials from EU member states and institutions in May 2010 and February, September and October 2012.
2 G8 is used consistently when referring to the 'political' G6/7/8 to avoid confusion with the G7, which only deals with financial and economic affairs. See also Chapter 10.
3 Since the entry into force of the Lisbon Treaty, the term 'European Community' no longer exists and has been replaced by 'European Union'.
4 Only the Belgian government made a slightly more critical contribution to the 2011 debate on global governance reform and the role of the G20. While acknowledging the complementary roles of the G20 and UN given their respective comparative advantages, Belgium called upon the G20 'to respect the autonomy and working methods of the international organizations and the United Nations system in particular'. Belgium also advocated a composition of the G20 based on constituency system, similar to the ones used in IMF and World Bank in order to strengthen the legitimacy of the group.
5 Internal preparatory note for the G20 Toronto summit of the European Commission, May 2010.
6 For more information, see www.imf.org/external/ns/cs.aspx?id=249.
7 On 19 February 2012 there was one informal G20 meeting of foreign affairs ministers under the Mexican Presidency at which the High Representative Catherine Ashton was invited. But the Mexican initiative was not broadly supported in G20 circles and will probably not be followed up.
8 For example, the Working Party of Agricultural Counsellors and the Working Party of Social Questions.

References

Alexandroff, A. and Kirton, J. (2010) 'The emergence of the G-20 Leaders' Summit', in A. Alexandroff and A. Cooper (eds) *Rising states, rising institutions*, Baltimore: Brookings Institution Press, pp. 177–95.

Attina, F. (2008) 'Multilateralism and the emergence of "minilateralism" in EU peace operations', *Romanian Journal of European Affairs*, 8(2): 5–24.

Bini Smaghi, L. (2006) 'Powerless Europe: why is the euro area still a political dwarf?', *International Finance*, 9(2): 261–79.

Carin, B., Heinbecker, P., Smith, G. and Thakur, R. (2010) 'Making the G20 Summit process work: some proposals for improving effectiveness and legitimacy', *CIGI G20 Papers*, No. 2, June 2010.

Chowdhury, I.A. (2010) 'The Global Governance Group ("3G") and Singaporean leadership: can small be significant?', *ISAS Working Paper*, No. 108: 1–13.

Cooper, A. (2010) 'The G20 as an improvised crisis committee and/or a contested "steering committee" for the world', *International Affairs*, 86(3): 741–57.

Council of the European Union (2008) *Follow-up of the European Council on 15 and 16 October 2008: preparation of international initiatives in response to the financial crisis*

184   *P. Debaere* et al.

– *Note of the Presidency on international financial architecture* (14838/08), Brussels, 31 October 2008.

Debaere, P. and Orbie, J. (2013) 'The European Union in the Gx system', in K.E. Jørgensen and K.V. Laatikainen (eds) *Routledge handbook on the European Union and international institutions: performance, policy, power*, London: Routledge, pp. 311–23.

Dutch Ministry of Finance (2009) *Report on Eurogroup meeting and Ecofin of 6 and 7 July 2009*. Online. Available www.rijksoverheid.nl/documenten-en-publicaties/kamerstukken/2009/07/09/verslag-eurogroep-en-ecofin-raad-van-6-en-7-juli.html (accessed 4 July 2012).

European Commission (2012) *A blueprint for a deep and genuine economic and monetary union*, COM(2012) 777 final/2, Brussels, 30 November 2012.

European Council (2009) *Agreed EU language for the Pittsburgh G20 summit*, 17 September 2009.

European Union (2011) *EU initial views on the role of UN in global economic governance and development*, 18 May 2011.

Eutrio.be (2010) *International forum on decent work*. Online. Available www.eutrio.be/files/bveu/media/Decent_Work.pdf (accessed 30 December 2012).

Fidler, S. (2009) 'The new G-20: as European as ever', *Wall Street Journal*, 1 April.

General Assembly (2009) *As financial crisis engulfs world economy, expert commission unveils plan for profound reform of global financial construct, in General Assembly*, (GA/10815, 26 March 2009). Online. Available www.un.org/News/Press/docs/2009/ga10815.doc.htm (accessed 30 December 2012).

Goodliffe, G. and Sberro, S. (2012) 'The G20 after Los Cabos: illusions of global economic governance', *The International Spectator*, 47(4): 1–16.

Grosche, G. and Puetter, U. (2008) 'Preparing the Economic and Financial Committee and the Economic Policy Committee for enlargement', *Journal of European Integration*, 30(4): 527–43.

Hodson, D. (2011) *Governing the euro area in good times and bad*, Oxford and New York: Oxford University Press.

Ickes, W. (2010) 'Global leaders mull joint governance ahead of G20', *AFP*, 18 October.

Isler, D. (2012) 'Could Poland join the G20?', *Polski Radio*. Online. Available www.thenews.pl/1/6/Artykul/97041 (accessed 30 December 2012).

Jørgensen, K.E. (2006) 'A multilateralist role for the EU?', in O. Elgström and M. Smith (eds) *The European Union's roles in international politics*, London: Routledge, pp. 30–46.

Jukela, J. (2011) 'The G-20: a pathway to effective multilateralism?', *UISS Chaillot Paper* No. 125, Paris.

Keukeleire, S. and MacNaughton, J. (2008) *The foreign policy of the European Union*, Houndmills: Palgrave Macmillan.

Kirton, J. (2010) 'Multilateral organizations and G8 governance: a framework for analysis', in J. Kirton, M. Larionova and P. Savona (eds) *Making global economic governance effective: hard and soft law institutions in a crowded world*, Farnham: Ashgate, pp. 23–42.

Kratochwil, F. (1993) 'Norms versus numbers: multilateralism and the rationalist and reflexivist approaches to institutions. A unilateral plea for communicative rationality', in J.G. Ruggie (ed.) *Multilateralism matters: the theory and praxis of an institutional form*, New York: Columbia University Press, pp. 443–74.

Lesage, D., Debaere, P., Dierckx, S. and Vermeiren, M. (2013) 'IMF reform after the crisis', *International Politics*. Advance online publication, 26 April 2013: 1–26.

Nagpal, S. (2009) 'EXTRA: EU middle-weights to complain G20 expansion, ministers say', *TopNews.in*. Online. Available http://topnews.in/extra-eu-middleweights-complain-g20-expansion-ministers-say-2133288 (accessed 30 December 2012).

Naím, M. (2009) 'Minilateralism: the magic number to get real international action', *Foreign Policy*, 1 July.

Nasra, S., Lesage, D., Orbie, J., Van de Graaf, T. and Vermeiren, M. (2009) 'The EU in the G8 system: assessing EU member states' involvement', *EUI Working Paper RSCAS 2009/45*.

Pop, V. (2010) 'Van Rompuy and Barroso to both represent EU at G20', *EUobserver.com*. Online. Available http://euobserver.com/news/29713 (accessed 19 March 2010).

Price, D. (2009) 'Recovery and reform', in J. Kirton, and M. Koch (eds) *The G8 2009: from La Maddalena to L'Aquila*, London: Newsdesk.

Putnam, R. and Bayne, N. (1987) *Hanging together: the seven-power summits*, London: Sage Publications.

Runningen, R. and Viscusi, G. (2008) 'Bush, Sarkozy to seek series of summits on financial crisis', *Bloomberg*. Online. Available www.bloomberg.com/apps/news?pid=newsarchive&sid=auipZhnYOZe0 (accessed 30 December 2012).

Strupczewski, J. (2009) 'EU must move to single voice in IMF: Almunia'. *Reuters*. Online. Available www.reuters.com/article/2009/04/06/us-eu-imf-idUSTRE5351NL20090406 (accessed 28 April 2013).

The Economist (2009) 'Talking-shop-on-Thames'. *The Economist*. Online. Available www.economist.com/node/13278766 (accessed 30 December 2012).

TWN (2009) 'G192 only credible body to bring about reforms', *Third World Network*. Online. Available http://twnside.org.sg/title2/finance/2009/twninfofinance20090405.htm (accessed 30 December 2012).

Van Haver, K. (2010) 'EU zoekt hefboom voor meer macht', *De Tijd*. 12 February.

Visser, M. (2010) 'De Jager geeft zetel in IMF nog niet op', *Het Financieele Dagblad*. 25 October.

WBJ (2010) 'Poland must enter G20, says Jarosław Kaczyński', *Warsaw Business Journal*. Online. Available www.wbj.pl/article-49808-poland-must-enter-g20-says-jaroslaw-kaczynski.html (accessed 30 December 2012).

12 Conclusion

The compatibility of internal and external reform

Edith Drieskens

Introduction

Drawing evidence from the contributions to this volume, this chapter aims to provide a balanced empirical picture of the realities of external and internal reform and their compatibility. It summarizes the main findings and lessons learned, and also explores the way forward. The main proposals developed by think-thanks in preparation for the European Council meeting of December 2013 provide the stepping-stones for this conclusion.

The second decade

The genesis of this volume coincided with reflection and debate on a potential revision of the ESS. In anticipation of the tenth anniversary of adoption of this document, and particularly in preparation of the European Council meeting of December 2013, practitioners and scholars examined its wording and relevance. The discussion was fostered by the informal meeting of the foreign ministers of the EU member states on 9 and 10 March 2012. Organized by the Danish Presidency, the meeting aimed to discuss human rights, EU foreign policy in times of economic crisis, as well as the nature of influence, sanctions and engagement, but the smaller member states managed to add the future of the ESS to the agenda (Drent and Landman 2012; Andersson *et al.* 2011). The most visible result of this gathering was that Poland, Italy, Spain and Sweden launched a debate on the development of a European Global Strategy. Going beyond security and defence and opting for a maximalist approach, the debate would be think-tank driven. More specifically, it would be organized and structured by a consortium led by the International Affairs Institute (IAI, Rome), the Polish Institute for International Affairs (PISM, Warsaw), the Elcano Royal Institute (RIE, Madrid) and the Swedish Institute of International Affairs (UI, Stockholm).

A first attempt to revise the ESS was made four years earlier in 2008, but the initiative fell flat because of a lack of political will (Biscop 2009; Andersson *et al.* 2011). France and former President Nicolas Sarkozy, in particular, advocated a profound review of the text. Germany and the UK were less keen about the idea, mainly because of the questions and answers that would arise when doing so. Given these different perspectives, the momentum faded away. It did not lead to a new strategic document, but remained limited to the adoption of the Implementation Report discussed in the Introduction of this volume.

Only time will tell if a second attempt will be more successful, yet the stars seem to be better aligned this time (see, for instance, Andersson *et al.* 2011; Lundin 2012; de France and Witney 2013). Potential facilitating factors that have been identified are the dynamics of the EU's budget cycle, the planned review of the EEAS, the implementation of the Lisbon Treaty (and the difficulties encountered in that regard), the changed external environment, as well as the strategic documents that have been adopted both inside and outside of the EU. The EU approved, for instance, a *Strategy for Security and Development in the Sahel* and an *Internal Security Strategy* in March 2011 and February 2010, respectively; both NATO and the US revised their strategic concept in 2010. Potential obstacles and barriers, however, are the increased number of EU member states, the increasing complexity and comprehensiveness of the security concept, and the fact that more institutions than ever will be involved in the discussions as a result of the entry into force of the Lisbon Treaty. Moreover, not all member states support a revision. Maybe most importantly, there may be impatience with the EU and its performance as an international actor, but a true sense of urgency, as in the aftermath of the Iraq crisis in 2003, is lacking.

The political and institutional dynamics that characterized the Iraq crisis also help explain the prominence that the ESS gives to effective multilateralism (see Introduction). At the time of writing, it was an open question whether and how the ESS would be revised before entering the second decade. Chances were thin, however, that a revised version would place the same central focus on effective multilateralism as the original. The two main reform proposals presented in the weeks before this volume was sent to the publisher support this conclusion. Indeed, while these proposals were quite broad in their language and content, they remained silent on effective multilateralism. They included few explicit references to multilateralism more generally and mentioned the reform of multilateral institutions only in passing.

Taking the lead, the *Think Global Act European* network formulated its recommendations in April 2013. Bringing together 16 think tanks, the network stressed the need for a 'strategic rebound' of the EU's external action (Notre Europe 2013: 16). Covering a kaleidoscope of topics ranging from migration to natural resources, the network's report briefly addressed the question of reform when discussing the EU's external representation in economic governance. According to the authors, the EU member states should understand that they are overrepresented within this field of governance. The *status quo* is 'unlikely to resist indefinitely', so the EU should 'anticipate these evolutions and organise so as to preserve its power' (Notre Europe 2013: 20). Pillorying the fragmentation of the EU's representation, they suggested the consolidation of its representation through the creation of a 'single voice' for the euro area in the IMF (Notre Europe 2013: 71). A caveat, nonetheless, is that this 'requires a reform, or at the very least a reinterpretation, of IMF Articles of Agreement, since officially only "countries" can be part of the IMF' (Notre Europe 2013: 73).

Opting for a maximalist approach, as well, the *European Global Strategy* consortium presented its input in May 2013. Under the heading 'Boosting international economic and environmental problem-solving', the consortium noted that the EU 'should aim not only to upgrade its own multilateral performance but also to empower and support international institutions per se' (European Global Strategy 2013: 15). More specifically, the legitimacy of the G20 would benefit from increased cooperation with other multilateral structures, as well as from 'a more inclusive approach to states and organizations with issue-specific expertise' (European Global Strategy 2013: 15). The consortium also touched upon reform when it discussed the need for further regionalization. Singling out the UNSC, it recommended that the EU should support the participation of other regional groupings in its work. Also, the EU should contribute to its reform. A collective seat on the UNSC was seen as a 'worthy long-term vision' in that context (European Global Strategy 2013: 17).

Both proposals recognize that the broader picture is one of increasing multipolarity, but their recommendations focus on the settings in which membership and proceedings have been questioned most (openly) by this new reality, namely the UNSC and the IMF. While acknowledging that these recommendations should be seen as input for discussion and not necessarily as a blueprint for change, a chance may have been missed to incorporate these settings into a broader, coherent strategy, translating the EU's principles, interests and objectives in terms of reform. In fact, one of the members of the European Global Strategy consortium, i.e. the Stockholm-based UI, suggested a more 'aggressive' reading of multilateralism in an earlier report (Andersson *et al.* 2011: 16). Such a reading would imply that the EU should improve its relations with international organizations and aims for enhanced participation of global actors, but also leads 'constructive reform endeavours'. To that aim, it should specify 'principles' and 'action points'. In what follows, we formulate some suggestions hereto by building upon the empirical work presented in this volume. Indeed, the cornerstone of any policy advice that is relevant for policy-making is a correct reading of the *status quo*.

Key findings

Concentrating on the decade following the adoption of the ESS, the contributions to this volume reveal that the EU and its member states did, in fact, operationalize the notion of effective multilateralism in terms of reform. Most often, however, they stayed away from high-level commitments on substantial reform and concentrated their efforts on procedural, administrative and technical issues. Importantly, the EU and its member states focused primarily on these issues, though not exclusively.

This volume includes numerous illustrations of the involvement of the EU and its member states in procedural, administrative and technical reform. For instance, they have played a rather active role in the reform of the working methods of both the UNGA and UNSC but have been less willing to consider the more fundamental questions that are on the table in New York, particularly the membership of the UNSC (Chapter 2). A similar story can be told about the WHO. Indeed, there has been no high-level commitment to strengthen the WHO as the leading organization on global health, focusing on its priorities and structure (Chapter 3). Rather, van Schaik and Battams discovered that the input of the EU and its member states has mainly focused on enhancing the organization's transparency and accountability.

More or less the same pattern can be observed at the IAEA (Chapter 7). The EU did not support the reform of the structure of the Board of Governors or the reform of the legal mandate of the Secretariat to enforce safety measures on the members; instead, Glavind demonstrates that the EU has supported smaller initiatives focusing on the enhancement of security, safety and safeguards. Likewise, van Willigen could not detect a grand strategy on the reform of the OSCE but found that the EU and its member states have taken a rather pragmatic stance and tend to focus their energy on concrete issues (Chapter 9). This pragmatic approach explains, for instance, why the EU supports bestowing legal personality upon the OSCE, but did not defend this position in ministerial council meetings. Likewise, Davis found that the EU and its member states are everything but united on the reform of the Rome Statute and the inclusion of the crime of aggression therein (Chapter 6). That being said, they have used a broad range of tools to foster universality, complementarity and cooperation.

Some of the cases presented in this volume, however, point at a more substantial reform role for the EU and its member states. Most visibly, Kissack found that they played a decisive role in the recent reform of the FAO, making negotiations possible in the first place and building bridges between the US and the G77 (Chapter 4). EU success can also be seen within the context of the reform of the G20, because Commission President Barroso played a key role in the upgrade of this forum to the level of the heads of state and government (Chapter 11). The finding that the EU does not support a further institutionalization of the G8 or the G20 but rather the strengthening of their informality may come across as counterintuitive; after all, the ESS took a rather institutional perspective on (effective) multilateralism. However, this apparent contradiction between (institutional) theory and (informal) practice may be explained by the simple fact that the EU benefits from the less institutionalized nature of these settings. The informality of the G8 allows for the EU to participate in the meetings as such, but also means that it does not need to define its presence, unlike in more formal settings (see Chapter 10). Such advantages may also explain why the Commission (like the larger member states) tends to prioritize the G20 over the IMF in terms of political steering (Chapter 11). Nonetheless, important obstacles to enhancing the EU's effectiveness within these bodies remain in place after Lisbon, like the inability to host summits and the perception of over-representation (Chapters 10 and 11).

The proposal of the *Think Global Act European* network hinted that the EU's perceived lack of engagement in substantial reform may be explained by a fear of losing the privileged positions that some of its member states enjoy within specific settings. These positions may have long stood the test of time, but their future is increasingly in jeopardy, particularly because of the shift towards multipolarity. In this regard, the reform of the IMF and the reduction of the number of European seats on the Executive Board can be seen as the proverbial 'writing on the wall' (Chapter 11). These less-than-rosy perspectives, as well as the EU's global ambitions – formulated by the ESS and the Implementation Report, and more recently confirmed by the intention to upgrade its status in various international settings (see Introduction) – may foster expectations of engagement from the EU and its member states in (discussions on) substantial reform. However, and perhaps stating the obvious, also after the entry into force of the Lisbon Treaty, the EU's foreign and security policy is a common policy, not a single one. If only for the reason that this policy represents 28 unique member states, the EU's performance cannot be compared with that of sovereign states like the US, China, Russia, Brazil or India. Indeed, leaving aside discourse and ambitions, the more logical reference points are the positions and policies of other regional players.

Declarations 13 and 14, which are both attached to the Lisbon Treaty, leave no doubt about what a common policy means for the EU's functioning in international organizations: the innovations introduced by the Lisbon Treaty do not affect the member states' representation of and participation in international organizations, particularly not the membership of the UNSC (see Chapter 2). Comparing theory with practice, many contributors found that the EU member states still tend to see both their membership and the topics covered by international organizations as a question of national competence, priority and action. This is, for instance, the case for sustainable development (Chapter 5), the crime of aggression (Chapter 6), disarmament (Chapter 7) and the status of Kosovo (Chapter 9).

Two nuances should be noted, however. First, differences of opinion do not always prohibit the EU member states from acting together. Van Schaik and Battams found that there are EU positions for almost all WHO-reform related topics, even if there is no obligation to work towards these positions and despite differences of opinion on global health governance, including on its organization (Chapter 3). However, the flipside of the coin is that their adoption is often a time-consuming process resulting in a rather technical and inflexible mandate. More importantly, the EU member states are only willing to adopt these positions when it suits them. For this reason, van Schaik and Battams conclude that the EU has been punching below its (financial) weight within the context of WHO reform.

Second, Delreux's analysis shows that differences of opinion do not need to be permanent and that political dynamics can change (Chapter 5). Arguing that one should go beyond the Copenhagen experience when evaluating the EU's role in environmental negotiations, and beyond climate change more generally, he shows that the EU managed to assume bridge-building and coalition-making roles at the follow-up conferences in Cancún, Durban and Doha. At first sight, the EU's role in Rio was somewhat less impressive. However, as explained above, the Rio+20 picture is much more positive when looking beyond the failed institutional upgrade of UNEP.

Contrary to what is often claimed by advocates of a single EU voice, this volume shows that a more united functioning of the EU in international settings is no panacea. Instead, a more united performance may be counterproductive for both the EU and the external context in which it operates. Discussing the EU's functioning in the G8, for instance, Huigens and Niemann conclude that EU unity may lead to polarization between the EU and the 'Rest'. Likewise, Kissack found that a more pronounced EU role in the reform of the FAO would have been detrimental to the reform process that started in late 2004 and was successfully concluded in early 2012 (Chapter 4). The EU member states may not have been very visible therein, but their diplomats were instrumental as bridge-builders and facilitators. In fact, the EU's overrepresentation was rather beneficial because it allowed for burden sharing.

Continuing on the same line, Davis states that a regional form of representation could endanger the effectiveness of the ICC. There is no guarantee that other regional actors, and the African Union in particular, are as supportive of the ICC as the EU (Chapter 6). A stronger EU voice, thus, could indirectly undermine the ICC's effectiveness. More generally, a stronger regionalization, notably a regional form of representation, may seem an obvious suggestion when envisioning a progressive EU foreign policy, but it is less obvious when taking into account the intergovernmental nature of most international settings in which the EU and its member states operate. For example, regional actors are excluded from budgetary negotiations in the FAO (Chapter 4). Moreover, the introduction of regional seats at the UNSC is not an option but an ideal that is more distant than ever, particularly following the EU's status campaign in the UNGA and the resulting stir the campaign created (Chapter 2).

Indeed, the genesis of this volume did not only coincide with discussions on a possible revision of the ESS, but also with the implementation of the Lisbon Treaty. Though it is too early to give a final evaluation of the EU's newest treaty, some first observations can be made. Like previous commentators, many contributors recognize that the Treaty may contribute to the EU's international presence and performance because of the continuity it offers in terms of representation. At the same time, they see important challenges and obstacles, both inside and outside the EU.

Practice shows indeed that the successful implementation of the Lisbon Treaty depends not only on internal factors, but also on external ones. This was particularly obvious at the UNGA, where the EU's intention to upgrade its status resulted in an unprecedented level of resistance, mainly from the Caribbean and African countries (Chapter 2). Similarly, though less visibly, Russia refused to accept a formal status for the EU at the OSCE unless the same privilege was extended to the Collective Security Treaty Organization and the Eurasian Economic Community. Similar status issues can be expected for the IAEA, which is high on the EU's priority list for a future upgrade (see Chapter 7). The *status quo ante*, as well as the yet to be completed implementation of the Lisbon Treaty, may explain why both Glavind and van Willigen sketch a rather positive picture of the impact of the Lisbon Treaty in Vienna (Chapters 7 and 9).

Importantly, the EU's implementation struggle cannot be reduced to New York. In Geneva, the EU's capacity to act within the WTO has been undermined by internal struggles over coordination and representation (Chapter 3). The relationship between the new delegation and the EU member states may have improved, but the latter still closely monitor the former, particularly to avoid a broad interpretation of the mandate. In fact, competences have been a problem in most organizations studied. A recurring observation is the outspoken position of the UK on the importance of respecting the distribution of competences. This has been the case in New York and Geneva, but also in The Hague (ICC), Rome (FAO) and Vienna (OSCE) and in international negotiations in the environmental sphere. As for the latter, the Lisbon Treaty does not provide a clear template for representation for issues of shared competences. Delreux's contribution shows, however, that the EU's failing leadership does not relate only to intra-EU reasons, but also to resistance from its external partners.

More generally, while the Lisbon Treaty streamlines the EU's external representation (see Introduction), it does not bring the distribution of competences into uniformity or the decision-making procedures. Also, it speaks for itself that the Lisbon Treaty does not change the external context in which the EU and its member states operate. This context helps to explain why there have been differences in implementation among the various cities discussed in this volume and why differences will remain after implementation. Compared to New York and Geneva, the impact of the Lisbon Treaty on the EU's functioning in Rome seems somewhat limited, especially within the context of the FAO. According to Kissack, this may be explained by the fact that the EC/EU has enjoyed membership in the FAO since 1991 (Chapter 4). That being said, the implementation has been no smooth sailing either, mainly because the UK advocated a continued presence of the rotating presidency. Quite interestingly and somewhat paradoxically, the successful pre-Lisbon FAO reform complicated the implementation of the Lisbon Treaty because the diplomats involved were reluctant to be marginalized by their EEAS colleagues.

Likewise, Davis found little impact of the Lisbon Treaty on EU's functioning within the context of the ICC (Chapter 6). After all, the main working party in Brussels remains chaired by the presidency and the exchange of information and coordination in The Hague remains a member state-driven process because no EU delegation is present. According to Davis, the new delegations may be an interesting tool for enhancing support from third countries for the ratification of the Rome Statute as well as for cooperation with investigations and prosecutions. Nonetheless, she expects other EU initiatives to be more significant for the EU's functioning.

In a similar vein, Drent writes that the broader trend towards informality rather than institutional decisions like the Lisbon Treaty have shaped the relationship between EU and NATO (Chapter 8). In fact, the Lisbon Treaty has

made the EU less effective when it comes to NATO. After all, the crisis management structures are integrated into the EEAS, but the decision-making remains
intergovernmental. More anecdotally – but probably also more visibly – Ashton
skipped some informal meetings of the ministers of defence, including when the
Secretary-General of NATO was present, as well as some gatherings of the
European Defence Agency.

Conclusion

Taking a comparative stance on the EU's functioning in international settings,
this volume investigated what has become of the EU's intention to make multilateral settings more effective. Exploring the realities of internal and external
reform, the contributions provided an empirical picture that is one of mixed
success. Covering the ten years since the adoption of the ESS, the authors showed
that the EU and its member states contributed to a more effective functioning of
multilateral settings. They played a part in the institutional reform of various settings but focused their efforts on administrative, procedural and technical initiatives. Unsurprisingly but significantly, national concerns about membership and
competences often resulted in a less developed focus on substantial reform.

The Lisbon Treaty aims to strengthen the EU's international profile yet its
implementation did not lead to a focus change. By concentrating almost exclusively on streamlining the EU's external representation, a chance may have been
missed to integrate this objective in a broader reflection on institutional reform.
In fact, the EU's wish for a more visible international representation could have
been a catalyst for launching discussions in that regard. Even more so because a
more coherent representation may make the EU's functioning more effective in
multilateral contexts – even in discussions on reform – but not when the message
is weak, insufficiently targeted or simply lost in delivery. Six years after the
adoption of the Lisbon Treaty and four years after its entry into force, it is
becoming increasingly difficult to justify missed opportunities by claiming
growing or transition pains, particularly given the EU's explicit status ambitions.
The argument that these ambitions intend to align institutional reality with the
Lisbon Treaty is not convincing either, especially when status enhancement
requests have become the rule rather than the exception, largely as a result of
changing polarities.

In the foreword to this volume, Laatikainen and Smith write that they find it
striking to see how rarely scholars investigate the EU's contribution to broader
multilateral processes, combining thus internal and external variables when
explaining the realities of effective multilateralism. A similar conclusion can be
drawn for the EU when it comes to institutional reform. This is illustrated by the
implementation of the Lisbon Treaty in multilateral contexts more generally, and
by the list of organizations within which the Commission and the EEAS favour
an EU status upgrade, more specifically. The existence of this document, its language and its tone all indicate that the EU is willing and able to think strategically about institutional reform, but that it still does so by taking an internal

perspective, focusing on the externalization of its own institutional reform efforts. In this light, the tenth anniversary of the notion of effective multilateralism provides a unique opportunity but also a critical moment for the EU to translate the dual perspectives introduced by Laatikainen and Smith into policy practice, especially because the more traditional road to international status is a two-way street.

References

Andersson, J.J., Brattberg, E., Haggqvist, M., Ojanen, H. and Rhinard, M. (2011) *The European Security Strategy: reinvigorate, revise or reinvent?*, Stockholm: Utrikespolitiska Institutet, Occasional Paper No 7. Online. Available www.euglobalstrategy.eu/upl/files/77715.pdf (accessed 1 June 2013).

Biscop, S. (2009) 'Odd couple or dynamic duo? The EU and strategy in times of crisis', *European Foreign Affairs Review*, 14(3): 367–84.

de France, O. and Witney, N. (2013) *Europe's strategic cacophony*, Brussels: European Council on Foreign Relations. Online. Available http://ecfr.eu/page/-/ECFR77_SECURITY_BRIEF_AW.pdf (accessed 1 June 2013).

Drent, M. and Landman, L. (2012) *Why Europe needs a new European Security Strategy*, The Hague: Clingendael Institute, Clingendael Policy Brief 9. Online. Available www.clingendael.nl/sites/default/files/20120706_research_policybrief9_llandman_mdrent.pdf (accessed 1 June 2013).

European Global Strategy (2013) *Towards a European global strategy: securing European influence in a changing world*. Online. Available www.euglobalstrategy.eu/nyheter/publications (accessed 1 June 2013).

Lundin, L.-E. (2012) *From a European Security Strategy to a European Global Strategy: ten content-related issues*, Stockholm: Utrikespolitiska Institutet, Occasional Paper No 11. Online. Available www.euglobalstrategy.eu/upl/files/84836.pdf (accessed 1 June 2013).

Notre Europe (2013) *Think global – act European IV: thinking strategically about the EU's External Action*, Paris: Notre Europe. Online. Available www.eng.notre-europe.eu/media/tgae2013.pdf?pdf=ok (accessed 1 June 2013).

Index

Page numbers in *italics* denote tables.

Taylor & Francis

eBooks

ORDER YOUR FREE 30 DAY INSTITUTIONAL TRIAL TODAY!

FOR LIBRARIES

Over 23,000 eBook titles in the Humanities, Social Sciences, STM and Law from some of the world's leading imprints.

Choose from a range of subject packages or create your own!

Benefits for you

▶ Free MARC records
▶ COUNTER-compliant usage statistics
▶ Flexible purchase and pricing options

Benefits for your user

▶ Off-site, anytime access via Athens or referring URL
▶ Print or copy pages or chapters
▶ Full content search
▶ Bookmark, highlight and annotate text
▶ Access to thousands of pages of quality research at the click of a button

For more information, pricing enquiries or to order a free trial, contact your local online sales team.

UK and Rest of World: **online.sales@tandf.co.uk**
US, Canada and Latin America:
e-reference@taylorandfrancis.com

www.ebooksubscriptions.com

ALPSP Award for BEST eBOOK PUBLISHER 2009 Finalist

Taylor & Francis **eBooks**
Taylor & Francis Group

A flexible and dynamic resource for teaching, learning and research.

For Product Safety Concerns and Information please contact our EU
representative GPSR@taylorandfrancis.com
Taylor & Francis Verlag GmbH, Kaufingerstraße 24, 80331 München, Germany

www.ingramcontent.com/pod-product-compliance
Lightning Source LLC
Chambersburg PA
CBHW050435280326
41932CB00013BA/2122

9 781138 377455